The True Story of

Pierre & Marie Mayeux, the Natchez Massacre and the Settlement of French Louisiana

by

KENNETH N. MYERS

Mayeux Press

Denison, Texas

1729
The True Story of Pierre & Marie Mayeux,
The Natchez Massacre,
And The Settlement Of French Louisiana

Myers, Kenneth Neal, 1959-

Cover design and maps by Michael Peterson

Cover pictures:

Le Commerce que les Indiens du Mexique Font avec les François au Port de Missisipi by François-Gérard Jollain, c. 1720; The Historic New Orleans Collection 1952.3. Used by permission.

John J. Egan, American (born Ireland), active mid-19th century; *Fort Rosalie; Extermination of the French in 1729; Grand Battle Scene; Mode of Scalping,* scene 14 from *Panorama of the Monumental Grandeur of the Mississippi Valley*, c.1850; overall panorama: 90 inches x 348 feet; Saint Louis Art Museum, Eliza McMillan Trust 34:1953

Published by Mayeux Press
561 Bailey Drive, Denison TX 75091

For Joan

and all the descendants of Pierre & Marie

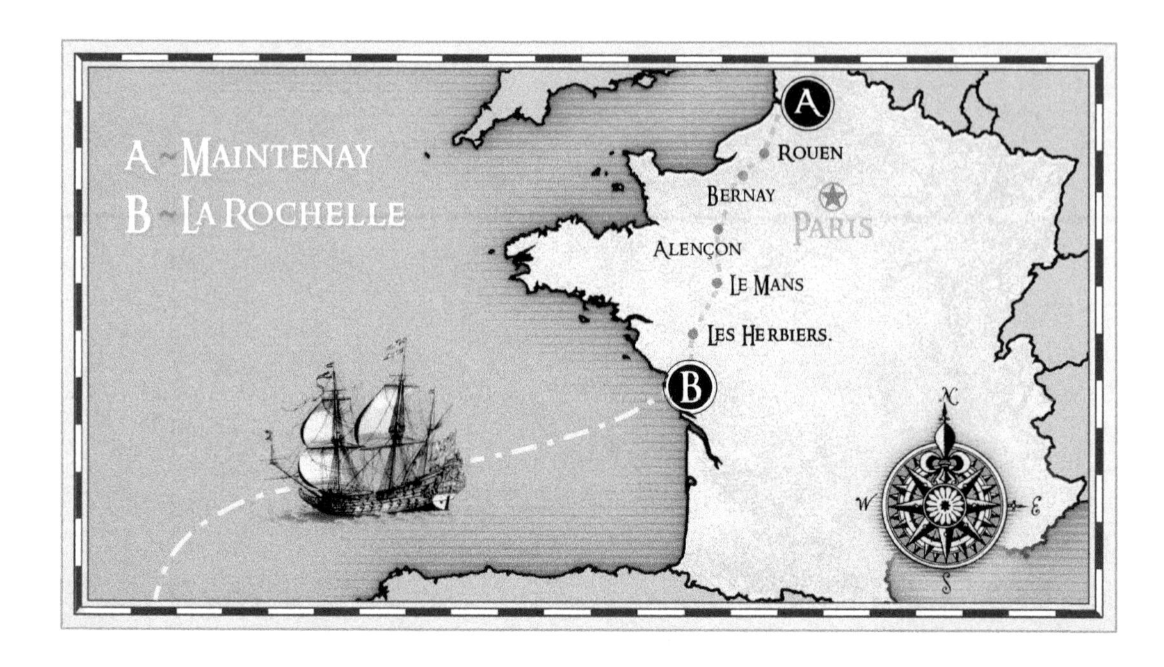
A ~ Maintenay
B ~ La Rochelle
Rouen
Bernay
Paris
Alençon
Le Mans
Les Herbiers.
A
B
N
W
E
S

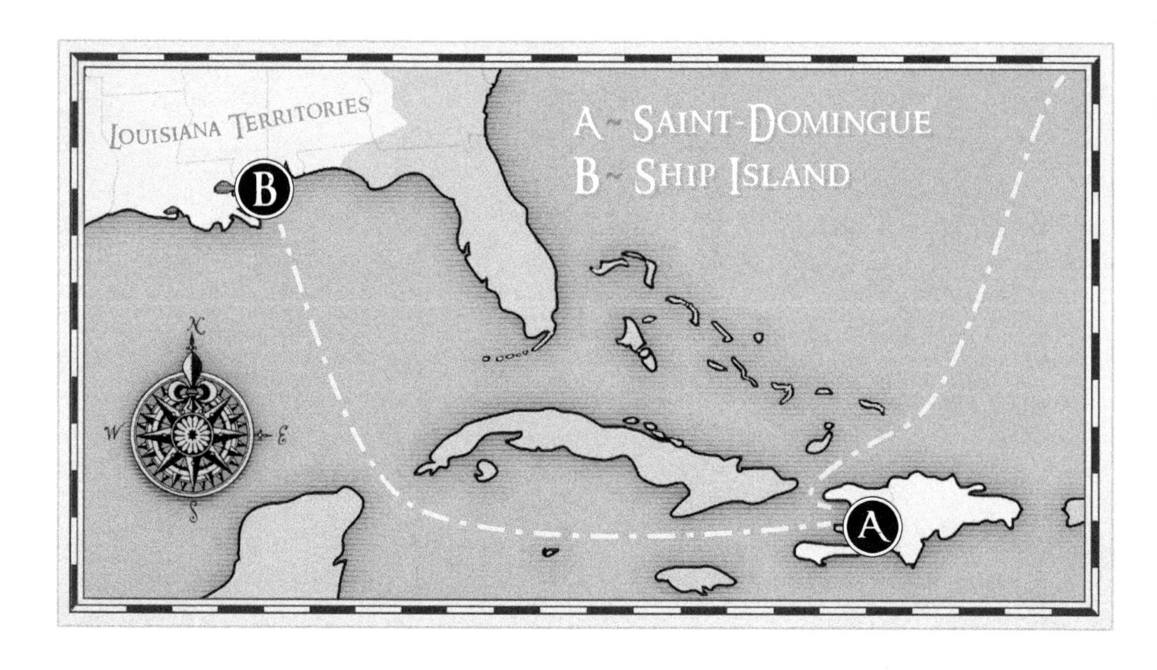
Louisiana Territories
A ~ Saint-Domingue
B ~ Ship Island
B
A
N
W
E
S

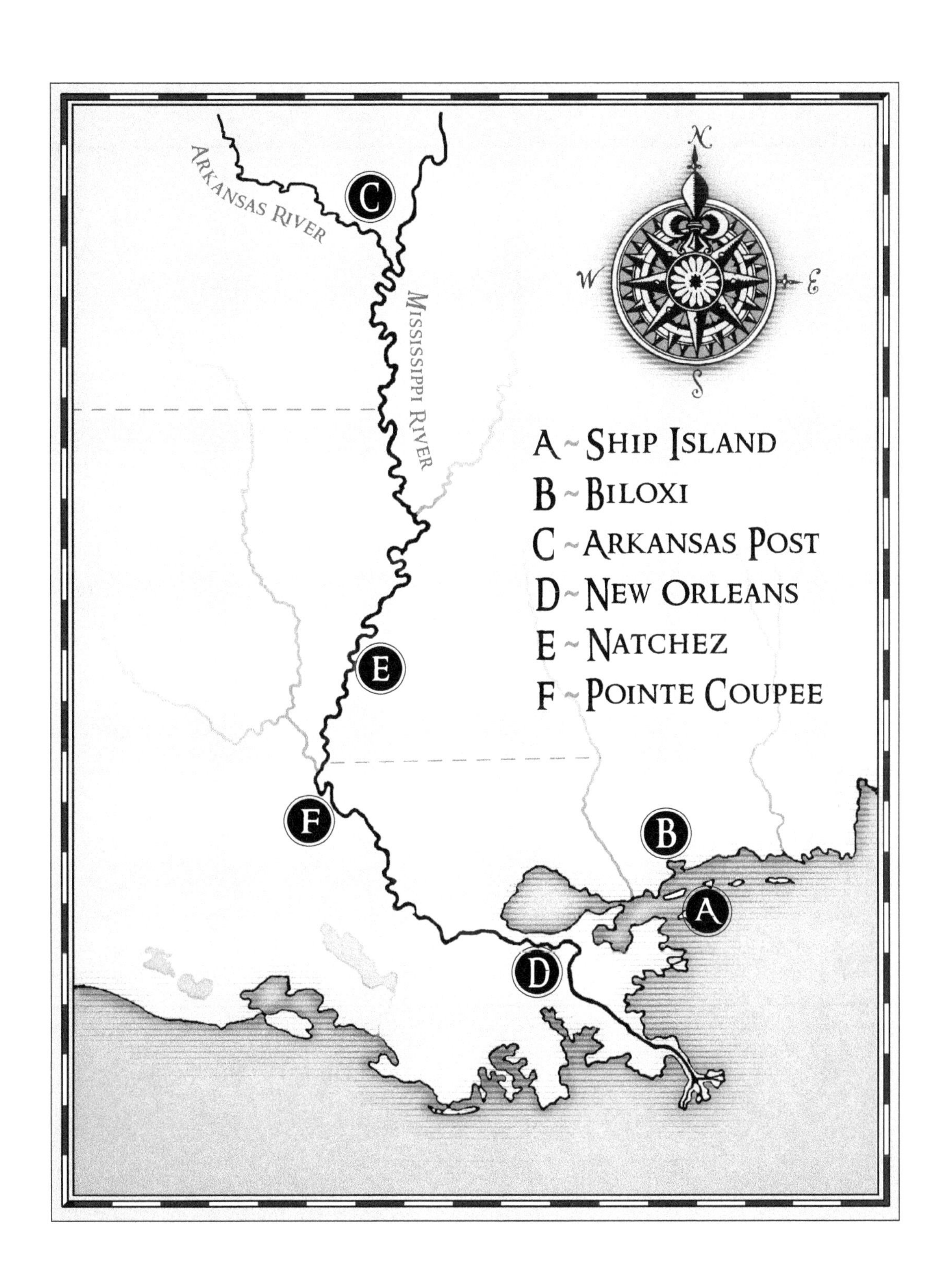
N
W
E
S
Arkansas River
Mississippi River
C
E
F
B
A
D
A ~ Ship Island
B ~ Biloxi
C ~ Arkansas Post
D ~ New Orleans
E ~ Natchez
F ~ Pointe Coupee

Table of Contents

Thank You

I am deeply indebted to so many people who helped make this book possible. First, my late wife Shirley, who stood beside me through ten years of research and traveled with me all over the globe as I pored over documents and books. My father and mother, Larry and Mary Myers, who encouraged my writing and helped fund travel and translation. My dear friends Victor and Debbie Leal, who also supported this endeavor and traveled with us to France to visit sites important to the book. The legendary local Natchez historian Smokye Joe Frank. The Avoyelles Parish Genealogy Research Group, whose members are nearly all distant relatives, and who have been so encouraging as I worked on this project. Kathy Lemoine Sturgell, who was very helpful with genealogical information and original source documents. Dave Cottrell, who translated the massive report of the massacre by Officer Delaye from barely legible 18th century handwritten papers (the first English publication of this document to my knowledge). Brian Costello, my friend, deep roots cousin, and historian *par excellence*. My friend Michael Peterson who designed the book cover, the maps, and helped with the illustrations. And finally, Rae Dickson, Heather Doucet, Bill Forsythe, Jack Holden, Debbie Leal, and Sheila Moore, all of whom read the manuscript, offered helpful critiques, and made this book better.

Preface

Pierre Mayeux left us no written records. There is no journal, no diary, no remembrances of his life. All we have are scraps of documentation here and there - a work contract, a ship's passenger list, a census, a marriage record. But, Pierre and his wife Marie Cellier were part of the sweeping history of the birth of Louisiana, and what we do know of them places them at locations and events which were seminal to Louisiana's existence. They were part of the (sometimes forced) migration of over 6,000 men and women who left their homeland in France to tame the wilderness of a new world. They were in the tent city of Biloxi when plague and famine killed over 1,000 settlers. They were in New Orleans when it was a brand new village of only a few hundred inhabitants. And they were in Natchez when the fort and adjacent village was destroyed in one of the most significant massacres in American history. And so, in a very real way, the story of this one couple is the story of the birth of Louisiana.

When I was in my late teens, I began hearing stories from "the old folk" that one of our ancestors had survived an Indian massacre. No one knew the details. No one knew where, or when, or who, exactly. We were the Myers family, with roots in Pointe Coupee and Avoyelles parishes in south Louisiana, and there were whispers and hints that our real name was Mayeux, but in a culture of illiteracy and short memory, even that reality was hazy. Jump forward a dozen or more years and through the efforts of various family members we discovered that John Henry Myers was really Jean Henri Mayeux, and that indeed our roots went all the way back to the French settlement of Louisiana in the early 18th century. Jump forward another decade or two and DNA tests confirmed all our research. Through the meticulous digging of uncles and aunts and cousins, especially my first cousin Joan Fowler, the full lineage of the Myers/Mayeux family was finally discovered and the story of "the grandparents of us all" began to emerge from the fog of lost history.

I have spent the last ten years researching exactly what our family's deep history was, and in the process discovered that it was actually the history of Louisiana itself. I read every book and article I could find on the time period and places involved in the story, including books on rural France, 18th century transatlantic travel, Biloxi, New Orleans, Arkansas Post, Pointe Coupee and Natchez. I traveled to the village of Mantaney in the Picardy region of France, as well as to La Rochelle, the port city from which the young couple departed their homeland never to return. I made multiple visits to Biloxi, New Orleans, Arkansas Post, Natchez, and the Louisiana parishes of Pointe Coupee and Avoyelles, piecing together the emerging story of their fascinating and tragic life. Pierre Mayeux and his wife Marie Cellier are my

7th great grandparents, but more importantly are the ancestors to approximately a million living descendants, and to virtually every living Mayeux and Bordelon in Louisiana and the rest of the United States today.

But perhaps most important, the story of Pierre and Marie is a micro-tale of Louisiana itself. These two persons represent thousands upon thousands of others who share similar stories full of adventure, danger, wonder, and tragedy; people who left behind all they knew in France and came to the territory of Louisiana with dreams of a new life. Deceived by propaganda from the Company of the Indies that they were trading lives of hardship for a new paradise (see the cover of this book which includes a reproduction of a 1720 picture used for advertisement throughout France. It depicts New Orleans as a beautiful harbor with palm trees, mountains in the background, French chateaus, and peaceful native peoples welcoming the French). Thousands died en route or soon after arrival. Thousands more lived out their lives in obscure poverty and never fulfilled the dreams that compelled them to cross a wide ocean and venture into uncharted territory. Only a handful actually achieved their visions of hope, and only after hardships that are unimaginable to their distant descendants. But because of their sacrifice, their tenacity, and their vision, Louisiana came into being. And so did I.

Here, then is the story of my ancestors, and the story of the birth of Louisiana.

Kenneth Myers
Denison, Texas
March 8, 2017

Prologue
New Orleans
1729

They heard the screams first. Not from one person, but from many, and not close, but at a distance. The men who were unloading cargo from the ships and the shopkeepers from Levee Street dropped what they were doing and ran to the river's edge, hardly believing their eyes and unable to comprehend what they were seeing.

On a cool morning in the first week of December Marc Caillot and his friends were taking a leisurely stroll along the new levee that kept the raging waters of the Mississippi River from flooding the new town of nearly 800 people. Caillot, a clerk for the Mississippi Company, recorded in his journal, "...the next day, about five o'clock in the evening, a group of us who were friends were walking together along the levee, otherwise known as the quay, and saw a little pirogue coming down the river. We would not have paid any attention at all to that boat if not for the fact that we noticed that it was being rowed, and that it was going very fast." After a moment of watching, the men continued their walk along the levee when they "saw that this pirogue had arrived at the river bank and that a great number of people were running there."[1]

Caillot was expecting supplies to arrive from upriver and thought the pirogue he saw headed to the bank might be his man. By the time he arrived on the scene he knew this wasn't his supplier. Making his way through the commotion of townspeople, he saw maybe half a dozen men and women climbing out of the flat bottom boat, none of them with more than a nightshirt on, some completely naked and all of them spattered with blood. Two men were so badly wounded they had to be helped out of the boat. The only words Caillot could make out between the screaming and the crying were spirited exclamations that "everything was on fire and covered with blood" at Natchez.[2] These boat people were convinced they were the only ones who had been able to escape.

The townspeople were shocked and confused, but certainly some among them found confirmation in this report from a rumor that was already circulating. Only the afternoon before a lone man had made his way into New Orleans, disheveled and weary, saying he had escaped from Natchez, or Fort Rosalie, a tobacco growing village 170 miles up the river from New Orleans. No one was prone to believe him when he reported that he alone had escaped a savage attack on the village by the nearby Natchez Indians.

Pierre Ricard had wandered into the parade grounds in the middle of town from the woods that crept up to the south side, scraped and bruised and claiming he had paddled downstream after narrowly escaping the edge of a tomahawk. At first the soldiers who found him thought he was drunk, or perhaps mad, and escorted him to the barracks, a low lying wooden building next to the parade square. Inside the dark room, the windows opened for light and fresh air, they sat the man down at a big wooden table and gave him some wine and leftover food from lunch. Calling for Commandant Louboey, the soldiers gathered round more out of curiosity than concern and began to ply the stranger with questions. As his story unfolded a few wondered if there was truth in his tale but most thought what he was saying was simply impossible. The Frenchman described a morning filled with craziness and confusion when the relatively friendly natives came to the homes surrounding Fort Rosalie bearing gifts of corn and chickens. Before anyone knew what was happening laid aside their ruse of kindness and began cutting throats and shooting the villagers. Ricard claimed he was at the river, unloading the ship that had just arrived, when about ten Indians came running down to the loading dock wielding their weapons and shouting their battle cries. Making his escape, Ricard dove into the river and swam toward the middle. Swimming out of range, he eventually attached himself to a floating log until he drifted to Rousseau's Camp, a few miles downriver from Natchez. Arriving at a cabin there, he knocked on the door and found Rousseau visiting with a group of Yazoo natives who were his hunting partners. When he told them the awful news about Fort Rosalie, they gave him a pirogue and some supplies to make the trip to New Orleans and report to Governor Périer."[3]

Commandant Louboey had the unenviable task of overseeing the troops - a handful of ill-trained, ill-clad and ill-fed soldiers who had come to the French colony of Louisiana with images in their minds of heroism and service to the King, only to discover a life of boring drudgery interrupted by the hard and unsoldierly work of digging ditches along the city's dirt streets to prevent destructive flooding when the hard winter and spring rains came. Most of them lived in barracks alongside the square, some lived with their wives in small wooden houses in town, and a few were unfortunate enough to live in tents pitched in empty lots where homes were yet to be built. He answered to the Governor Périer, and would make his report of Ricard's ravings to him, but in all likelihood the bedraggled stranger would be held in suspicion or dismissed as mad.

The Governor's Mansion, if a two story shipboard home with no glass in the windows can be called a mansion, lay adjacent to the parade square, and only a few hundred feet from the levee and the river. Whether Louboey had the opportunity to make his report before the ruckus arose on the riverbank is unknown. But when the crowd descended from the levee, dockworkers and storekeepers carrying with them a small group of men and women who looked like they had just gone through living hell, there was no question as to the truth of Ricard's story.

Commandant Périer sent soldiers to fetch the nuns from the new Ursuline hospital. There were only eight sisters in residence, and they spent most of their time teaching young girls and only hesitatingly tending the sick. The sisters' house on the edge of town served the triple purpose of being their quarters, a home for six or seven orphans, and a boarding house for a dozen residents. The hospital was at the other end of town and like everything else in New Orleans, its name betrayed the reality of the place. To call it a hospital was being too generous; it was actually only a large house, quickly thrown together, with several rooms to treat the constant stream of townspeople struck with a variety of maladies ranging from malnutrition to malaria. The sisters hadn't even come to New Orleans to be nurses. They were a teaching order from a convent in Rouen, and had agreed to the nursing role only because it was a requirement for their relocation to Louisiana. When mother superior Sister Saint-Augustin first saw the hospital that would be her new place of ministry she wrote, "There is neither stable nor cattle shed that does not present more agreeable and commodious lodging. They say that there is very little sickness that would force one to this miserable shelter." [4] As the nuns arrived to give medical aid to the survivors, word began to spread throughout the town. No longer the ravings of a suspicious madman, there was now news of a verifiable massacre.

Governor Etianne de Périer was not a man to be trifled with. He arrived in New Orleans on March 15, 1727 with fresh appointments from the King as Governor of all Louisiana, as well as holding the office of Commandant General for the Company of the Indies, or, "The Mississippi Company," financier John Law's private enterprise that held complete power over the developing territory. Périer had been in the city only two years and had already begun to transform it from a backwoods outpost into the capital that it was to be. Under his watch a levee that was over a mile long and 18 feet across the top was built in front of the city to protect it from the flooding Mississippi. He created the first city park, brought the Ursuline nuns to establish their hospital, built the first church, the shipboarded parish of St. Louis the King situated just behind the parade grounds, mandated that ditches and sidewalks be created to alleviate the flooding of the dirt streets, and established a conservatory for the development of the arts. If anyone could transform swampland into a new Paris, it was Périer. He ruled with an iron fist. And he had no place in his heart or his schemes for the Native Americans who populated his world.[5]

Unlike Jean-Baptiste Le Moyne, Sieur de Bienville, the Montreal born first governor of the French territory of Louisiana, Périer did not respect or appreciate the Indian nations which surrounded him, and the news he had just received only served to confirm his sentiments. Interviewing the survivors and hearing their tales of terror he wasted no time in executing a plan. He sent a pirogue to the Choctaw nation to inquire if they had been involved in the massacre. There were rumors floating in the air that a general conspiracy of the tribes was afoot to drive the French from the land. No sooner had that pirogue departed than he sent another with an additional message: if the Choctaw were not part of a conspiracy, would they join the French in combatting the Natchez who were their sworn enemies? With the launching of the two parties to the Choctaw, Périer ordered Louboey to prepare men to head north toward Natchez, then he set about making sure New Orleans was protected from the same fate.

Word of the attack spread through New Orleans instantly. Many of the townspeople had been at the scene when the survivors were brought from the river, and before nightfall everyone had heard the news. Some of the local residents were intimate with many of the dwellers in Natchez. Jaques Cantrelle, one of the few survivors of the massacre and likely one of the men in the piroque, was friends with Pierre Thomelin, a master carpenter in New Orleans. Cantrelle and his wife Marie Francienne had arrived in Louisiana nine years before aboard the ship *Le Profond*. Either aboard the ship, or before leaving France, Jaques and Francienne Cantrelle had become friends with Pierre and Marie Mayeux,[6] a couple in their early twenties who were seeking a new life in a new world. In the likely event that the carpenter Thomelin visited with his friend Cantrelle, he would have discovered that Francienne had been murdered by the Indians, and in all likelihood so had the young Mayeux couple. As far as anyone knew, everyone else in the fort town of Natchez was dead.

---

[1] Mark-Antoine Caillot, *A Company Man*, The Historic New Orleans Collection, New Orleans, 2013, p. 123.

[2] *Ibid*, p. 124

[3] Dumont gives details of Ricard's escape, Jean-Francois-Benjamin Dumont de Montigny, *The Memoir of Lieutenant Dumont, 1715-1747*, University of North Carolina Press, Chapel Hill, 2012, p. 238. Swanton writes that Ricard was the warehouse keeper at Natchez, and was with Commandant Chepart in his debaucheries the night before the attack, John R. Swanton, *Indian Tribes Of The Lower Mississippi Valley, Dover Publications*, Mineola, NY, 1911 (1988), p. 234; French also details Ricard's arrival in New Orleans, Benjamin Franklin French, *Historical Memoirs Of Louisiana*, Lamport Blakeman & Law, New York, 1853, p. 74.

[4] Giraud describes in detail the conditions the nuns faced in their attempt to serve God and people. Several sisters found New Orleans too dire and returned to France, while some opted to leave behind their habits and take up domestic life; Marcel Giraud, *A History of French Louisiana, Volume Five: The Company of the Indies, 1723-1731*, Louisiana State University Press, Baton Rouge, 1987, pp. 303ff. For a detailed history of the

Ursulines in New Orleans, including the correspondence from Marie Tranchepain, see Emily Clark's *Masterless Mistresses*; the quote is from page 55.
[5] For details of Périer's character, achievements and foibles, see Giraud, *in toto.*
[6] The French convention of the time was to list the wife by her maiden name, i.e., "Pierre Mayeux and Marie Cellier." However, for the sake of modern readers, the couple will be referred to in these pages as "Pierre and Marie Mayeux."

Chapter One
La Rochelle
1720

Pierre Mayeux and his wife Marie Cellier climbed their way from a small boat onto the deck of the flute ship *Le Profond*, and paused long enough at the railings to look back on the city of La Rochelle and with it France. One of the thousands of young couples to risk all for the chance of a new life in a new world, they were leaving behind everything - their families, their friends, their histories, and the only way of life they had ever known - for the promise of bounty awaiting them in Louisiana.

Little is known of the ancestry of Pierre Mayeux. Records indicate he was born in 1697,[1] and lived in the northern French town of Maintenay, a small hamlet in the district of Pas-de-Calais bordering the Picardy region along the Somme River. With evidence of prehistoric human dwellings, the area was populated by a succession of Celts, Romans, Germanic Franks and

Alemanni, and Saxons, the language of the region being as fluid as the succeeding waves of conquerors. Nestled in the rolling hills north of the Somme River, the small village which never had a population of more than about 300 was established in the 11th century by the monks of the nearby Abbaye de Volloires when they built a mill on the L'Authie River which served to grind meal and cut lumber for the growing religious center. The community that grew up around the mill was intimately related to the abbey and most of the residents earned their living supplying it with crops from the surrounding fertile fields.

The deceptively idyllic beauty and peaceful countryside of the region was often the scene of warfare of epic proportion. In August, 1328, King Edward III of England led a devastating *chevauchée* through the region, his soldiers pillaging and burning the villages on their route until the campaign culminated in the Battle of Crécy on August 28. With his an army of more than 10,000 men, including 3,000 longbow archers, Edward faced a significantly larger French army. But the recent innovation longbows in warfare tipped the scale in favor of the English, and the battle ended with over 4,000 French knights killed, compared to the astonishingly low 300 dead among the English. After the battle, Edward's army continued its devastating march through the countryside to the port city of Calais, only 93 kilometers north of Maintenay, which fell after a year long siege and remained under English rule for over 200 years, until 1558.

Eighty seven years later the hills around the village were once again the scene of English invasion when in 1415 Edward III's great grandson, King Henry V, led his troops from Normandy through the countryside of Pas de Calais and confronted the French in the legendary Battle of Agincourt, thirty three kilometers northeast of the Maintenay, where the English again overwhelmingly defeated the French using the same tactics they had employed at Crécy. Immortalized by Shakespeare in his play *Henry V*, the battle saw an English army of 10,000, 7000 of whom were longbow archers, confront a French army of between 20,000 and 30,000. But just as at Crécy, the archers gave the English the advantage and the result was an English victory with between 5,000 and 10,000 French killed, as opposed to only about 100 Englishmen.

The region continued throughout history as the scene of massive battles of global significance. In World War I the Battle of the Somme took place about 130 kilometers southwest of Maintenay, where in 1916 the Allied forces faced Germany in one of the deadliest battles in human history with over a million men dying in the course of the five month campaign before a victory for the Allies. Like the longbow of the 14th century, another martial innovation, the tank, was first used in the Battle of the Somme. A generation later World War II saw Maintenay and the whole of Pas de Calais occupied by Nazi forces until it was liberated by the Allies after the D-Day invasion of Normandy in June, 1944.

Pierre Mayeux married Marie Cellier sometime before 1720, when at the age of 20 she joined her husband aboard *Le Profond* for a journey across the sea to Louisiana. Although the license of their marriage is yet to be discovered, the couple was likely married in Maintenay, where the ceremony would have been performed in the thirteenth century parish church, *Iglese Saint-Nicolas*.

Compared to the bellicose centuries that preceded and followed it, the time in which Pierre and Marie lived was relatively peaceful in Maintenay, but the early eighteenth century was a difficult time to begin a new family in France, and thousands of people were looking for any opportunities for a new life, however far flung or risky. King Louis the XIV, the Great, the Sun King, had died five years earlier, in 1715, after reigning an incredible seventy two years. During his reign, France was engaged in no less than five wars, the final and most devastating being the War of Spanish Succession which lasted thirteen years and brought France to the edge of social and economic bankruptcy. At the same time, between 1693 and 1710, during Pierre Mayeux's childhood years, the nation endured two severe famines which left over two million people dead.

During his long reign Louis the Great was noted for his bellicose attitude, extravagant lifestyle, personal vainglory, and ill treatment of the people and is seen by some historians as having planted the seeds of the French Revolution of the late eighteenth century. The Sun King's great grandson, Louis XV, was only five years old when he came to the throne and the vacuum left by the death of the Sun King was quickly being filled by every opportunistic and self-serving henchman in the royal halls of Versailles. Until the new king reached the age of succession in 1723 holding together the fragile country of France would fall to his older first cousin twice removed, Philippe II, Duke of Orleans. The first order of the day for Philippe was to save France's crumbling economy, brought on by the wars and famines of the previous decades.

When the Duke came into power, he discovered that things were far worse than he had imagined. The national debt was over two billion livres, with an interest of over 90 million livres each year. The corrupt and antiquated tax system found itself incapable of securing monies to repay the interest on the debt, let alone any of the principle, and even the King's holdings had been consumed in financing the war. To curb the rampant corruption, Philippe instituted the Chamber of Justice, designed to ferret out any businessmen, tax collectors or officials who had abused the system. The Chamber promised a one-fifth bounty for anyone exposing corruption, a policy which left in its wake a wide swath of treachery and betrayal, with disgruntled enemies or mistreated servants reporting sometimes innocent people who saw their property and money confiscated. As a result, many of the wealthy packed their belongings and fled the country. The policy backfired, and caused the economic conditions to worsen even more.[2]

Like most commoners of their time, Pierre entered the world of adulthood with dim prospects of success. While the elite were blindly living their lives in an artificial extravagance, the ordinary man hoped at best to subsist. Even providing food for the table was a difficult task. While the extreme measures which were taken to secure monies for the payment of France's national debt drove many of the wealthy to flee the country, only to be arrested at the borders and returned for trial, imprisonment and the stripping of all their wealth to fill the Crown's coffers, the typical French family just hoped to scrape together enough to buy meager food and housing.

Into this morass walked a Scotsman named John Law. Born in Fife in 1671, Law was 23 when he killed a man in a sword duel over a woman's honor, was arrested and sent to prison in London, and sentenced to death by hanging. A debonair and daring man, Law was loved by the ladies, himself loved gambling, and had a brilliant mind for all things monetary. Through the help of friends he escaped from his cell in the Newgate fortress and made his way to the Continent where he lived a comfortable and profitable life of gambling.

Eventually John Law made his way into the court and the friendship of Philippe II, Duke of Orleans and regent of France. His ideas for economic change charmed Phillippe and outraged the old guard. Paper money? Who had ever heard of such a thing? Until now exchanges were made in coin - gold or silver minted by the government, and the economy was limited to the amount of coinage in existence. The very idea that money could be *printed* was new and to many minds ludicrous. But it might just be, Philippe thought, the very thing that would save France. Law was given permission to establish a private bank, the *Banque Generale,* and issue notes backed by precious metal. Initially the project floundered, but soon people were standing in line to buy stock in the new bank, depositing their gold and silver, and walking away with a pocketful of paper.

By 1718 the bank was such a success, and held such promise for the recovery of the French economy, that the Crown gave it the highest honor of making it the official bank of France, changed its name to the *Banque Royale,* and instantly catapulted Law to the position of, after Philippe, the most powerful man in the country.

But the bank was not the only jewel in John Law's crown. He was convinced that vast new resources were to be had in the far off French territory of Louisiana, and in 1717 founded "The Company" - the Company of the West - specifically to exploit those New World riches. In 1719 the Company of the West merged with the East India Company and was renamed The Company of the Indies, or as everyone called it, The Mississippi Company[3].

The American continents were discovered by Europeans in 1492 when the Spanish-backed explorer Christopher Columbus landed on an island he named San Salvador, now part of the Bahamas. The New World soon became a target and a playground for European expansion, offering unimaginable new resources and opportunities for land-locked and cash strapped European nations. Spain, Portugal, England and France all vied for dominance of the new land. In 1682 René-Robert Cavelier, Sieur de la Salle, navigated the Mississippi River to the Gulf of Mexico and claimed the territory for France, naming it Louisane in honor of the Sun King, Louis XIV. France's territory on the North American continent now reached from the Great Lakes to the swamps of Louisiana, from the coastline of Quebec to the piney woods of Texas. The tiny English colonies along the eastern seaboard were dwarfed in comparison.

The only problem was, discounting that the land was already populated with Native Americans, from France's perspective the Louisiana territory was empty. In 1701, when Jean-Baptiste Le Moyne, Sieur de Bienville became governor of Louisiana, the entire territory had a population of only 180 French men and women. As late as 1715 the population was under 300, half of them being soldiers. If its natural resources were to be of any benefit to the motherland, Louisiana had to be populated, cultivated, and domesticated. John Law, with his eye for opportunity and his penchant for a gambler's risk taking, saw this vast empty empire as the opportunity of a lifetime. Using his favor with Philippe, he established the Company of the West for the express purpose of establishing "concessions," massive plantations along the Mississippi River which would provide valuable crops for France, especially the much coveted crop of tobacco. Until now England held the upper hand on tobacco production, the fine leaf from Virginia being in demand across the European continent. But the fertile land along the Mississippi, Law believed, would produce a crop that would at first rival and eventually displace England's corner on the market.

Law, who himself never set foot in Louisiana, was given complete control of its development and a twenty five year lease on the project. He was lord, not only of the concessions, and of the economic development, but also of the military and government of Louisiana, having authority to name governors and military commandants, and to appoint and remove judges.[4]

The French Jesuit priest Pierre de Charlevoix, in his *History of New France* published in 1744, lists five arrangements granted to Law by the Crown:

1. Trade with Canada in regard to cultivation and plantations.
2. To carry on exclusively for the space of twenty-five years "trade in the province and jurisdiction of Louysiana, and in perpetuity all the lands, ports, coasts, harbors and islands which compose that province."
3. "The power to treat and form alliances in his majesty's name...with all nations of the country [in other words, the Native American tribes], not dependent on other European powers, and in case of insult, to declare war against them, treat of peace or truce."
4. The "absolute possession of mines" opened by the Company during the 25 year contract.
5. "Permission to sell and alienate the lands within said grant, to erect such forts, castles and strongholds as it shall

> deem necessary for the defence of the territory granted; to place garrisons there, to raise troops in France with his majesty's concert, and to appoint such governors, majors, officers and others as shall please it, to command the troops."[5]

John Law was, in short, the king of the territory. And he was convinced that among the war and famine ravaged poor people of France he had a ready made population for his schemes.

In exchange for these benefits from the Crown, the Mississippi Company was obligated to bring a minimum of 6,000 settlers and 3,000 African slaves to Louisiana.[6] In the first four years of the Company's endeavor to populate Louisiana, from 1715 through 1721, 43 ships sailed from France filled with 7,020 colonists. Two thousand people either died on the trip across the Atlantic, defected to Spanish or English territories in America, or quickly found ways to return to France.[7] Approximately half of those who survived the voyage died shortly after arrival due to cholera epidemics, starvation or Indian attacks. In 1726 the census listed 1,952 French citizens in Louisiana, and even that low number would shrink in the coming years.[8] By 1721 there were also 533 African slaves in the colony, a number which skyrocketed to 3,600 by 1732, more than doubling the 1,720 French settlers in Louisiana that same year.[9]

The initial attempt to populate Louisiana was one of forced relocation. Charlevoix wrote that the people, "are wretches, who being banished from France for their crimes or ill-behaviour, true or supposed, or who, in order to shun the pursuits of their creditors, listed themselves among the troops, or hired themselves to the plantations...looking upon this country as a place of banishment only, were consequently shocked with every thing: they have no tie to bind them, nor any concern for the progress of a colony of which they are involuntary members."[10]

An army of archers was raised with the sole purpose of scouring the streets of Paris and other cities to find undesirables unlucky enough to be captured and sent away. These archers, most of them ruffians themselves, combed the streets of Paris arresting street people for little or no cause and carting them off to the prisons. The archers were paid a hundred livres for each person arrested, and even honest people were not safe from them. Sometimes completely innocent people found themselves ensnared by the archers, imprisoned for no other reason than being unemployed. Wives who tired of their husbands falsely reported them and suddenly found themselves free to pursue new lovers. Unscrupulous businessmen reported their partners. Prostitutes were rounded up and sent to the infamous Salpétriére prison, where they were often chained to madwomen and forced to survive in rat infested cells, and it was not uncommon for families to dispose of unruly and unwanted members by reporting them to the authorities as prostitutes or thieves. The case of Anne Francoise Roland serves as an example. Born about 1700 in Paris, she became the victim of the archers' schemes when at the age of 18 she was reported by her father as having taken up a life of prostitution. The evidence suggests that she was, rather, simply a "wild child," uncontrollable by her strict father and perhaps jealous stepmother. In 1719 she was arrested, sent to the Salpétriére, and later to New Orleans where she lived out her years as a well-respected and well-married woman, becoming an ancestor of many founding families of Louisiana[11].

It is estimated that in Paris alone more than 4,000 vagrants, prostitutes, smugglers, orphans,thieves and other criminals were collected from the streets, jail cells, mental hospitals and orphanages, loaded onto boats, and sent to Louisiana in an ill conceived ploy to bring civilization to the swampy frontier.[12] Following the lead of England, which sometimes offered the sentence of "transport" to the colonies in lieu of a death sentence, French courts often exiled criminals to Louisiana as penalty for their crimes. In September, 1719, eight months before Pierre and Marie Mayeux set sail for their new life, eighty criminals who received pardons in lieu of agreeing to relocate to Louisiana were shackled to eighty prostitutes, married in a mass ceremony, and marched through the streets of Paris, then sent to La Rochelle and from there to Louisiana.[13] This was not the only occasion for mass weddings. It happened again shortly thereafter, but because of the public scandal of seeing couples marched through the streets in chains, the subsequent wedding found the couples linked with garlands of flowers, yet still under the watchful eyes of the archers. Of the thousands who were sent to Louisiana during this time, over half either died en route or returned to France as quickly as they could bribe their way onto a ship, and many who remained succumbed to famine, pestilence, or hostility from Native Americans.

Clearly this was an exercise in futility. If France hoped to bring actual civilization to its New World colony, it was guaranteed failure by sending criminals. When they arrived in Louisiana, many of the prostitutes quickly abandoned their husbands, made their way to any reasonable facsimile of a city - New Orleans, Biloxi, or Mobile - and continued to ply their trade. Venereal diseases plagued the territory. Men who weren't in the habit of honest work in France didn't, by and large, find the habit once they arrived in Louisiana. Many criminals simply resumed their old ways of life. After repeated complaints from officials in Louisiana and protests from the people in France, forced deportations were halted in May, 1720. From then on the only emigrants would be people who of their own free will chose to make the journey. *Le Profond*, the ship on which Pierre and Marie Mayeux would sail to their new home, left port a month later bound for a new and prosperous life in a beautiful, peaceful, and bountiful far away land.

The Company crafted articles and took out ads in newspapers all across France and Germany, and produced colorful flyers describing the riches awaiting everyone willing to start life over in the new territory. One magnificent painting, reproduced in full color and distributed throughout France, depicted what awaited the lucky pilgrims: a verdant land with French castles resting on mountains in the background, ships filling the peaceful harbor, palm trees swaying in the breeze, while elaborately adorned natives warmly embraced the French newcomers. Never mind that the highest point in what is now the state of Louisiana is only 535 feet above sea level. This picture of paradise was surpassed only by the print in the advertisements: "a land of milk and honey in which the climate was temperate, the soil fertile, the woods replete with trees suited to building and export, and the countryside populated with wild yet benign 'horses, buffaloes, and cows, which however do not harm but run away at the sight of men.'"[14] Another brochure stated "the abundance of the country cannot be easily imagined. There is also game, which every person is permitted to kill: leopards, bears, buffaloes, deer, whole swarms of Indian hens, snipe, turtle doves, partridges, wood-pigeons, quail, beaver, martens, wild cats, parrots, buzzards and ducks." The deer were so plentiful they could be killed with ease, and the Indians would readily purchase the skins of any animals killed by the new settlers.[15]

The land, a veritable paradise, also promised wealth for the literal picking - the region was described as being filled with emeralds, copper and silver, all easily accessible to anyone industrious enough to scrape the ground. As if the natural environment was not beckoning enough, the cities were described as places of refinement and culture. In an advertisement from 1719 the unwitting French people were told that the new city of New Orleans was home to "nearly 800 very comfortable and well appointed houses, each one of which has attached 120 acres of land for the upkeep of the families." The reality is that New Orleans, founded a year before the propaganda piece was circulated, was a destitute outpost of four houses, all built on land below sea level that tended to flood, and a breeding ground for malaria carrying mosquitoes and all kinds of snakes and wild animals.[16]

Whether Pierre Mayeux discovered the Louisiana opportunity by way of brochure, advertisement or gossip at the local tavern is not known, but like thousands of other young couples, in the cold springtime of 1720 Pierre and Marie found themselves in such dire straits that they had little option but to say goodbye to family and friends, look into the eyes of their loved ones one last time, rid themselves of practically all their possessions, and make their way across France to the port city of La Rochelle on the west coast. Somewhere along the journey to La Rochelle, most likely in Paris, Pierre signed a contract with John Law's Company of the Indies to serve as an *engage*, an indentured servant, for a term of three years.

He was promised 400 livre per year for a salary[17], which was meager indeed, but there would be almost no expense in living. His travel from Maintenay to the coast, and passage from there to Lousiana, would be fully covered by the Company. Once settled in Louisiana he could build his own house without cost, raise and hunt most of the food, and gain additional income from the sale of deerskins and other items to the nearby Indians. His appointment was not to just any concession, but to John Law's personal concession at Arkansas Post, over 600 miles upriver from mouth of the Mississippi.

The trip from Maintenay to La Rochelle took a week or more, with stops in Rouen, Bernay, Alençon, Le Mans and Les Herbiers. The couple would have taken in the sights and tried to commit to memory every building in every town, every face in every inn, taking with them as much of France as they could hold in their hearts. When they arrived in La Rochelle they were taken to the Company housing along the docks to await boarding the flute ship *Le Profond*. What they found was dismal.

The conditions in the company housing were not much better than the notorious prisons like the Salpétriére. Although there were no chains or shackles, the dwelling was deplorably cold and infested with rats. Beds were stacked two or three high and there was no privacy for couples within the damp and cold stone walls. It must have run through their minds that back in Maintenay even the farm animals fared better in lodging. For a month or more Pierre and Marie would share their temporary home with hundreds of others bound for Louisiana. The weeks of waiting would have been spent walking along the wharfs, wandering the streets in the city, visiting at the fountains with others waiting for the voyage, and enduring days of rain and cold wind blowing in from the sea.

Though they probably didn't realize it, the couple was fortunate to have been sent to La Rochelle instead of the port city of Lorient, two days up the coast and the official port for the Company of the Indies. Most of the company ships sailed from there, where the living conditions in Lorient made La Rochelle seem like a holiday escape. With inadequate housing for the mass of people making their way to a new life in Louisiana, tent cities were pitched in the squares and parks of Lorient. There was not enough food or medicine to care for the travelers, and of the 3,991 *engages* known to have arrived in Lorient, nearly 2,000 died from a cholera epidemic that swept through the "holding pens" of the city. [18] While most of the passengers leaving Lorient were French, a sizable number of Germans and Swiss also made the journey. The ship *Deux Frères*, which left Lorient in November 1720 after a five month delay brought on by the epidemic, unwittingly brought the disease on board and saw half of its passengers die in transit, with only 160 reaching Louisiana.[19] Of the 1300 Germans who boarded the ships bound for Louisiana, 500 died at sea, and another 500 died after arrival, leaving only 300 workers who actually made it to their appointed concessions.[20]

While Pierre and Marie waited in La Rochelle, the ship was fitted and readied for the long journey across the Atlantic. Preparing a ship for a transatlantic voyage was no small task. First, the captain and crew had to be chosen. The Company hired the Brigadier of the Marine Guards at Brest as its commander, Captain M. De Guermeur,[21] and a crew of 56 men, including sixteen ship's boys who were all fifteen years old.[22] *Le Profond* was a 350 ton flute style ship, flat at the bottom and built for hauling cargo. The tons did not refer to the weight of the ship itself, but to the amount of cargo it could transport. A ton, or tun, was a cask of wine holding 252 gallons at 2,240 pounds, and tonnage became the standard volume measurement for the tall sailing ships of Europe. Approximately 120 feet long and 30 feet wide, the ship was fitted with sixteen cannon for protection against pirates and unfriendly navy ships, particularly the English. In addition to supplies and cargo, *Le Profond* carried 263 passengers to Louisiana.

After the captain and crew were secured, the ship had to be careened. This involved removing all the vessel's ballast, then using cables and pullies attached to the lower masts, and gently pulling the ship down on one side. Workmen replaced any damaged or rotting planks, filled the seams with oakum, a loose fiber made by untwisting old ropes, and then coated the entire hull with pitch and tar to waterproof it. When one side was repaired, the ship was hoisted upright, lowered to the other side, and the process repeated.

When the careening was completed, the ship was refloated and workers scraped and painted the surface of the hull. Finally, the ballast, usually rocks, gravel and old iron, was again loaded into the bottom of the vessel. Cargo also served as ballast, so as fresh water and wine were consumed on the trip, the casks were refilled with seawater to provide weight.

Finally, the ship was packed with cargo. In the case of *Le Profond*, the cargo consisted of materials bound for the concession of Diron Dartaguette, in what is now Baton Rouge but was at the time nothing more than a few tents pitched along the river. Careening, ballasting and loading the ship usually took about a month[23].

All the while *Le Profond* was being readied for sail, Pierre and Marie would have spent their time watching the progress, walking along the piers, and making acquaintance with others who, like themselves, found life in France so desperate that they were willing to leave it behind and sail to Louisiana. When the day of sailing arrived, the passengers were assisted by the ship's boys who loaded their minimal cargo, perhaps a single trunk, into the dark caverns below deck. They had all been briefed on what to expect at sea, and with the the tendency of desperate people to hope for better days to come, they would have thought that anything would be better than the hell hole they had been enduring for the last month. They couldn't have been more wrong.

---

[1] The 1745 Pointe Coupee census lists him as 48 years old.

[2] For details of the economic and social unrest following the death of Louis XIV, see Janet Gleeson, *Millionare: The Philanderer, Gambler, and Duelist Who Invented Modern Finance*, Simon & Schuster, New York, 1999, pp. 103-117.

[3] cf. James F. Barnett, Jr, *The Natchez Indians*, University Press of Mississippi, Jackson, 2007, p. 81; Gleeson, p. 137.

[4] Morris S. Arnold, *Colonial Arkansas*, University of Arkansas Press, Fayetteville, 1991, p. 127.

[5] Pierre F.X. de Charlevoix, *Charlevoix's Louisiana: Selections from History and the Journal*, Louisiana State University Press, Baton Rouge, 1977, p. 37f.

[6] Ellen C. Merrill, *Germans of Louisiana*, Pelican Publishing Company, Gretna, 2005, p. 20.

[7] Gwendolyn Midlo Hall, *Africans In Colonial Louisiana*, Louisiana State University Press, Baton Rouge, 1992 p. 7f.

[8] *Ibid*, p. 8.

[9] *Ibid*, p. 10.

[10] Charlevoix, p. 282.

[11] John Hanno, *The Settlement Of The German Coast Of Louisiana And The Creoles Of German Descent*, The German American Historical Society, Philadelphia, 1909, p. 18;

Gleeson, p. 174. Anne Francoise Roland is the author's 7th great grandmother. Details of her life, including transcripts of the court records detailing her arrest, are available from his personal files.

[12] Barnett, p. 77; Gleeson, p. 172f.

[13] Gleeson, p. 176.

[14] *Ibid*, p. 167f.

[15] Hanno, p. 18.

[16] Gleeson, p. 169.

[17] The typical wage for an indentured servant was 400 livre; Gleeson, p. 262.

[18] Merrill, p. 21.

[19] *Ibid*, p. 22.

[20] Merill, p. 22.

[21] French, p. 78

[22] Details of the crew and passengers are found in the official Company records (http://www.memoiredeshommes.sga.defense.gouv.fr/indes/sous-serie_2/2P/inv2P/20/III/D/1721), as well as in a private journal kept by a surgeon on board now held by the Chicago History Museum (http://www.worldcat.org/title/page-du-pratz-manuscripts-1720-1724/oclc/712673693).

[23] For details of fitting the tall ships, see Gilles Prouix, *Between France and New France - Life Aboard the Tall Sailing Ships*; Dundurn Press, Toronto, 1984, p. 42ff.

Chapter Two
The Atlantic
1720

When *Le Profond* left the port of La Rochelle in June of 1720, the crew and passengers knew they might not see land again for more than three months, and this was an optimistic guess. Any number of variables from storms at sea to pirates to windless days or weeks could extend the trip to as long as six months.

Le Profond was a flute style ship, designed not for battle but for transporting cargo, with a flat bottom which allowed it to maneuver waters as shallow as thirteen feet.[1] While its exact dimensions are unknown, a flute of 200 tons was usually no more than 75 feet long.[2] With a cargo hold of 350 tons, *Le Profond* may have been as long as 120 feet. This vessel, no more than about one third of a football field in length, would become a traveling home for Pierre and Marie, 261 other passengers, and 56 crewmen. As if this were not crowded enough, the ship also had to transport enough fresh water, wine, and foodstuff for the journey including live animals such as pigs, chickens and cattle, as well as supplies destined for the Mississippi Company's Dartaguette concession, at the tent town of Baton Rouge.

Getting under way from La Rochelle was itself a test of endurance. The week before departure Pierre and Marie joined the other passengers for a briefing of the rules for life on board the ship. The passengers were assigned quarters either in one of the storerooms where three tiered cots with mattresses were attached to the walls, or in the between decks where hammocks were suspended from the beams. Sometimes a piece of canvas would be strung between the hammocks or cots to provide a slight measure of privacy for the passengers.[3] One traveler who made a similar trip to Canada in 1734 wrote, "We were crammed into this dark, foul place like so many sardines; it was impossible to get into bed without banging our heads and knees twenty times. A sense of propriety prohibited us from undressing, and after a while our clothes caused us appalling discomfort. The motion of the vessel would dismantle the apparatus, slinging people into each other's cots. Once I was dropped, still in my bed, upon a poor Canadian officer, descending upon him like the Angel of Death. I lay there for five or ten minutes, unable to extricate myself from my cot, with the officer half suffocated and barely able to summon the strength to swear."[4]

The instruction-filled briefing would continue: the days would begin at seven with breakfast served on deck when weather permitted. Dinner would be served at six and passengers were to bring their bowls and cups on deck for the meals, and clean them afterwards. Portals were to be kept closed during high seas. Candles and lanterns were strictly forbidden because of the danger of fire at sea, and pipe smoking was permitted only on deck.

By the 18th century, the harbor at La Rochelle had become so filled with silt that large ships were unable to dock there and instead had to weigh anchor in the bay, where the passengers and cargo were ferried to make ready for departure. After several days of waiting for the right winds, the word would spread among the passengers that the captain had ordered the anchor to be raised and had hoisted a flag on the topmast to signal that they were finally getting under way. He would also order the cannon fired to hurry anyone who might not yet be on board. This cannon blast also signaled a flurry of activity as the sailors unfurled the topsail. Soon the passengers would feel the ship lurch beneath them and begin moving slowly through the bay and out toward the sea[5]. It was traditional for the captain to order a seven cannon salute to the city and then direct that the rest of the sails be unfurled.[6] As the passengers gathered along the rails of the ship and felt the wind catch the sails they watched the city of La Rochelle begin to shrink in their sight, and with it France.. The ships from La Rochelle sailed up the coast to Isle Dieu or Belle-Isle, then set the course westward for the open sea.[7]

The joke that air travel is hours of tedious boredom interrupted by moments of sheer terror was no joke for the seafarers of the 18th century. For them it was weeks of tedious boredom sometimes interrupted by days of sheer terror.

The boredom consisted of monotonous days passing time on deck playing card games and visiting with fellow passengers, or in rough, cold or rainy weather waiting below deck in the bunks or hammocks. Sometimes the boredom was tempered by passengers gathering on deck and singing songs accompanied by flute or fiddle or any other musical instruments that passengers may have brought along. The food, too, was monotonous. The live animals were slaughtered, generally early in the trip and usually only for the officers or company officials on board, for soups and stews. For passengers the standard fare consisted of two ship's biscuits a day, 3/4 pint of wine to be mixed with water, three pints of water for drinking and cooking, and perhaps a vegetable stew or broth. In inclement weather when cooking was impossible the diet was reduced to biscuits.[8] Not infrequently, the water or food would go bad. Marc-Antoine Caillot, who sailed from France to Louisiana in 1729, nine years after Pierre and Marie, recalled, "The pint of water we received had little worms wriggling in it and was stinking and greenish besides. Moreover, it was very hot, but nonetheless, we drank this nectar with pleasure."[9] He also recounts a humorous story showing how precious meat was on board a ship: "I saw a little drama between some sailors to whom a goose had been given that had immediately fallen into the sea. They jumped in after it. They not only had trouble catching it but also had to fight off sharks, which were out to get both the game and the hunters."[10]

For the religious among the passengers the boredom was somewhat assuaged by Catholic ceremonies. Most of the ships from France had a priest on board who, when weather permitted, would lead mass on deck on Sundays and holy days, and offer masses of thanksgiving after enduring a particularly harrowing event.

The first terror of the sea to be experienced by the previously land-bound passengers was sea sickness, usually striking immediately after setting sail. Caillot recorded in his journal,

> "We left the port with favorable winds. I began to take pleasure in finding myself on board a ship that sailed quite well, and also in seeing most of the passengers sad and pale and subject to unending dizziness. I was feeling overjoyed not to have their deplorable luck, when, as I lost sight of land and the ship started to move in a more agitated manner, I began to feel certain sensations that made my delight turn to dolefulness. Nevertheless, this passed, while all the others with whom I was traveling just got sicker and sicker. I would have preferred to be in the same predicament as my fellow passengers because of the vexation I suffered from not being able to talk to them and seeing them continuously vomiting in the most awful manner. A few days passed in that way, then a few passengers regained their appetite; the others vomited only rarely and recuperated with the passing of each day. Unfortunately for me, there came a wind that was stronger than ordinary, which put us all in a sorry state, especially me, who had not yet had that bad time of it. For seven days I was unable to drink or eat or sleep and I always had dizzy spells and awful disgorgements."[11]

Even veteran seafarers were not immune. Jean-François-Benjamin Dumont who made his second voyage to Louisiana aboard the *Portefaix* in March, 1721 recorded in his memoir, "We set sail, but the ship had barely passed Belle-Isle when I began to suffer seasickness as if I had never been to sea before."[12]

Perhaps the most terrifying events at sea were weather related. Caillot records a frightening calm that hit them early in their journey. "A completely flat calm came upon us, and that made me more anxious than the storm we had just gotten through. For not seeing a breath of wind, and because a ship at sea without movement is a sorry sight, plus seeing that it was unlikely we would have any wind anytime soon. I fell even more deeply into my thoughts than I had before. Besides this, I heard the seamen swearing they were mortal enemies of the calm because, ordinarily, as long as it endures, their rations are cut back in order to make sure they will last."[13] Dumont recorded that on the final leg of his journey, between Cap Francais (modern Cap Haitien, on the north coast of Haiti) and Biloxi, a passage that might take as little as a week to make, "We tried to round Cabo San Antonio but were held up there for two weeks by calms, a result of sailing too close to the island of Cuba, which doubtless blocked our wind." The primary threat of the calms was the consequent food shortage. But doldrum days also left the ships open to the attack of pirates who in their smaller and faster corsairs could often take advantage of the unmoving flutes and frigates. Dumont continued, "There was there a small corsair that, hoping to capture a larger prize than the small boat it already held, came out to engage us. But she paid dearly for her courage and curiosity. The one cannonball that we fired at her hit its mark and forced her to abruptly reverse course and flee to the nearest port on the coast."[14]

The French ships that sailed the Atlantic were threatened by a variety of pirates. English, Spanish, and Moroccan pirates and privateers sailed the seas in search of vulnerable ships that could be commandeered for their cargo and for taking the crew and passengers captive during times of war. The privateers, working under the auspices of the King of England or Spain, were allowed to sell any captured ships or goods, giving a percentage of their gain to the Crown. They were also handsomely rewarded for any prisoners taken, who would in turn be used in wartime negotiations or held for ransom until their freedom was purchased by France. France, of course, had its own arrangement with pirates, and during the 18th century offered 50 livre for every prisoner captured.[15]

To fall into the hands of the English or Spanish pirates was bad enough, but the worst threat was the Moroccan pirates based along the Barbary Coast of of North Africa who plied their craft as far away as the Atlantic coastline of the Americas. To fall into their hands rarely meant being held as hostage until purchased by a European homeland, but instead to be sold into slavery in the Ottoman Empire. It is estimated that between 1530 and 1780 over a million Europeans suffered the fate of a life of slavery at the hands of the Barbary pirates.[16]

When pirates actually were sighted, the ship went into full alarm including the passengers. The decks were cleared, and everyone was ordered to bring any bedrolls or other padding above deck to line the walls of the ship as a precaution against an attack. The sailors manned the cannon - *Le Profond* had 16 on board - and the passengers were given firearms, swords, spears and axes. Sometimes the crew and passengers would spend the entire night on guard, prepared to battle for their lives if necessary. 17

Worse than the calms and the pirates were the storms at sea which could arise unexpectedly and toss the ship like a matchbox. Sometimes the calms were literally "the calm before the storm," and people aboard the still and lifeless ship would helplessly watch the horizon as a bank of dark, lightning-filled clouds tumultuously rolled toward them, causing the waves to mount, foreboding the approaching chaos. No part of the journey was protected from the threat of possible storms, and storms could be not only inconvenient and unsettling, but even life-threatening. At best, an approaching storm guaranteed a day of being tossed in the waves and thrown off course; at worst a storm might leave a wake of destruction and death, lightening hitting and destroying the mast, sailors being washed overboard, or even the entire ship going down in the walls of waves that battered it.

Caillot described many storms in the account of his 1731 transatlantic voyage. Describing dinner after the first storm at sea which struck soon after they had left France, he wrote,

> "We went below to take our places at the table, but we were not there two minutes when a second blast of wind struck us broadside and made the ship lean so much that it made us fall down upon one another. Not a single dish stayed on the table, even though they had been secured. Everyone got up as best they could, one with two broken teeth, another completely covered in sauce, and they came to tell us that we had almost lost our mast because of the shock of the wave. That cruelly gave me pause to think about the rest of the voyage and what might be in store for us, since we had barely left the roadstead and were having such bad weather."[18]

When a storm approached, all passengers and nonessential crew members were ordered below deck and consigned to their bunks where they tied themselves down and waited out the winds and rain, sometimes for days on end. The remaining sailors manned their stations, tied to the ship with ropes to protect themselves from being swept overboard.

When most people imagine a storm at sea, they envision waves of five, or ten, or even twenty feet high. But modern oceanographers and meteorologists have calculated the statistical possibility for an Atlantic storm to produce waves of up to 200 feet high. The storm made famous in Sebastian Junger's book, *The Perfect Storm,* was estimated to have produced a wave over 100 feet high. Being caught in the trough of such a giant wave would mean certain destruction for the ship. The water pressure at the bottom of the wave would give it the force of a fast moving wall of concrete[19], guaranteeing the loss of all souls aboard any ship unlucky enough to be caught in its angry path. Seafarers have described being tossed about in their bunks, not knowing which way was up or down or sideways. Describing another storm later in his journey, Caillot writes, "our ship plunged into abysses that were surrounded by waves like mountains." Awaking in the night to the taste of salt water, his body drenched and being completely disoriented, he cried out to the chaplain, "We are lost, Lord have mercy on us." Stumbling his way onto the deck, he saw that, "the sea was extraordinarily agitated and all on fire. The rain and the lightening seemed to throw their light for the soul purpose of showing us the chasm. The wind and darkness of the heavens were horrible." The storm continued in its fury for three days.[20]

Another meteorological threat on the sea is the waterspout, the ocean's version of a tornado. Unlike a land-based tornado, in which the winds are filled with dirt and debris, a waterspout is a fast moving whirlwind filled with water. If a sailing ship was struck by a waterspout, there was the danger of the ship breaking the connection between the sea and the spout, causing the circling fury of airborne water to collapse onto the boat, instantly plunging it to destruction. To avoid such a fate, when caught in the path of an approaching waterspout the captain would order cannonballs fired into it, with the goal that enough metal would break the spout's connection to the sea so it would collapse a safe distance from the ship.[21]

But there was more than boredom and terror to life at sea. There were also wonders to be seen. Caillot recounted seeing, "a huge number of flying fish, some of which got caught up in our sails and fell to the deck."[22] There were whales breaching the surface and shooting geysers of water from their blowholes, dolphins playfully racing along the sides of the ship, Portuguese men of war bobbing in the surf, an array of colorful tropical fish, and as land was approached, unfamiliar sea birds. And there was the completely unexpected pageant of "baptism" played out when a ship crossed the Tropic of Cancer.

The drama would begin a few days before reaching the Tropic as officers and crew began to whisper suspiciously and cast knowing glances at one another, leaving the passengers curious and suspecting that something might be wrong. Any concerns expressed by the passengers would be dismissed as empty imaginations or the result of mind tricks from being at sea too long. At dinner, the day before the event, a strange figure dressed in colorful rags would balance himself on the ropes of the sail and proclaim, "I am the messenger of *Bonhomme Tropique,* god of the sea! He sends me to announce that you approach the Tropic of Cancer and tomorrow you shall cross it."

As the confused passengers looked on in wonder, the messenger would continue, "My Lord Neptune, for that is another of his names, informs me that this fair ship is called *Le Profond* and aptly it is named for it plies the deep waters of the sea. And the commander of the vessel is Captain Guermeur, a man of noble character and great skill. I am ordered to welcome the good captain and all souls on board to the kingdom of Lord Tropique. He is delighted that such an honorable company arrives in his realm and he deigns to welcome you himself on the morrow."

As the passengers and many of the crew stood listening in amazement and delight, the messenger of the god would continue, "My Lord also requests that those who have not before visited his realm be made ready for baptism, and bids the good captain to make preparations for the celebration to come."

Suddenly another voice would boom from somewhere on deck, "We give good greetings to your master." The passengers would turn to see the captian, in the case of *Le Profond,* Captain Guermeur, standing on top of the forecastle where the officers quartered. Holding a brass speaking trumpet to his mouth the captain would shout, "Please inform Lord *Bonhomme Tropique* that we gladly anticipate his visit among us, and will make due preparations for his arrival." When the passengers looked again to the top of the mainmast, the messenger of the god would have appeared to vanish.

The rest of the daylight hours was a scurry of activity as the crew maneuvered two large wooden tubs into place, one on the starboard side of the ship and the other port side. Across the top of each tub was placed a long plank to serve as a seat for the baptismal candidates. Smaller tubs were placed on either side of the large ones, and then the crewmen would hoist up buckets of sea water and fill the tubs. As night fell the passengers were bidden a good nights sleep and told to prepare themselves for baptism on the next day.

After breakfast in the morning the door of the forecastle would fling open and out would spill an entourage of creatures, men or gods or demons, no one could be sure. The passengers would begin to laugh at the site of half a dozen crewmen dressed in all kinds of colorful clothes, some in women's dresses, others with bright red and yellow and blue scarves wrapped around their necks and flowing down their backs. A few would have elaborate hats with bright feathers, and all of them had their faces painted red or blue or green. As they pranced along in parade they banged pots with spoons and clanged cups together to make as much noise as they could. Perhaps one would carry a violin and play it wildly as he followed the procession toward the mainmast.

Suddenly a voice would be heard from among the sails as the passengers looked up to see a sailor disguised as the much anticipated *Bonhomme Tropique*. He had long white hair and an even longer beard made from the unraveled cords of an old rope, and beneath his patchwork robe of many colors he had a pillow on his shoulders to give him a hump on his back. On his head he wore both a red night stocking and a well worn tricorn hat with at least a dozen brilliantly colored feathers sticking out in all directions.

As soon as the procession stopped at the base of the main mast, several of his attendants climbed up to assist the god onto the deck, and someone placed a large trident in his hand which he carried like a bishop's crozier. The crowd of passengers would laugh and applaud when again there boomed the voice of the captain greeting the newly arrived deity. "We welcome you kind sir! And we bring you the good news that you have many new children to add to your family!"

The old god would make his way to the captain and embrace him, and then turn to the few others who had made past journeys across the tropic line and greeted them as dear children. "And who do we have to add to our family today?" the disguised sailor would ask in a deep voice. As the captain escorted him around the deck introducing him first to one group and then another, Lord Tropique would leap and dance with excitement. "Let the waters of baptism be prepared."

The servants of the god seated him on a large chair which was set on a makeshift platform midship between the two tubs, and the captain gave him a list off all the passengers and crew yet to be baptized. One by one the names were called out by Neptune, and each person stood before the seated god who held a kitchen pan which served as a collection plate. They were bidden to make some offering and then to be seated on the plank above the tub. If the offering was a few coins, only a trickle of water was poured over the candidates wrists, but if it was nothing at all, a bucket of water was dumped on the top of the candidates head, soaking that person, whether man or woman, while all the onlookers laughed and cheered.

When the last of the passengers and crew had been baptized *Bonhomme Tropique* would rise from his throne and call for the uninitiated officers to stand before him. After the men appeared before the god and made their offerings to him they were seated on the planks aboard each large tub and faced toward one another. When *Tropique* gave the signal, the planks were jerked forward and the officers fell butt first into the tubs. The crowd would roar with laughter and begin to clap their hands and cheer when suddenly from every direction it seemed, torrents of water would splash on everyone. Some crewmen climbed into the sails above and others were strategically scattered throughout the crowd, and they all unleashed their buckets of water at the same time. Passengers scattered, going in every direction, bumping into one another and slipping on the wet deck. Grabbing pails themselves and filling them at the tubs they would sling water back onto the crewmen. Before the fiasco came to a close there would not be a single man or woman who was not soaked to the bone.[23]

After more than two months at sea, *Le Profond* reached its only stop before continuing to Louisiana. At the cry of, "Land Ho," the passengers quickly rose from their places on the deck and rushed to the sides of the ship in hopes of sighting that thing they had all nearly forgotten - dry land. It would be a while later before their naked eyes could see the dry brown hills of Saint Domingue. Called La Isla Española by the Spaniards, the island had been controlled by them since Columbus' ships arrived there in 1492. But a hundred years before *Le Profond* arrived, French pirates began to use the western part of the island as a base for their plundering, and within a generation or two Spain had ceded to France the entire land mass, nearly 400 miles from east to west and 150 from north to south.

As the ship approached the bay of Cap Français, the captain fired a cannon to summon a harbor pilot to guide it through the rocks and sandbanks to port.[24] By the time ship dropped anchor, the passengers' minds were filled with fantasies of their first baths in over two months, fresh water, fresh vegetables and meat, good bread and wine, clean clothes, and long walks on dry land. Ships from France would lay in port in Cap Français for at least a week for restocking food and supplies, and sometimes as long as a month or more if repairs needed to be made or calms kept them from sailing.

Anchored in the harbor, the passengers were unloaded into smaller boats and brought ashore where they were guided to their simple lodgings which, compared to their cramped hammocks and cots seemed like stepping into a palace. Here on this Caribbean island the passengers would have their first experience with a non-European culture.

The first thing that caught their attention was the exotic beauty of the Creole people who populated the city, their dark and smooth skins contrasted with the dazzling white clothes they wore. The women wore long white muslin skirts and matching blouses, having, "the appearance of goddesses, capable of ravishing all of the proudest of hearts,"[25] and many of the men wore lightweight white shirts, some with equally light jackets, white breeches gathered at the knee and white stockings. Most of them were accompanied by slaves who were similarly dressed, the first black people ever seen by many of the newly arrived French travelers. Caillot described the scene on the streets: "These Creole women have many slaves, and this is the reason they are so lazy, even to the point that if they drop something on the ground, they have the patience to call a slave five or six times to come pick up what is just at their feet."[26]

With a population of about 6,000 French and four times as many African slaves, Cap Français wasn't large compared to Paris or La Rochelle, but it dwarfed the Mayeux's hometown of Maintenay. Passengers from the ships strolled through the town, sightseeing along the way. Coming to the edge of the town, some would follow dirt roads into the countryside where the buildings were no longer board, brick or stone, but cane walls with thatched roofs. Those who ventured beyond the town were startled to see African men and women walking in broad daylight naked as the day they were born. Nakedness was the common chosen attire among many of the resident Africans who thought the white man's clothing to be nothing less than silly in the sun soaked hot climate of the island.[27]

Instead of the stale biscuits that had been their mainstay for the last two months, the temporary residents of Cap Français would dine on grilled chicken, rice, beans, fresh bread, and plates of fruits they had never encountered before: coconuts, oranges, bananas, guavas, pineapples, pomegranates and mangoes[28], leaving them to dread resuming their journey to Louisiana.

On Sundays during their stay, many passengers attended Mass at the church on the edge of town. Making their way toward the church they heard the bell ringing and were surprised to see the bell tower was nothing more than an oak tree in front of the church with a bell hanging from a limb. Streaming into the church, and walking along the streets of the town were many men and women, some French, some Creole, and some African, all dressed in brilliant white, the women carrying so many white parasols that it looked like a field of moving lilies before their eyes[29].

Inevitably, the passengers would soon have to exchange this brief stay in a tropical paradise for life resumed on board ship, but the short remainder of the trip, anywhere from a week to a month, was made more bearable with clean clothes, fresh food and water, and the hope of arriving soon in Louisiana. Making their way to the water's edge, they waited their turns to climb into the small boats that transported them back to the ship, and back to the personal hell holes they had called home since leaving La Rochelle. Once all passengers were on board, the captain fired a cannon in salute to the city, raised the anchor and hoisted the sails, waiting for a gentle breeze to push the ship back to sea.

If the weather was favorable, the next day they would pass between the two large islands of Jamaica, under English rule, and Cuba, under Spain, separated by about sixty miles of water. On a clear day the passengers could just make out the outline of the mountains on either side of the ship. Rounding the western tip of Cuba, they entered the Gulf of Mexico. Little did the passengers know that the worst seas of the entire trip were likely to lie ahead of them. Late August in the Gulf of Mexico could be fickle. It might be smooth sailing all the way to the coast of North America, or it might just as well be a hurricane.

On Monday, September 16,[30] the weary passengers of *Le Profond* once again heard the shout, "Land ho!" At last Louisiana was within sight. Climbing to their feet and gazing out past the bow of the ship, they saw in the distance a small spit of land. Because the waters of Biloxi were too shallow for ships to enter directly, they instead dropped anchor at a small island, five miles to the south, where cargo and passengers were unloaded into smaller boats and taken to Biloxi, the capital of Louisiana. The passengers tried to imagine what the place must be like, with the painting from the brochure flashing in their minds - the beautiful bay, the palm trees along the beach, the hillsides dotted with chateaus, the friendly natives greeting the Frenchmen. But Biloxi would have to wait. Their first stop in this paradise would be the desolate, plague stricken, rat infested Ship Island.

[1] Gilles Proulx, *Between France and New France: Life Aboard the Tall Sailing Ships*, Dundren Press, Toronto, 1984, p. 20.
[2] ProulxIbid, p. 25
[3] *Ibid*, p. 100f.
[4] *Ibid*, p. 102.
[5] *Ibid*, p. 47f.
[6] Dumont, p. 97.
[7] Proulx, p. 47.
[8] *Ibid*, p. 106f.
[9] Caillot, p. 46.
[10] *Ibid*, p. 21.
[11] *Ibid*, p. 18.
[12] Dumont, p. 137.
[13] Caillot, p. 20.
[14] Dumont, p. 138.
[15] Proulx, p. 72.
[16] Robert Davis, *Christian Slaves, Muslim Masters: White Slavery in the Mediterranean, The Barbary Coast, and Italy, 1500-1800,* Macmillan, New York, 2004, pp. 3-26.
[17] Caillot, p. 25f.
[18] *Ibid*, p. 20f.
[19] Sebatian Junger, *The Perfect Storm: A True Story of Men Against the Sea,* Norton, NY, 2009, p. 119.
[20] Caillot, p. 24.
[21] *Ibid*, p. 63.
[22] *Ibid*, p. 23
[23] Dumont, p. 97ff; Caillot, p. 29.
[24] *Ibid*, p. 100.
[25] Caillot, p. 52.
[26] *Ibid*, p. 53.
[27] *Ibid*, p. 51.
[28] *Ibid*, p. 51.
[29] *Ibid*, p. 53.
[30] French, p. 78.

Chapter Three
Biloxi
1720

When Pierre and Marie Mayeux arrived on Ship Island on September 16, 1720, Biloxi was the third in a succession of French capitals for Louisiana. The Quebec born explorer, ship captain, soldier and later governor Pierre Le Moyne d'Iberville, recognized as the Father of Louisiana, had been tasked by the French government with discovering the mouth of the Mississippi River and establishing a fortress/capital there. When he located the mouth of the river with the help of local Indians who remembered the French explorer La Salle, he found there was no suitable site in the delta to build a fort. Instead, he moved east and built Fort Maurepas in 1699 in what is now Ocean Springs, Mississippi, two miles east of present day Biloxi.

In 1702 Iberville and his men discovered a more suitable and healthy site for the primary fort on the Mobile River and built Fort Louis. The new site was more strategically located, allowing the French to keep eyes on the Indians, the English to the northeast in the Carolinas, and the Spanish in Florida. As settlers began to build around Fort Louis, the town of La Mobile was born. Dauphin Island, off the coast of Mobile, became the anchoring point for French ships, and when its channel became choked with sand in 1717, the capital was moved once more, this time to a new site across the bay from Fort Maurepas, and was named Nouveau-Biloxi, New Biloxi.

Biloxi in 1720 was nothing more than a tent city with a few wooden buildings situated immediately adjacent to the beach. Charlevoix who spent a month there in March, 1722, wrote, "A worse place than this could not have been chosen for the general quarters of the colony."[1] He described the weather in extremes. The early part of the month was bitter cold with winds blowing off the Gulf, only to be replaced by mid-month with scorching heat: "The heats were very troublesome in Biloxi, from the middle of March; and, I imagine, when once the sun has taken effect upon the sand, the heat will become excessive."[2] In the months before *Le Profond* arrived, more than 4,000 company workers arrived hoping to be dispersed to the various concessions throughout Louisiana.[3] The conditions awaiting them were in many instances worse than those faced during their voyages.

Ship Island, not much more than a spit of sand sitting in the Gulf of Mexico south of Biloxi, offered a relatively deep harbor on its north side, but the twelve miles between the island and the capital averaged only between 12 and 15 feet deep, making it impossible for large ships to dock near the mainland. Ships would anchor at the island, passengers would disembark, and supplies would be unloaded to be transported to the mainland by smaller boats. Le Page Du Pratz, the French historian and naturalist who spent from 1718 to 1734 in Louisiana and whose journeys somewhat mirrored those of Pierre and Marie, wrote,

> "Biloxi is situate opposite Ship Island, and four leagues from it. I could never guess the reason, why the principal settlement was made at this place, nor why the capital should be built at it; as nothing could be more repugnant to good sense; vessels not being able to come within four leagues of it; but what was worse, nothing could be brought from them, but by changing the boats three different times, from a smaller size to another still smaller; after which they had to go upwards of an hundred paces with small carts through the water to unload the least boats."[4]

Even the short trip from Ship Island to Biloxi could be filled with danger. Jean-François-Benjamin Dumont, who arrived in March, 1721, records,

> "At two in the afternoon on the day following our arrival in this port, the officers among the ship's passengers, eight of us, set off from the ship in a shallop with our trunks and wine chests…For the moment, we enjoyed a calm sea, and so it was the power of the oars of the seamen on board that had to carry us to the mainland of New Biloxi. But as we were about to arrive at that settlement, there came up a sudden blast of wind from the west so furious that, with the tide ebbing at the same time, it drove us back into the open sea, in spite of all the efforts we could put to the oars. It threw us, I say, beyond the passage used by ships, and what

was worse, the night was so black that we could scarcely make out the far end of our shallop. One could see only by the lightning, which struck repeatedly, accompanied by furious rolls of thunder. At the same time, the waves, swollen and angry, promised us nothing but shipwreck and inevitable death...We were pounded again and again by mountains of water hitting the side of our shallop and seeming to want to sink it in the sea...Finally, however, the storm ceased, the clouds lifted, the sun appeared overhead, and in the light, what did we see? No land in any direction. We were in the open sea." After finding a compass and sailing for an hour and a half they finally caught sight of land, the deserted Cat Island several miles southwest of their destination.[5]

Some passengers had the misfortune of having to spend weeks or months on Ship Island, and some never made it off the island. In the spring of 1721 an epidemic raged through Biloxi killing so many people that the priest responsible for record keeping was unable to keep an accurate account.[6] During these dangerous seasons, newly arriving passengers were not allowed to leave Ship Island for fear of contracting the disease. Instead, they remained on the island, continuing their diet of ship's food, sleeping in the sand, and fighting off rats, the only animal inhabitants of the place. Those who died while still on the island were incinerated in a furnace.

How long Pierre and Marie Mayeux remained on the island is not known. If they were among the lucky, it was only a matter of days. But life in Biloxi was not much better. Once ashore, Pierre and Marie discovered that the promises portrayed in the advertisement pictures were works of pure fiction. Biloxi may have been the capital of the Louisiana territory, but in reality it was nothing but a mosquito infested tent city. The great majority of inhabitants were, like them, passers-through, eventually headed to one of the Mississippi Company's inland concessions. The permanent residents were a motley mix of about 300 people including military men who despised their assignments, laborers who made their living dealing with the people in transit, and slaves. No one liked living in Biloxi. No one *wanted* to be there. This created an environment ripe for corruption, laziness, and a general sense of uncaring and despair. Although Biloxi was the designated point of arrival for the thousands of French workers, there was absolutely no infrastructure to provide for their care or health. It was an oversight of epic proportions. There were no arrangement for securing foodstuffs from inland, no hunters designated to provide wild game, and no farmers working crops - the sandy soil was unsuited to such an enterprise. The entire population lived off what could be secured from the nearby Indians, from fishing, or more dependably, from the unscrupulous pilfering of the supplies aboard the ships arriving from France, goods intended for the various Company concessions. As a rule of habit, the local authorities took the incoming supplies by force and used them to feed the soldiers, leaving the sea worn travelers dependant on whatever fish, crabs and oysters they could catch or harvest from the beach shores, and whatever crops the natives might trade.[7]

Three months after Pierre and Marie Mayeux arrived in Biloxi, in January, 1721, the population of Biloxi was counted at 1,249 people. That winter an additional 880 arrived from France. Sometime in the spring of the year another boat filled with African slaves arrived in Biloxi and conditions were so severe that the slaves were sold for a very low price to anyone who could feed them. The Company kept most of the slaves for its own enterprise, and during the food shortage many of them died of starvation, along with many of the French and Germans immigrants.[8] Of the 2,000 people in Biloxi at the time, nearly half of them died before arriving at their concessions.[9] By August of that year food began to be in extreme shortage. Dumont, who arrived in Biloxi in June, wrote, "The soldiers of the Company had to go to the Indian villages, both the Biloxis and the Pascagoulas. These inhabitants of the forest received them very well, furnishing them with supplies of corn, which they cooked for them along with plenty of deer or buffalo meat or, if meat was not available, with bear grease. As for the rest of us, we remained in our barracks, with our soldiers reduced to beans and peas with a little salt meat, but no bread and very little eau-de-vie."[10]

Du Pratz, who was in Biloxi about this time, described the land there as,

> "...nothing but a fine sand, as white and shining as snow, on which no kind of greens can be raised; besides, the being extremely incommoded with rats, which swarm there in the sand, and at that time even ate the very stocks of the guns, the famine being there so very great, that more than five hundred people died of hunger; bread being very dear, and flesh-meat still more rare."[11] The famine, Du Pratz commented, was the result of "the arrival of several grantees all at once; so as to have neither provisions, nor boats to transport them to the places of their destination, as the company had obliged themselves to do."[12]

While the famine was laying waste to the town, the corrupt commandant had secretly hidden eight barrels of good flour commandeered from the arriving ships - each barrel being enough to feed a family for four months - and was planning to sell them to the highest bidder. The barrels were seized by the royal lieutenant and distributed to the starving soldiers.[13]

Conditions were so severe that mutiny was not uncommon among the soldiers, some abandoning their posts and joining with the English in the Carolinas, others arrested and punished "in Indian fashion," having their heads crushed as a warning to anyone else who might be entertaining similar ideas.

The scene, then, during the Biloxi stay of Pierre and Marie, was one of utter chaos and destitution. Thousands of workers were arriving on the ships from France, what food they had was being hijacked by the local authorities, a plague of rats infested the whole town, disease (most likely cholera) was sweeping through the tented camps, people were forced to resort to fishing and oyster hunting (many dying from tainted oysters), hundreds were starving and dying all around them, and there were no boats to take them to their destination.

Assigned to John Law's personal concession at Arkansas Post, Pierre and Marie spent their time in Biloxi surviving, scrounging for food, battling sickness, and working on building their own boats for the trip upriver. With them from the time of their departure from La Rochelle was another young couple, Jaques and Marguerite Cantrelle, whose story would parallel that of the Mayeux's for the next nine years.

Pierre and Marie stayed in Biloxi from September, 1720 until April or May, 1721. Their journey up the Mississippi River would hold sights, wonders and experiences that caused everything that had happened to them since leaving La Rochelle to pale in comparison. These country folk from France, who had endured such hardships in their crossing the Atlantic and arriving in Biloxi, were about to step into a new world as foreign to them as a distant planet would be to modern explorers. They were about to become real pioneers.

---

[1] Charlevoix, p. 182.
[2] *Ibid*, p. 187f.
[3] Hanno, p. 21.
[4] Du Pratz, p. 78.
[5] Dumont, p. 139f.
[6] Hanno, p. 23.
[7] *Ibid*, p. 22.
[8] Dumont, p. 147.
[9] Caillot, p. 144, footnote 12.
[10] Dumont, p. 144.
[11] Du Pratz, p. 78.
[12] *Ibid*, p. 79.
[13] Dumont, 145.

Chapter Four
The Mississippi River
1721

Arkansas Post, the promised paradise in the making that was to be the first colony of the Mississippi Company's campaign to populate and civilize France's Louisiana territory, lay more than 600 river miles upstream from the mouth of the Mississippi River where it dumped into the Gulf of Mexico. To make the journey took between three and six months, depending on weather conditions, stops along the way, and disruptions of the trip brought on by a host of possible setbacks including unfriendly Native Americans. But, before Pierre and Marie Mayeux and their company could make the journey, they first had to assist in building and loading the boats that would carry them up the river.

Louis-Elias Stutheus, the agent responsible for establishing the colony on the Arkansas River, arrived in Biloxi in early April,

1721, eight months after *Le Profond*, and died a few days later on April 12, leaving Jaques Levens to succeed him as director. Levens organized the expedition and was appointed as the civil judge for the Arkansas territory[1], but he never actually went to Arkansas himself.[2] The company of 80 *engages*, along with a handful of soldiers to provide protection and possibly a few slaves to add manpower for the hard work ahead, left Biloxi sometime in late April or early May in a flotilla of five large pirogues. The boats were on average 40 or 50 feet long by five feet wide, and each could carry thirty men or up to fifty tons of supplies. The pirogues had seats for the rowers and were guided by a rudder manned by the coxswain.[3] Sails were useless on the river because of the constant turns, but could be used during the initial stages of the journey along the coastline of the Gulf of Mexico.[4]

Setting sail from Biloxi, the entourage first traveled sixty miles along the coastline, past Bay St. Louis, and into what is called Lake Borgne, a lagoon of brackish water where fresh water from the Pontchartrain Basin flows into the salt waters of the Gulf. Due to erosion, Borgne is now part of the Gulf, but in the 18th century it was separated from the salt water by wetlands. Once on Lake Borgne, the *engages* rowed northwest and crossed into Lake Pontchartrain. In the dry season, portage was necessary to enter into Pontchartrain, but in the wet spring months it was possible to row through the riverlets of the marshland that divided the two lakes.

Lake Pontchartrain, formed 4,000 years ago by the constantly shifting soil deposits of the Mississippi River Delta, is a shallow lake, about fifteen feet deep, that covers over 600 square miles and was called by the Indians, "Otwaka" - "Wide Waters." It would have been here, in the shallow waters of Pontchatrain, that the

French settlers caught their first sight of Louisiana wildlife, including alligators, snapping turtles, and paddlefish. Skirting along the southern shoreline of the lake, the pirogues could use sails if the winds were favorable. Otherwise, the hard work of rowing commenced, and would not stop until their arrival at Arkansas Post four months later.

On the southern shore of Lake Pontchartrain the travelers encountered their first point of civilization since leaving Biloxi, if New Orleans in 1720 can be thought of as civilized. Founded two years earlier by Jean-Baptiste Le Moyne Bienville under the authority of the French crown and John Law's Mississippi Company, the city was established in perhaps the poorest possible choice of locations along the Mississippi, slightly above sea level but surrounded by swampland which were beneath sea level and prone to flooding, wild animals, poisonous snakes, and disease. But Bienville saw potential here and had personal designs on the area, and after being appointed *commandant générale* in March, 1718, he took a ragtag band of about fifty convicts and began the hard work of clearing brush and building the first shack on the site.[5] Exactly a year later, Bienville awarded himself two large tracts of land where his proposed city would be (in what is now the French Quarter of New Orleans), hired engineers Pierre Le Blond de La Tour and Adrien de Pauge to lay out a plot for a city eleven blocks wide by four blocks deep, and set out to convince the authorities that the capital of Louisiana should be moved from Biloxi to New Orleans. However, the relocation of the capital did not happen until the middle of 1722, a year after Pierre and Marie and their company of travelers passed through Bienville's little swamp village, and at the time of their visit the town consisted of nothing more than a few wooden staked houses with thatched roofs and perhaps a few dozen inhabitants.

Skirting along the southern shore of Pontchartrain, the flotilla of five boats loaded down with eighty people and their supplies entered into a narrow and still stream known as Bayou St. John. Fort St. John, really nothing more than a small wooden shack housing a few soldiers, was situated at the mouth of the bayou and served more for assisting travelers than for offering any kind of protection. Rowing due south, after two or three miles the boat party came to the end of the bayou and had to portage the last mile or two toward the village. Jean-Francois-Benjamin Dumont, who made a similar journey from Biloxi six months before Pierre Mayeux, recorded in his journal,

> "We entered it [Bayou St. John] and rowed upstream for two leagues to a portage, where there were some sheds that served as a depot…To reach this river [the Mississippi, called by the French the St. Louis River] on a well prepared trail with carts to carry all our cargo through the forests and brush might have been a simple matter, a pleasure even. But no, we found upturned trees blocking the path, which our soldiers had to cut up and remove, and then a small ravine that was swollen with rainwater that had flooded the area and made the ground muddy and the trail very bad. It was no small matter to transport the supplies and the equipment for the troops We had even more trouble transporting our five boats, which, as soon as we got to the post known by the name of New Orleans, were put into the water of the beautiful Saint Louis River. All this required only a few days, after which we reloaded our boats once again, embarked the soldiers in them, and left behind this little outpost, where there were then only four or five houses all

separated from one another, belonging to various habitants."[6]

The men and women traveling to Arkansas Post were not afforded any luxuries in New Orleans, not even lodging. As with the rest of the trip, they pitched tents and built cook fires, and after reloading the boats, they began the hardest part of their journey: going *up* the mighty Mississippi River. In September, 1721, four months after the Mayeux's visit to the future capital, what little there was of the village of New Orleans was destroyed by a hurricane and the undauntable Bienville had to rebuild his dream from scratch.

The L'Authie river that ran through Pierre Mayeux's hometown of Maintenay was almost small enough to jump across, no more than 20 feet across at its narrow points. Even the nearby Somme, whose name is derived from the Celtic word meaning tranquility, is a gently rolling river that in some places is only a few dozen yards wide. Nothing they had seen before could have prepared Pierre and Marie for the sheer magnitude of the Mississippi River.

With its headwaters at Lake Itasca in Minnesota, the Mississippi River winds its way for over 2,500 miles through the middle of the North American continent, growing in size as each major tributary along the way feeds into it - the Missouri, the Ohio, the Arkansas and other rivers - with a watershed of 1.2 million square miles reaching from the Allegheny Mountains in the east to the Rocky Mountains in the west. Only twenty or thirty feet wide at its source, by the time it reaches the Gulf it is over a mile wide, and flowing between three and five miles an hour. In New Orleans it delivers 600,000 cubic feet of water per second.[7]

John Barry, in his book *Rising Tide,* describes the dangerous complexities beneath the surface of the river:

> "The Mississippi never lies at rest. It roils. It follows no set course. Its waters and currents are not uniform. Rather, it moves south in layers and whorls, like an uncoiling rope made up of a multitude of discrete fibers, each one separetely and together capable of snapping like a whip. It never has one current, one velocity…The river snakes seaward in a continual series of S curves that sometimes approach 180 degrees. The collision of river and earth at these bends creates tremendous turbulence: currents can drive straight down to the bottom of the river, sucking at whatever lies on the surface…For the last 450 miles of the Mississippi's flow, the riverbed lies below sea level - 15 feet below sea level at Vicksburg, well over 170 feet below sea level at New Orleans. For these 450 miles the water on the bottom has no reason to flow at all. But the water above it does. This creates a tumbling effect as water spills over itself, like an enormous ever-breaking wave."[8]

The river is home to over 260 species of fish, 50 species of mammals, 145 species of reptiles and amphibians, and is the flight path for over 60% of the migratory birds of North America.[9] The patriotic French named it the St. Louis River, but the more apt Indian name is what stuck: Mississippi, "The Big River."

How does one go *up* the Big River without sail, steam or electrical power? The method is called *cordelling,* and it was common practice on the river into the mid 20th century. With twenty men manning the oars of the large pirogues, a few men worked their way ahead and along the banks in smaller boats, pulling ropes attached to the main vessel. These men would tie the ropes onto trees or stumps or any other stationary objects, thus preventing the larger boat from drifting backward with the current. As difficult as this task may seem, it was made all the more arduous by the drifting logs and trees that the travelers often encountered. Dumont described the perilous situation:

> "There are always snags of dead trees caught up on one another, which one has to paddle around with great effort, taking care that the force of the water doesn't grab the bow of your boat and force it broadside to the current, which is called being knocked down and can send you downriver in spite of yourself, losing more than a league [about three miles] of progress. And if you allow yourself to be knocked down into these snags, you run the risk of filling your boat with water and being forced down under them, so you must have good foresight and take precautions when making such voyages."[10]

Sometimes, if the river was in flood stage, the boats could cut through flooded woodlands, avoiding large loops in the river and saving as much as an entire day of hard rowing. Using this cordelling method, travelers in the 18th century were able to maintain an upstream speed of up to ten to fifteen miles a day, a remarkable feat by any standard.[11]

Each day started at sunrise, when breakfast was cooked and camp broken, and ended in the late afternoon when the travelers made camp and cooked dinner before darkness set in. Sometimes camp could be pitched in comfortable settings such as a grassy meadow alongside the river or a large sandbar. Other times, if the river was too high or there was no suitable landing place, the traveling parties would have to spend a miserable night on the boats, anchored to a tree on the river bank. Dumont described the experience:

> "So, when one can make five or six leagues between morning and nightfall, it is a good pace, given the rapid current in this river. And when the sun is about to disappear below the horizon, we stop the boats in the most convenient place to sleep. Some go into the forest in search of firewood to heat the kettle...others pitch the tent for the commandant, and still others try to kill something to sate their appetites. When the kettle is ready, each eats from his own dish, and then after sharing a pipe, we go to bed."[12]

In addition to these nightly stops, there were along the way to Arkansas Post several villages belonging either to the French or to friendly Native Americans. Baton Rouge, which at 100 river miles above New Orleans was about a week's journey, was the first French post for travelers to stop in. Begun as another concession of the Mississippi Company, in 1721 Baton Rouge was nothing more than one wooden cabin and a few tents pitched on a bluff. But it provided a place for rest, for catching up on news, and for stocking new supplies if necessary, including game such as buffalo and deer sold to the trading post by nearby hunters. Dumont, who passed through Baton Rouge a few months before the Mayeux group, recounted a story that well depicts the rough and tumble ways of Louisiana in its early years:

> "We finally arrived at Baton Rouge, which was then beginning to be settled by M. Diron d'Artuguiette's concession...the same day we arrived in this place, it happened that one of our boat captains had stolen a barrel

> with more than twelve pots of eau-de-vie [brandy] and was constantly drunk. He was discovered as he went to tap the barrel again, and being thus caught in the act, when we arrived at the concession and went ashore, a council of war was summoned. He was dismissed from his command, reduced to the rank of sailor, and condemned to a whipping. He was attached to a large tree, with his shoulders bare, and each soldier in turn gave him a lash on the back. He was not treated lightly, given that his theft had reduced the supply of eau-de-vie for the soldiers, who, angry at this thief, left on him the marks of their thirst."[13]

Dumont's company, as was the custom of river travelers, stayed in Baton Rouge for three days, hunting buffalo and bear, enjoying fresh food, and resting for the next leg of the journey.

Thirty miles upriver from Baton Rouge, Pointe Coupee ("Cut-Off Point") served as the next layover village. Although Natchitoches, established in 1714 on the Red River, is recognized as the oldest city in present day Louisiana, Pointe Coupee has a history reaching back to 1708 when French traders from the upper Mississippi River territory established a little village and intermarried with the local Native Americans.[14] Just a backwoods village, a decade later Pointe Coupee would become a fort offering protection to travelers destined for places up the Mississippi River, or for Natchitoches on the Red River.

In between the relatively civilized French villages, the travelers would take breaks from their journey to spend a few days resting and hunting. Coming so recently from France, and from lands that had been tamed and cultivated for a thousand years, their forays into the wilds of Louisiana offered them sights and experiences they had never before encountered, some delightful, some puzzling, and some very dangerous. A traveler might be hunting in the woods and hear the clear sound of someone rapidly hammering only to discover a large woodpecker, a bird foreign to their homeland.[15] Another animal new to the freshly arrived Europeans was the seemingly beautiful black and white bushy tailed animal seen scurrying through the underbrush. After only one close encounter with the skunk the Frenchmen learned to keep their distant from what they called the *bête puante,* "stinky animal." Other creatures new to the French people were raccoons, or *chats sauvages* - "wild cats," coyotes, large wood rats, and bobcats. This is to say nothing of the snakes, crawfish and reptiles they had never encountered in France.

Deer were plentiful, but perhaps the most abundant wild animal, and the most easily hunted, was the buffalo. Thought of now as an animal of the American West, the buffalo were so plentiful in the Mississippi Valley that one explorer wrote, "the bison and cows are so numerous that you cannot lack provisions if you have powder and balls."[16] Although more plentiful above the Arkansas River, buffalo were common all the way to the Gulf of Mexico, and provided a staple of survival for both the French and the Indians. Sometimes, instead of hunting for deer and buffalo themselves, the weary travelers were able to trade with friendly Indians in the villages along the river.

On his trip between Baton Rouge and Pointe Coupee, only a few months before the Mayeux's made their voyage, Dumont experienced a buffalo hunt during which hunters killed two of the animals.

"The five men could not carry even one entire carcass between them. Each loaded up and returned to our camp to inform us of their success. A detachment of soldiers was sent out to fetch the rest of this excellent provision, for ever since our departure from New Orleans, we had lived on lard and salt beef. Hence this fresh meat gave us great pleasure."[17]

Dumont also recounts a bear hunt - of sorts:

"After two days in this place [Baton Rouge], on the third, at the first light of day, we all embarked again and continued on our route upstream. It was then that we had the pleasure of killing some bears that were swimming across the river. A boat would break off to pursue them, shoot them, and then pull them on board. One day in particular, the boat commanded by M. Petit de Livilliers (who was a very good shot), having spotted one of these animals crossing over, set out to catch up with it by the power of their arms. The officer, who was standing in the bow, shot at it. But because of the movement of the boat, he only hit the animal in the ear, which caused the bear, who was surprised by this blow, to turn and come back toward the boat rather than continue swimming toward land. Having grabbed the boat with its large, handlike paws, it climbed in. All the soldiers who were rowing were seized with such fear that they threw themselves under their seats. There was not a single one among them who did not prefer to be suffocated by the body of his comrade rather than be left on top of him. But the animal, having climbed on board, rather than express rage and anger, only looked around to one side and the other, and then, walking over the backs of

> the men, passed by the boathouse and threw himself into the water. But at the sound of the splash, the guns were taken up again, and he did not make it far before he paid dearly for his good nature, for he was killed and brought dead on board the same boat he had just passed across alive."[18]

Bears and cougars were also plentiful. Marc Caillot, the French company clerk who lived in New Orleans in 1729, wrote in his memoirs, "The bears and tigers are very big, but not very bad." By what standards he measured badness is unclear, for he continued, "Nevertheless, when you shoot at these animals you must take good care not to miss them, for otherwise they will charge you and devour you."[19]

Describing the plentiful bounty of wild animals on his trip north from New Orleans, Le Page Du Pratz, who had a farm at Fort Rosalie from 1720 to 1728, wrote,

> "I had a barrel of powder, with fifteen pounds of shot, which I thought would be sufficient for the voyage: but I found by experience that this was not sufficient for the vast plenty of game that is to be met with upon that river, without ever going out of your way. I had not gone above twenty-eight leagues [about 75 miles, or just south of Baton Rouge] to the grant of M. Paris du Vernai, when I was obliged to borrow of him fifteen pounds of shot more. Upon this I took care of my ammunition, and shot nothing but what was fit for our provision; such as wild ducks, summer ducks, teal, and saw bills. Among the rest I killed a carancro [vulture], wild geese, cranes, and flamingos; I likewise often

killed young alligators; the tail of which was a feast for the slaves, as well as for the French and Canadian rowers."[20]

Although travelers up the river encountered bear and cougar, poisonous snakes and other dangerous animals, two creatures in particular were the most dreaded, one being the largest animal in the waters, and one being the smallest insect above the waters: the alligator and the mosquito.

While the French were somewhat familiar with crocodiles because of French holdings in Africa, South America and the Caribbean islands, none of the immigrants had actually experienced them. However, the near relative to the crocodile, the American Alligator, was nearly ubiquitous in the lakes and rivers of Louisiana. When New Orleans experienced heavy rains, residents would have to fend against alligators that had come up out of the swamps and into the muddy streets and yards of the city. Passengers would sometimes have to fight off the creatures as they attempted to crawl into the boats that traversed the lakes and rivers of the area. Camping along the Mississippi required the posting of guards at night, not only to protect the provisions from thieving Indians or unscrupulous Frenchmen, but also to guard against the huge alligators that might wander into the camp and drag away an unsuspecting sleeping man, woman or child. Marc Caillot reported hunting these "crocodiles" soon after his arrival in Louisiana. "I killed one that was nineteen feet long. There were some that were quite a bit larger and were monstrous."[21]

Recounting his time in New Orleans, Caillot wrote,

"There are a huge number of them, and they are monstrous in size...There are some in the river that have pulled cattle into the water, which they devoured. This is why the Negroes who lead the livestock to drink take great care to look and see if there are any around. They killed one that, after it had pulled in a woman who was doing her wash along the edge of the water, came back for her baby, who was crying, and ate the baby too. They killed it, and upon weighing it they found that it weighed seven hundred fifty pounds."

He continued by describing his own encounter with an alligator on Bayou Saint John:

"...we got into a little pirogue with our provisions. We were only halfway when, all of a sudden, a huge crocodile came and put his two front feet on the edges of our little boat, which he almost turned over, to get our meat. We were in a great deal of trouble, so, in the meantime, having loaded our muskets, together we all shot him in the head and blasted out his eyes. He left us, making a dreadful turbulence in the water. Not knowing where he was going anymore, he beached himself on the bank. The Negroes from the plantation, seeing that he had been wounded, ran and pulled him out of the water. We measured him and discovered that he was twenty-two feet long."[22]

The largest modern era alligator on record was killed in Mill Creek Alabama in August, 2014, measuring fifteen feet, nine inches, and weighing 1,011 pounds. Estimated to be between 24 and 28 years old, the alligator was killed only after five members of the Stokes family wrestled with it from their boat for over five hours. Before the advent of European settlers, that is, before guns and bullets, alligators had no natural predators and the bows and arrows of the Native Americans were practically harmless to them. Consequently, in the 18th century when the French began settling along the swamps, rivers and lakes of Louisiana, the older alligators dwarfed even the record setting specimens of modern times. One might dismiss a single report of a nineteen or twenty foot alligator as fanciful, but various reports from multiple sources confirm the enormous size of the animals in that time. Du Pratz describes a kill he made:

> "Among other things I cannot omit to give an account of a monstrous large alligator I killed with a musquet ball, as it lay upon the bank, about ten feet above the edge of the water. We measured it, and found it to be nineteen feet long, its head three feet and a half long, above two feet nine inches broad, and the other parts in proportion; at the belly it was two feet two inches thick; and it infected the whole air with the odor of musk. M. Mehane told me, he had killed one twenty two feet long."[23]

Dumont described the animal for readers back in France, writing, "There are some that are monstrous, at least fifteen or twenty feet in length. They have, in truth, the shape and appearance of a lizard, but whereas the lizard with its small size, is not at all unpleasant, by contrast, this creature with its massive size is terrifying.." He continued his description by recounting an incident at Bayou Saint John.

> "Its body is armored, as it were, with thick, strong scales, to the point where, if hit by a ball fired with the force of powder from a gun, it will not injure him at all, and the ball even bounces off. It is very hard to wound unless it is hit in the eye. When it is, it comes out onto land, since it

would lose all its blood if it remained in the water. But when out of the water, it is quite easy to kill with a blow from a club, the more so because its body is long, and, when it wants to turn around its tail, which is extremely long, has to turn with its head in one motion. It is highly carnivorous. A poor soldier from Bayou Saint John, at a post near the entrance of the bayou where there is only a small corps of guards, was sleeping on the ground in the shade of a tree, and one of these animals caught him by the foot and dragged him to the bottom of the water, where the poor, unfortunate man was eaten as he drowned. The alligator could easily pull this soldier in, since they truly are strong enough to carry off a buffalo drinking water at the edge of a river."[24]

The only creatures more dreaded than the alligators were the tiny mosquitoes which were to be found *everywhere* in Louisiana, and from which escape was impossible. Diseases carried by the mosquitoes were a deadly threat to the settlers . Describing the conditions of early New Orleans, Marcel Giraud wrote, "The entire population, in fact, suffered to one degree or another from the illnesses that were propagated by the more or less polluted water that soaked the soil of New Orleans. This water became especially baneful during the hot season, when it became a breeding ground for swarms of mosquitoes that might carry malaria, or other tropical fevers, mostly yellow fever."[25]

River voyagers awoke in the mornings only to be greeted by clouds of mosquitoes which followed them the entire day as they made their way in the boats. Sleeping along the river during hot weather, which could hit any time of the year in Louisiana, offered a choice between two hells. It was unbearable to close up a tent in the stifling heat, but even more unbearable to leave it open and suffer the bites of the swarming mosquitoes. One traveler wrote that, in comparison to the ever present swarms of mosquitoes everything else seemed "only a recreation." He was certain that the "little insect had caused more swearing since the French came to the Mississippi than had been done before that time in all the rest of the world."

After enduring weeks of dangers, discomforts, and the back breaking labor of traveling up the Mississippi, Pierre and Marie Mayeux and their companions were treated to one final layover before heading into the Arkansas territory. Fort Rosalie, high on a bluff on the east bank of the river 120 river miles above Pointe Coupee, was a veritable paradise compared to the swamps through which they had just passed. Located at what is present day Natchez, Mississippi, the fort was established in 1716 at the close of the First Natchez War. As part of the peace negotiations, Bienville demanded that the Indians provide building material and labor for building a stockaded fort. As peace settled in, settlers surrounded the fort with houses and began successfully growing tobacco and other crops, befriending and trading with the Natchez Indians in nearby villages. When the travelers bound for Arkansas Post stopped in Natchez in 1721, Natchez was the largest, most civilized, most beautiful, and most peaceful town they had experienced since leaving France. Biloxi had been a death trap of disease and starvation, New Orleans a few shacks in a swamp, Baton Rouge a single cabin and a few tents, and Pointe Coupee nothing more than a way station for hunters and trappers. By comparison, Fort Rosalie, and the surrounding town that was now being called Natchez, was a veritable metropolis. While New Orleans and Baton Rouge were still struggling to take root and survive, Natchez had a French population of nearly 500 farmers and workers peacefully coexisting with the surrounding Native American population of about 5,000 men, women, and children. Called by Bienville "the Jewel of the Mississippi," and beautifully situated high on the bluff above the river where cooler breezes relieved the stifling stillness of the river bottom, Natchez offered a final respite before the travelers continued north. It was the last French habitation on route to Arkansas Post. Between Natchez and their new home lay more than 250 river miles of nothing but wilderness.

---

[1] Arnold, *Colonial Arkansas*, footnotes 30 & 31, p. 183f.

[2] Morris S. Arnold, *Unequal Laws Unto A Savage Race: European Legal Traditions in Arkansas, 1686-1836*, University of Arkansas Press, Fayetteville, 1985, p. 14.

[3] Nancy Maria Miller Surrey, *The Commerce Of Louisiana During The French Regime, 1699-1763*, Columbia University Press, New York, 1916, p. 57f.

[4] Dumont, p. 140.

[5] Lawrence N. Powell, *The Accidental City: Improvising New Orleans*, Harvard University Press, Cambridge, 2012, p. 43.

[6] Dumont, p. 149.

[7] For perspective, a semi-trailer holds 3,600 cubic feet; the Mississippi delivers 166 times that amount of water *every second*.

[8] John M. Barry, *Rising Tide: The Great Mississippi Flood of 1927 And How It Changed America*, Simon and Schuster, New York, 1997, p. 38f.

[9] Statistics from the National Park Service, http://www.nps.gov/miss/riverfacts.htm.

[10] Dumont, p. 207.

[11] Surrey, p. 76.

[12] Dumont, p. 150.

[13] *Ibid*, p. 150f.

[14] No author given, *Biographical and Historical Memoirs of Louisiana*, Goodspeed Publishing Company, Chicago, 1892, v. 2, p. 194.
[15] Dumont describes getting lost in the woods as he followed the sound of a woodpecker at night, p. 123.
[16] Morris S. Arnold, The *Rumble Of A Distant Drum: The Quapaws And Old World Newcomers, 1637-1804,* University of Arkansas Press, 2000, p. 30.
[17] Dumont, p. 151.
[18] *Ibid*, p. 151f.
[19] Caillot, p. 116.
[20] Du Pratz, p 71.
[21] Caillot, 66.
[22] *Ibid*, p. 114f.
[23] Du Pratz, p. 71.
[24] Dumont, p. 389f.
[25] Giraud, p. 214.

Chapter Five
Arkansas Post
1721

Not all men are cut out for the sacrificial demands of Catholic priesthood. Some think they are, but after a season of training come to realize the life is not for them. René-Robert Cavelier was such a man. Born in 1643 on a family estate near the Normandy capital of Rouen, René grew up with all the comforts and privilege a wealthy home can provide. At the age of 17 he renounced all his family's wealth and any inheritance that might come his way, took a vow of poverty, and entered the Jesuit College in Rouen to prepare for a life of priestly ministry. Several years later, before taking his final vows and being ordained a priest, Cavelier had a change of heart and was released from his vows due to, in his words, "moral weaknesses."[1] Whatever these moral weaknesses were, his real reasons for abandoning the priesthood may have been his sense of wanderlust and desire for adventure more than any unseemly or unacceptable proclivities.

Unable to recover his forfeited wealth and inheritance, he did receive a seigneury or lordship from the King and, following the footsteps of his brother Jean, a Sulpician priest who had left for New France a year earlier in 1666, René-Robert made the difficult journey across the Atlantic to Quebec. Assigned a small tract of land in the newly founded city of Montreal, the young adventurer took as his title the name of his family estate back in Rouen: he was now René-Robert Cavelier *Sieur de La Salle*, forever more to be known in history simply as La Salle.

La Salle worked his land, living among the local Indians, learning their language, and hearing tales of a great river to the south which they called "The Father of Waters." After three years he sold his property and began exploring the unknown wild lands in the heart of the continent. In 1669 his first expedition ended in failure when his men rebelled against him on the Ohio River near what is now Louisville, Kentucky and abandoned the mission.

In 1673, before La Salle could mount another expedition, two more men, the French Jesuit priest Jacques Marquette and the Canadian explorer Louis Joliet, became the first Europeans to travel down the Mississippi River, although they turned back after reaching the mouth of the Arkansas River for fear of hostile Indians and a rumored Spanish presence moving in from Spanish-controlled Texas. La Salle regained his place in history when in 1682 he and his trusted lieutenant Henri de Tonti led a group of explorers down the Mississippi River to the Gulf of Mexico and on April 9 with much fanfare buried a cross in the delta dirt of the mouth of the Mississippi, claiming for France all the lands that drained into this Father of Waters, and in honor of King Louis XIV named the territory *Louisiana*.

As La Salle, de Tonti, and their crew paddled down the Mississippi to where it is joined by the Arkansas River, they heard the faint sound of drums in the distance, and caught sight of Indian life along the western bank of the river. Not knowing whether the natives were hostile or friendly, the Frenchmen made camp on the far bank and sent two scouts to the Indian village to make clear their peaceful intentions. Shortly afterwards, the scouts returned with a delegation of Indians, including several village chiefs, who presented La Salle with the calumet, or "peace pipe," and escorted the exploring party back to their main village where a grand celebration was held to welcome them.[2] This friendly tribe who called themselves the *Ug' akh pa* or *Quapaw* were referred to by the French by the same name given them by the Algonquin speaking tribes to the north and east: the *Arkansas*, that is, "the downriver people." The hospitable tribe not only welcomed the French explorers, but implored them for protection from the nearby Chickasaw tribe, recognized King Louis XIV as their own Great Father, and began a close friendship that would last until the French ceded Louisiana to the United States in the Louisiana Purchase of 1803. Before moving further downriver La Salle built a pillar in the village painted with a cross and the arms of France, and the inscription, "Louis the Great, King of France and Navarre, rules. 13th March, 1682.[3]

On their return trip up the Mississippi River, while again stopped at the Quapaw village of Kappa, La Salle's trusted Lieutenant Henri de Tonti asked for rights to establish a village nearby which would serve as a trading post halfway between the upper Mississippi region and the Gulf of Mexico. La Salle agreed, and gave de Tonti the first land grant and trading rights in French Louisiana. Envisioning a future city of flourishing commerce and growing population, de Tonti returned to the confluence of the Mississippi and Arkansas rivers four years later in 1686 with six Frenchmen and built a house with a fence near the Quapaw village of Osotouy, naming it *Poste aux Arkansas*, that is, Arkansas Post, or as he presumptuously called it, "The City of Tonti." It was the first European settlement in the lower Mississippi valley. Although he never lived in Arkansas Post for any length of time, de Tonti did return several times, attempting to shore up the fledgling village that constantly struggled for survival. While on yet another expedition in the southern part of French Louisiana, de Tonti contracted yellow fever in the rustic seaport and former capital of Mobile and died in September 1704. His beloved "city" never had a population of more than six men during his life, and never materialized into the hub of commerce he had envisioned.

Of all the Native American tribes along the Mississippi River, the Quapaw were the most favored and respected tribe among the newly arrived French. De Tonti wrote of them, "it may be affirmed that these are the best-formed Savages we have seen." Others wrote that they were more physically attractive than other Indians, "all so well formed and proportioned that we admired their beauty," and, "far better made, honest, liberal and gay" than the other tribes. Father Pierre Charlevoix wrote that the Quapaw were, "reckoned the largest and handsomest of men of all the Indians of this continent, and are called by way of distinction *les beaux hommes*, or the handsome men."[4] The disposition of this tribe matched their physical attractiveness, and they were noted by French visitors of the time as friendly, mild, peaceful, warm, and brave.

The French men were also attracted to the Quapaw women who were industrious, hard working, independent, and good cooks.[5] In fact, intermarriage between the French and the Quapaw became relatively common in the 18th century. The most famous of the Quapaw chiefs, Chief Saracen, was the son of the French interpreter Francois Sarazin[6] and the grandson of the "wild child" Anne Francoise Roland who had been sent from the Salpetriere prison to Louisiana.

With roots along the Atlantic seaboard, the Quapaw were part of the Dhegiha Sioux people and are related to the Osage, Omaha, Kansa and Ponca tribes.[7] Moving from the seaboard into the Ohio valley in the 15th century, tribal warfare with the Iroquois pushed them further southwest into the region of the Arkansas River in the 16th century.[8] By the time Joliet and La Salle first encountered them, they had been settled along the Arkansas River for a hundred or more years, and had five villages along the Arkansas and on both banks of the Mississippi. With a combined population of between five and ten thousand, more than 1,500 of them were warriors[9], a necessary force to guard against nearby hostile tribes, particularly the Chickasaw to the east.

On every level, from religion to culture to roles of the sexes to general disposition, the Quapaw were markedly different from the other Native American tribes, including their distant Siouan cousins. With no formal religion, that is, no temples or priesthood or liturgies, the Quapaw believed in a force called Wakondah which filled the whole world and held everything in balance, a belief perhaps more philosophically akin to Chinese Taoism than the Supreme Being called the Great Spirit by other tribes. Wakondah came into being when the primordial male and female life forces were joined in the beginning of time. This life force emanated out through other entities; the sun, the moon, thunder and lightening, and other natural forces were all seen to be manifestations of this power. Even plants and animals contained the spirit of Wakondah on some level. Prayers were made to the sun and moon, and some animals were seen as guardian spirits.[10] While there were no religious centers, there were ceremonies throughout the year calling on the spirit beings for favor in planting and harvesting and for rites of passage such as birth, marriage and death, and for healing.[11]

In keeping with the dualistic nature of Wakondah, the Quapaw divided themselves into two interrelated groups, the Sky People and the Earth People. Each village had members of both groups dwelling together, and all marriages were required to be between a man and a woman from each group. A man from the Sky People married a woman from the Earth People and vice versa. The union of husband and wife, then, symbolized the union of heaven and earth, and the life force of Wakondah which flowed through all things.[12]

The villages contained several longhouses which were dwellings for multiple families, built by driving poles in the ground and tying them toward the center to form a roof. The longhouses were arranged around a central plaza with a large partially covered raised platform where tribal meetings and ceremonies were held.[13]

The political structure of the Quapaw was also markedly different from other tribes. Each village had a chief, who inherited his office through the male line, but the chief of the Kappa village, located twenty miles north of the Arkansas River along the west bank of the Mississippi, was recognized as the Great Chief.

However, neither he nor any other chief had actual authority to rule or demand anything of the people. It was a chiefdom of convincing, not coercion. So, the decision to go to war could not be arbitrarily decided by a chief or a council, but each warrior had the freedom to decide for himself whether or not to join the campaign.[14]

This somewhat egalitarian style of political leadership was also reflected in the relationships between men and women, husbands and wives. The men were the hunters, fishermen, warriors and political leaders. The women were the gardeners, wild food gatherers, cooks, housekeepers and child rearers. And yet the women were not subservient to the men, had a certain measure of independence and held ownership and control of their own lives.[15]

While the men hunted for buffalo, deer, bear, turkey, and other animals, the women harvested wild nuts and berries. Both men and women shared in the cultivation of corn, pumpkins, sunflowers, beans, peaches and plums on farms of massive proportion, one being five square miles in size.[16] In terms of dress, the men wore leather loincloths during seasonable weather, and the women wore knee length deerskin skirts and wore their hair loose if married, or braided and coiled behind their ears if unmarried.[17]

With their new encounters with the Europeans, this somewhat idyllic scene was devastated by a smallpox epidemic in 1698 that killed eighty percent of the population. When Tonti visited in 1700, the population of between 5,000 and 10,000 had dwindled to no more than 800 people. A priest passing through the country recorded that in one of the villages, "there were not a hundred men; all the children and a great part of the women were dead."[18]

A little over twenty years later in 1721, another smallpox epidemic swept through the villages, initiated by a sick Frenchman passing through the area. Father Pierre Charlevoix who visited shortly afterwards wrote, "the burial place appeared like a forest of stakes and posts."[19] That same year Pierre and Marie Mayeux and their companions stepped out of their pirogue after a long journey upriver to Arkansas Post, their promised paradise.

After months of travel on the open sea, surviving the abysmal conditions of Biloxi, and a four month journey rowing up the most powerful and unpredictable river on the North American continent, in August Pierre and Marie Mayeux finally arrived at their destination: a little French trading post on the Arkansas River that boasted no more than half a dozen soldiers barely surviving in the middle of the wilderness. They had agreed to give up three years of their lives in exchange for a minimum wage and the promise of owning their own little strip of land by working the personal concession of John Law. Law was the Scottish entrepreneur, director of the French Company of the Indies, and most powerful man in France, who planned to succeed where Henri de Tonti had failed: to transform Arkansas Post from a backwater hovel into a thriving city of commerce perfectly situated halfway between the Great Lakes and the Gulf of Mexico.[20] Here, at last, they would find their land of plenty as promised in the brochures and newspaper advertisements back home in France. Here they would find an abundance of game, valuable minerals like gold, silver and copper easily mined from shallow veins, and land so fertile that it practically produced gardens without back breaking labor.

The tiny garrison itself was situated near the mouth of the Arkansas River where it flowed into the Mississippi adjacent to the Quapaw village of Ouyapes, but the workers for Law's concession chose a spot for the new settlement about twenty miles up the Arkansas River on its right bank, less prone to the floods of the Mississippi and situated on a "beautiful plain surrounded by fertile valleys and a little stream of fine clear wholesome water,"[21] directly across the river from the main Quapaw village of Kappa.[22] Within a month of the arrival of the workers, Lieutenant Avignon Guérin La Boulaye arrived at the soldiers' post and took up the task of building new housing for the garrison with designs for building a fort and larger trading post.[23] Because of the recent flooding, La Boulaye relocated the military post to a spot adjacent to the concession village where it could provide protection and assistance to the workers, leaving a single soldier at the old location to inform trappers and traders of the new post.[24]

Pierre Mayeux's job, specifically, was to serve with a crew of men clearing timber and building houses for a group of several hundred German immigrants who were due to arrive the following year.[25] But the first order of business would be to clear a small spot to build his own home and plant a garden, no small task considering there were no plows, cattle or mules to work the land. Everything had to be done by hand and hard labor.[26] The plan would have been to depend on trade with the Quapaw for foodstuff during the initial months, however their villages were so devastated by smallpox and war with the Chickasaw that the Indians were themselves in survival mode when the French arrived. Less than a month after the Mayeuxs arrived, a great hurricane hit New Orleans and worked its way up the river flooding everything in its path. The aftermath of the hurricane brought heavy rain to the Arkansas area as well. During their first year the settlement was plagued with torrential rainfall and flooding along the Arkansas River, preventing much work and the direly necessary planting of gardens.[27] There was no harvest that year, and the Quapaw, far from having enough food for trading with the French, were so desperate that they weren't even able to save seed for the next year's planting.[28] When the Jesuit priest Fr. Pierre Charlevoix visited the settlement a month later, he reported that the people there were living lives of "*tristes débris*," lives of sorrowful wreckage, lives of melancholy ruins.[29] Even at the beginning of their endeavor, things were a disaster.

What none of the concessioners could have possibly known was that, while they were trying to scratch out a new life in the promised paradise of Louisiana, their "boss," the illustrious John Law, had become a fugitive to the law and had fled France for fear of his life. Even before Pierre and Marie set sail for Louisiana, John Law's Mississippi Company and the Bank Royale were on shaky financial grounds. Because of the overprinting of paper money and removal of coin, shares in the company began to fluctuate wildly, dropping 25% in value in a single month from 10,000 livre to 7,500 livre, and then bouncing back to 9,400 livre less than two weeks later.[30] In an attempt to avoid a run on the bank, where people were exchanging their paper for gold and silver, Law made the radical move of abolishing gold and silver coins altogether, converting the entire French economy to one of paper.[31] In May, 1720, while Pierre and Marie were preparing to depart La Rochelle for Louisiana, Law's bank issued new banknotes and doubled the amount circulating. That same month Law announced that by December the value of company shares would be cut in half.[32] People went into a frenzy, protesting and rioting in the streets of Paris. In an attempt to remedy the situation, Law had a change of heart. He would remove banknotes and shares from circulation and begin reintroducing hard coin. In a theatrical act of flamboyance, 400,000 shares owned by the company and the crown were burned in public bonfires witnessed by thousands.[33] Far from building confidence, this act caused the people to trust paper money and shares even less and to redouble their attempts to acquire silver and gold coins.

On July 17, while Pierre and Marie were somewhere in the middle of the Atlantic Ocean, a crowd of 15,000 people stormed the Bank Royale at 3 o'clock in the morning and over a dozen people were crushed to death in the chaos. Six thousand soldiers were called in to restore calm, but to no effect. More mobs gathered in the street and one marched to Law's house with the intention of lynching him. In September, values of banknotes and shares had plummeted to around 20% of their high value. Law's grand schemes had failed, and the "Mississippi Bubble" had burst. On October 10, the Crown announced that as of November 1 France would abolish all paper and return to a coin economy.[34] The French philosopher Voltaire wrote, "Thus ends the system of paper money, which has enriched a thousand beggars and impoverished a hundred thousand honest men."[35] On December 14, while Pierre and Marie and the other *Le Profond* passengers were trying to survive the food shortages and rampant diseases of Biloxi, John Law and his family quietly escaped France never to return.[36]

John Law was gone and the Mississippi Company was undergoing restructuring, but news traveled slowly to Louisiana, and the inhabitants of Arkansas Post did not hear about it until more than a year after the fact. In March, 1722 Bertrand Dufrense, the newly appointed director of the reorganized Mississippi Company, arrived at Arkansas Post to replace Jacques

Levens, who, coincidentally, had never actually been to the post, although he was technically the director. What Dufrense found was shocking. When the hundreds of expected German immigrants who had been sent by the Mississippi Company to inhabit the newly created Arkansas Post village heard about Law's fiasco, they all opted to forego the difficult trip up the Mississippi and instead settled just north of New Orleans in what became known as the German Coast. Even the priest who had been appointed to Arkansas Post did not arrive; he died en route from New Orleans.[37] Only about half of the original workers assigned to Arkansas Post remained, less than three acres of land had been cleared and only twenty rough cabins had been built. Dufrense immediately released half of the remaining workers from their contracts and gave them their promised acreage in hopes they would cultivate it and produce a good harvest in the coming year.[38] The promise of three years salary at a minimum wage had vanished along with John Law.

1722 was another miserable year in regard to weather. Le Page du Pratz, who lived in Natchez at the time, recounted a hurricane that hit the area in March:

> "Some time after my return from New Orleans to the Natchez, towards the month of March 1722, a phenomenon happened, which frightened the whole province. Every morning, for eight days running, a hollow noise, somewhat loud, was heard to reach from the sea to the Illinois, which arose from the west. In the afternoon it was heard to descend from the east, and that with an incredible quickness; and though the noise seemed to bear on the water, yet without agitating it, or discovering any more wind on the river than before. This frightful noise was only

the prelude of a most violent tempest. The hurricane, the most furious ever felt in the province, lasted three days. As it arose from the southwest and northeast, it reached all the settlements which were along the Mississippi; and was felt for some leagues more or less strong, in proportion to the greater or less distance: but in the places, where the force or height of the hurricane passed, it overturned every thing in its way, which was an extent of a large quarter of a league broad; so that one would take it for an avenue made on purpose, the place where it passed being entirely laid flat, whilst every thing stood upright on each side. The largest trees were torn up by the roots, and their branches broken to pieces and laid flat to the earth, as were also the reeds of the woods. In the meadows, the grass itself, which was then but six inches high, and which is very fine, could not escape, but was trampled, faded, and laid quite flat to the earth...As this hurricane came from the south, it so swelled the sea, that the Mississippi flowed back against its current, so as to rise upwardly of fifteen feet."[39]

On September 12, 1722, almost exactly a year after the concession workers arrived at Arkansas Post, the newly founded town of New Orleans was destroyed by another powerful hurricane which continued up the river where it left a devastating path of wind damage and flooding.[40] In his journal, Fr. Charlevoix recorded,

"At New Orleans, the church, hospital and thirty houses or log huts were thrown down; all other edifices were injured. No lives were lost, but some of the sick in the hospital were wounded. A number of boats, periaguas

> [pirogues], canoes and sloops were crushed in the port; three ships anchored there were very much damaged, and found themselves high ashore on the bank of the river, which had risen eight feet. In the settlements above and below the city there was not a building standing...several periaguas, coming down to New Orleans loaded with provision and poultry, were wrecked. The vegetables that were mature were destroyed, and the continual rains which came on spoiled a good part of what was still green."[41]

The same hurricane completely destroyed Biloxi and although Arkansas Post was too far inland to take the brunt of the storm, it did not escape the inundating rains of the dying storm. Just at the time the settlers should be preparing fall gardens they were instead enduring torrential downpours which bogged the fields and prevented the work so necessary for their survival.

That winter, du Pratz wrote, "was so severe, that a colder was never remembered. The rain fell in icicles in such quantities as to astonish the oldest Natchez, to whom this great cold appeared new and uncommon."[42]

On February 25, 1723 the inspector general of the reorganized Mississippi Company, Diron d'Artaguiette, made an official visit to Arkansas Post and also conducted a census. The workers who had been released by Dufresne, which included Pierre's friend Jaques Cantrelle and his wife, relocated with the soldiers about five miles up the river, built cabins and attempted to raise crops and also hunt and trap game. The inspector general recorded in his journal,

"The same day at 2 o'clock in the afternoon we embarked in a little Indian pirogue and arrived at about 4 o'clock in the evening at the post, where are the troops commanded by Sr. La Boulay. There is no fort at all. The commandant there has only a little hut. There is also a sort of barn which serves as lodging for the soldiers, who are very badly equipped in every respect. There are also in the vicinity of this post, on the banks of the river, many French habitants, who are all men dismissed from the concession belonging heretofore to M. Law. The Jesuit father baptized there two French children and performed two marriage ceremonies."[43]

Earlier that day he had visited the original site of the concession, and wrote,

"We embarked…in a little pirogue to go to see the settlement of M. Law…We did not notice anything in particular. There are only three miserable huts, fourteen Frenchmen and six negroes, whom Sr. Dufrense, who is the director there for the company, employs in clearing the land. Since they have been on this land they have not even been able to raise Indian corn for their own nourishment, and they have been compelled to trade for it and to send even to the Illinois for it."[44]

The inhabitants along the river, who were freed from their concession obligations, were listed in the census by name, and although their friend Jaques Cantrelle is listed there along with his unnamed wife (Marie Francoise), Pierre and Marie Mayeux are absent from that list. The census from the concession itself did not name the individuals, and simply recorded a generic, "14

Frenchmen, one woman, and six Negro slaves." It is possible, and perhaps even likely, that the one woman mentioned was Marie Mayeux, and that she and Pierre remained at the original concession when the group of workers was divided. What is known is that in 1723 while still in Arkansas Post, Marie gave birth to her first child, Francois Pierre Mayeux.[45]

Le Page du Pratz, who was a contemporary of the Mayeuxs and Cantrelles, wrote regarding the dissolution of Arkansas Post, "...and but a few of those who engaged in the service of that grant, remained at the Arkansas; they were afterwards all dispersed and set at liberty."[46]

The post continued to dwindle in size. No longer under contract to work there, the inhabitants began to wander off either to the nearby countryside - some settled on a nearby lake and became hunters and fishermen - or to completely different areas altogether.[47] In 1726 the government shut down the military outpost and relocated the soldiers to other locations.[48] With the removal of the thin protective barrier offered by the soldiers, Arkansas Post acquired one more reason for people to leave. While the remote village was never as safe as, say, New Orleans or Biloxi, what little security the settlers possessed now vaporized and left them exposed, not to the friendly Quapaw, but to those other tribes that even the Quapaw feared. By 1727, when Fr. Paul du Poisson moved into the commandant's old cabin to serve as a missionary to the Quapaw, there were only three married couples and eight unmarried men in residence there. Fr. Poisson secured an assistant who died of sunstroke two years later, and on his trip to New Orleans to find a new helper, Fr. Poisson was murdered by Natchez Indians who found him praying by the side of the river.[49]

The frustration and disappointment these people experienced is unimaginable. Like a line of dominoes, every dream, every hope, came tumbling down. Around every new corner waited new heart-wrenching disappointments: leaving home and family with no hope of ever seeing them again; traversing the wide ocean in a dirty, dangerous and crowded ship; surviving disease and famine in a primitive port city where nearly half the people died; enduring the months long journey against the currents of the most powerful river they had ever seen; and then, discovering it was all for nought, that the paradise so deceitfully promised had turned into a miserable hellhole. Lives of *tristes débris* indeed. Sorrowful wreckage. Melancholy ruins. Miserable fragments of shattered dreams.

There was nothing to do but go back down the Mississippi River. To the new town of New Orleans. To start all over again.

---

[1] Alan Axelrod, *A Savage Empire: Trappers, Traders, Tribes, and Wars That Made America*, Macmillan, New York, 2011, p. 89.

[2] Roger E. Coleman, *The Arkansas Post Story*, Eastern National, National Park Service, Department of the Interior, Fort Washington, PA, 2009, p. 8.

[3] Arnold, *Unequal*, p. 2.

[4] Arnold, *Rumble*, p. 3f.

[5] Ibid, p. 7.

[6] Francois Sarazin was the son of Nicholas Sarazin and the "wild child" Anne Francoise Roland, whose story is referred to in Chapter One.

[7] Jeannie M Whayne, *et al*, *Arkansas: A Narrative History*, University of Arkansas Press, Fayetteville, 2003, p. 53.

[8] Larry Johnson, T*ar Creek: A History of the Quapah Indians, the World's Largest Lead and Zinc Discovery, and the Tar Creek Superfund Site*, Tate Publishing, Mustang, OK, 2009p. 25.

[9] *Ibid*, p. 35.

[10] George Sabo, *Historic Indians of Arkansas*, Fayetteville, Arkansas Archeological Survey, 1992, p. 33.
[11] *Ibid*, p. 34.
[12] Whayne, p. 54.
[13] Sabo, p. 36.
[14] *Ibid*, p. 36.
[15] Arnold, *Rumble*, p. 7.
[16] *Ibid*
[17] Whayne, p. 55f.
[18] Arnold, *Rumble*, p. 157.
[19] *Ibid*
[20] Arnold, *Colonial*, p. 9.
[21] Coleman, p. 20.
[22] Arnold, *Unequal*, p. 212; Arnold *Colonial*, p. 12.
[23] Coleman, p. 21.
[24] Arnold, *Unequal*, p. 8; Cole, p. 20.
[25] Arnold, *Colonial*, p. 11.
[26] Hano, p. 50
[27] Coleman, p. 20.
[28] *Ibid*, p. 21.
[29] Arnold, *Unequal*, p. 9; Arnold, *Colonial*, p. 12.
[30] Gleeson, p. 179.
[31] *Ibid*, p. 192.
[32] *Ibid*, p. 196.
[33] *Ibid*, p. 206.
[34] *Ibid*, p. 216ff.
[35] *Ibid*, p. 225.
[36] *Ibid*, p. 230.
[37] Arnold, *Colonial*, p. 89.
[38] Arnold, *Unequal*, p. 9.
[39] du Pratz, p. 80f.
[40] Charlevoix, p. 69.
[41] *Ibid*, p. 69, footnote.
[42] du Pratz, p. 86.
[43] Diron d'Artaguiette, in *Travels In The American Colonies*, Macmillan of Canada, Toronto, 1916, p. 56.
[44] *Ibid*, p. 56.
[45] In the marriage records of his daughter, Francois Mayeux states his place of birth as Arkansas Post.
[46] du Pratz, p. 79.

[47] Arnold, *Colonial*, p. 17.
[48] Coleman, p. 21.
[49] *Ibid*, p. 23.

Chapter Six
New Orleans
1725

New Orleans has been called "the accidental city," but there was nothing accidental in the ambitious and conniving mind of Jean-Baptiste Le Moyne Sieur de Bienville. When his father Charles Le Moyne came from France to Montreal in 1641 he had visions of grandeur and some would say illusions and a penchant for official titles. Receiving a land grant near Montreal from the governor of the province, he named it Longueull after a village in his native Normandy. Assuming the title, "Sieur de Longueull," Charles founded a village there and sired two daughters and twelve sons. Although he came by his siegneury honestly, having received it from the Governor General of New France, he assigned his sons a similar titles, each named after a town in his beloved Normandy.[1]

Whether because of the prodding expectations of their father, the personal character possessed by each son, or some combination of the two, nearly all of Charles Le Moyne's sons achieved a measure of fame and honor through their military or civil service, or their achievements as explorers and founders of new cities. Because of their bravery and accomplishments they are called "The Maccabees of New France."

In 1661 Charles' wife gave birth to his third son, Pierre Le Moyne, who was given the title of d'Iberville. After a distinguished career in the military, including service in the Hudson Bay expeditions and King William's War, in 1697 the twenty six year old d'Iberville was ordered by the French Minister of Naval Affairs Louis Phélypeaux, compte de Pontchartrain, to seek out the mouth of the Mississippi River. Leaving Brest, France with four ships, d'Iberville sailed across the Atlantic, around the peninsula of Florida, and into the birdfoot Delta of the Mississippi River. Leaving there and returning eastward, he built a small fort on the Gulf shores among the Biloxi Indians to serve as protection of French interests from the Spanish presence in Florida. D'Iberville's first claim to fame, then, is "Father of Biloxi." Two years later, on his third exploratory voyage from France, he founded the fort and town of Mobile. In 1706, while on a military voyage with designs to attack the English colony of Carolina, he died of fever in Havana.

Charles Le Moyne's eighth son, born nineteen years after d'Iberville, was given the name Jean-Baptiste Le Moyne and the title Sieur de Bienville. Following in the footsteps of his brother, Bienville also devoted his life to exploring and establishing a civilization in the wild Louisiana territory. Joining d'Iberville as he sailed along the coast of the Louisiana territory, Bienville later journeyed up the Mississippi River as far as Pointe Coupee. In 1701 he was appointed governor of Louisiana when the total French population of the entire province was 180 people. And so it was with great hope that Bienville welcomed the visionary plans of John Law and his Mississippi Company to populate and civilize the vast Louisiana territory, and perhaps even more importantly, to create wealth not only for the Crown and the investors in France, but also for the industrious and far-sighted Bienville himself. In March, 1717 Bienville's fortune changed for the better when he was appointed Commandant Général of Louisiana, making him the highest royal official in the colony, and was also named to the Council of Commerce, the local board of directors of John Law's Mississippi Company.[2]

Recognizing that as Louisiana grew in population and industry a capital city on the great waterway of the Mississippi would better serve the enterprise than either the present capital of Biloxi or the even further removed Mobile, Bienville began secretly scouting a favored spot for a new capital city. Any site at the mouth of the river was out of question with the constantly shifting delta establishing one stretch of land or removing another, and since that area consisted entirely of soil deposits from upriver, there were no places stable enough to hold a city. A location too far up the river would eliminate the possibility of sailing vessels docking at port for unloading goods from France and returning to Europe laden with furs, foods and tobacco from the colony. Only two weeks after being appointed Commandant Général Bienville quietly led a group of convicts, mostly salt smugglers who had been sentenced in France to life in Louisiana, to a crescent in the river where the waters were deep enough for an inland port, close enough to the Gulf for the ships to sail to it, and inland enough to serve as a more central place of commerce with the planned concessions that would supply tobacco, cotton and rice, not to mention fur trade from the upper Mississippi area. His men began clearing the trees and swamp brush, and in June built the first shacks on the site. Only then did he inform Paris, "We are working at present on the establishment of New Orleans thirty leagues above the entrance of the Mississippi."[3]

Bienville had chosen the best and worst place to build the city of his dreams. It was best for all the obvious reasons already mentioned: accessibility to the gulf, central location on the river, and deep waters for a port. It was the worst possible location because it was low in elevation, only five feet above sea level, and in a bowl between the river and Lake Ponchartrain and thus prone to severe flooding, had a bedrock of clay covered by up to seventy feet of sandy soil, was in the vicinity of unfriendly or untrustworthy Native American tribes, and was close enough to the open waters of the Gulf of Mexico to suffer the full onslaught of severe hurricanes.[4] In 1718, against all odds and with the fierce determination that was a Le Moyne family trait, Bienville continued scratching out a village in the river crescent and making his arguments to Paris that the capital should be relocated to New Orleans. In June of that year he wrote in his journal, "We are working at Nouvelle Orleans with as much zeal as the shortage of men will permit…I am grieved to see so few people engaged in a task which requires at least a hundred times the number."[5] Capital city or not, John Law saw the logistical advantages to this new town and ordered a Company garrison, a director's building and staff housing to be built at the location, giving Bienville a much needed boost of confidence in his decision. That same year Bienville secured the services of two engineers, Pierre Le Blond de La Tour and his assistant Adrian de Pauger, to begin designing a proposed city plan which could be presented to the authorities as enticement to relocate the capital.

Bienville's dreams were almost dashed in the summer of 1718 when he received word from France that the capital would not be built in New Orleans, but at Bayou Manchac, a waterway near Baton Rouge which offered direct access from the Mississippi to Biloxi and Mobile via Lake Maurepas and Lake Pontchartrain. Never one to surrender a passionately held idea, Bienville continued to develop his new town, and awarded himself two large tracts of land at its center stretching from the riverfront all the way to the swamp behind the planned city.[6] Hearing the news that Lake Pontchartrain was too shallow for major shipping, the Company directors in France once again changed their minds and decided, in September, 1720, that Biloxi would indeed remain the capital, Bienville continued arguing for New Orleans. In spite of the indecisiveness of the directors, Bienville kept developing his beloved city, pointing newly arrived settlers in its direction, and working with La Tour and Pauger on the city plans.

Two things happened in 1721 that gave New Orleans the boost it needed. First, John Law's enterprises collapsed in scandal and the entire Mississippi Company was forced into reorganization with an entirely new board of directors in Paris, men keen on making the best decisions to keep the Louisiana enterprise afloat. Second, Pauger completed his plans for the new city and sent them to officials in Biloxi, which at the time was suffering from an epidemic, a food shortage, and an unmanageable influx of settlers including Pierre Mayeux and Marie Cellier. On December 21, 1721 orders were sent from France, finally, to relocate the capital to New Orleans.[7] It would take five more months before news reached Louisiana, but in 1722 Biloxi was abandoned and the capital was relocated to Bienville's New Orleans.

Exactly when Pierre and Marie departed Arkansas Post after the miserable failure of trying to establish that concession is not known. We know they were in at the post in 1723 when their first child, Francois Pierre, was born, and were in New Orleans by 1726 when Arkansas Post was closed. In 1727 Marie gave birth to their second child, Genevieve, in New Orleans. In March of that same year Pierre stood as a witness in the wedding of Pierre Thomelin and is listed as a "resident of New Orleans."[8] Records indicate that another of the Arkansas concession workers, Jean-Baptiste Homard was married in New Orleans in December, 1724 and had several fellow concession workers as witnesses. Homard, too, was clearly a friend of the Mayeuxs, as his son Jean Louis would later marry their daughter Cecile.[9] Since travel up the Mississippi River was no easy matter, it stands to reason that these workers had already relocated to New Orleans by 1724. In short, sometime between late 1723 and 1726 Pierre and Marie moved to New Orleans and began to rebuild their lives after the Arkansas Post debacle.

When they had passed by New Orleans in 1721 the town consisted of nothing more than a dozen or two men and an unorganized scattering of pole cabins with thatched roofs. Two years later in 1723 the population was 380. Now it was the bustling capital of Louisiana and on its way to becoming a great city. Due in part to the influx of settlers from the failed Arkansas Post, the 1726 census records a population of 650 French people including sixteen carpenters, and 106 slaves.[10] Work was readily available in this growing town to the degree that some projects had to be postponed for lack of a sufficient number of skilled workers.

Not only were there houses to be built, but also a church, a hospital, and several government buildings including barracks and officers quarters across from the central *Place d'Armes* square. A year later, the 1727 census showed that within one year the population had increased by only 150 people, but the number of carpenters in New Orleans had doubled.[11]

Adrian de Pauger, the engineer who laid out the plan for the city, had the initial ground clearing part of his work done for him by the forces of nature when a devastating hurricane destroyed New Orleans on September 12, 1722. Nearly everything was blown away. The wooden church was completely destroyed along with most of the haphazardly situated pole cabins. The hurricane, in effect, gave Pauger a clean slate from which to start. His plans called for a garden city eleven blocks wide and six blocks deep, fronted by the quay along the river. Each block was subdivided into twelve squares with enough space in each for a house and garden. Since there was no stone to quarry for several hundred miles, the structures were to be built in the traditional Normandy style of steep pitched hip roofs and walls of *briquete entre poteaux*, brick between posts.[12]

The reality differed from the plans: the first buildings to go up were barracks for the workers themselves, followed by the military barracks, the royal warehouse, a military hospital and the private residences of those who could afford to build homes.[13] These were all built from wood and had wooden floors placed directly on the ground. The homes were made of wooden slats placed upright and driven into the ground. Since nails were scarce, most beams were tied together with rope, but this was complicated by a shortage of rope in the area.[14] Nails and rope were not the only items in short supply. There was no glass available for windows, so instead the windows were shuttered and kept closed to keep out mosquitoes, or the better buildings might have windows covered in plastille, a fine mesh cloth that served as a screen which allowed air and light to enter.[15] Because of the dampness of the ground, the wooden floors and outside walls quickly began to rot, and most of the buildings lasted no more than a few years.

Immediately behind the Place d'Armes was a square designated for a church and future cathedral. Although it was decided in 1723 to have the church build on contract, there was not enough money to pay workers and purchase supplies. Instead, the governing council traded newly arrived slaves for cypress wood. The contract went to Michel Seringue, recognized as the best carpenter in New Orleans, who in turn subcontracted the work to other competent carpenters. The weatherboarding contract fell to Pierre Thomelin, a close friend to fellow carpenter Pierre Mayeux[16], and it may be that Pierre also worked weatherboarding the church. The main part of the structure was not completed until November, 1726, and it took another year before the interior was finished enough for services to be held. The church was dedicated on Christmas Eve, 1727, with a nave that was 112 feet long, thirty two feet wide and twenty four feet high, and filled with eighteen pews which were auctioned to the highest bidders, two L-shaped pews reserved for the Superior Council, and a special armchair for the governor.[17]

The beautiful plans drawn out by Pauger were a fantasy compared to the reality that emerged in New Orleans in the 1720's and 1730's. The orderly plots laid out on the map were in reality patches of thick weeds, snakes, and free wandering pigs and cattle. [18] The nicely paved roads were actually muddy trails prone to flooding every time it rained. In 1724 the residents were ordered to dig three feet deep ditches around their property with wooden bridges going across them at the front of the houses and at each intersection. The results were catastrophic. A heavy rain would fill the ditches and cause them to become rolling streams of muddy water which crashed into one another at the corners and destroyed the wooden bridges. When the rainfall stopped the ditches became long pools of stagnant water that were perfect for breeding mosquitoes.[19]

With these unsanitary conditions disease was rampant. Death was so common that in August of 1723 there were on average eight or nine funerals a day.[20] Practically everyone in New Orleans suffered from malaria or yellow fever brought on by the mosquitoes, or from dysentery caused by the polluted water, or from scurvy brought on by a lack of good food. Add to this the real famine that occurred the first years. Several years saw severe shortages, but because of war with the Natchez and the hurricane of September, food in 1723 was particularly sparse. Then, the spring of 1724 saw six weeks of uninterrupted rain.[21] Food brought in pirogues from places to the north alleviated the shortages ever so slightly as makeshift markets were set up on the quay. Only in 1725 did things begin to turn around with a relatively good local harvest and the arrival of three ships loaded with food from France, but the food supply did not stabilize until 1728.[22]

Marcel Giraud describes the scene as one of,

> "disorder and filth…Everything, moreover, contributed to strengthening that impression: the uncleared land in too many of the blocks; the absence of enclosures around these sites, against which the Conseil Supérieur protested again and again; and the farm animals, especially pigs, that

wandered freely about the town, causing permanent damage to the banks of the ditches and to the inhabited areas."[23]

In his book *The Accidental City* Lawrence Powell sums up the scene as looking, "like a manmade bog with intersections. By the time the Company of the Indies surrendered its charter in 1731, New Orleans had scarcely emerged from its land-clearing stage, its notional neatness still only visible for a few blocks back from the river."[24]

The culture of New Orleans was as abysmal as the living conditions. Louisiana's first French inhabitants, other than soldiers, were men and women who had been forced to come either because they were in desperate straits or because they were criminals and prostitutes loaded onto the boats in chains. Consequently, as many as one quarter of New Orleans original inhabitants were criminals.[25] Added to this motley crew were the survivors of the failed concessions such as Arkansas Post, many without a trade to ply or any plans other than going to New Orleans in hopes of finding a new life.

Illegal taverns served patrons wine, brandy and beer until they were inebriated and easy prey for unscrupulous gamblers, causing the streets to be filled with violence and "an atmosphere of general delinquency." When the authorities shut down a tavern in one part of town in a matter of days it would open again in another location. To complicate matters, New Orleans became a prime location for prostitution. In an attempt to kill two birds with one stone, clean the streets of Paris and populate Louisiana, the French Crown arrested prostitutes, sent them to the Salpetriere prison, then shipped many of them to Louisiana. Some were forced into marriages with convincts, loaded onto ships handcuffed to their husbands, and sent to Louisiana to make a new life for themselves. As can be expected, most of these marriages did not last, and the prostitutes went back to doing what they knew to do. Because of a quirky law in the colony, any woman arrested for prostitution was ordered to be sent to New Orleans for punishment and rehabilitation.[26] The punishment for the worst offenders was public flogging, but after enduring the humiliation and pain, the women simply resumed their trade, staying in New Orleans rather than making the trip back up the river to wherever they had come from. The drunkenness, gambling and prostitution led Governor Périer to report, "Idleness and vice prevail here more than in any other country in the world."[27]

It may have been that the Mayeux family went back to New Orleans in hopes of actually returning to France. Thousands of *engages* attempted exactly that, but few were able to afford the trip home and ended up settling in the crescent city or in some other place in the colony. Whatever the case, Pierre would have easily found work as a carpenter in the growing city, and in 1727 their second child, Genevieve, was born to them. But clearly, New Orleans was no place to raise a family. With a five year old son and a newborn baby girl, Pierre and Marie began making plans to leave the dangerous and dirty city of New Orleans for a more pastoral setting. They had passed through Natchez twice, on their way to and from Arkansas Post, and after experiencing life in Biloxi and on the river, must have appreciated the peaceful setting high up on the bluffs above the river, the orderly conduct of the village that was more like their hometown than anything else they had experienced in Louisiana, and the opportunity not only for Pierre to work as a carpenter, but also perhaps to become a gentleman farmer. Natchez was becoming known as a tobacco producing area, the very crop France was eager to consume.

Sometime in late 1727 or early 1728 Pierre and Marie bundled up their belongings and their two little children, and along with Jacques and Francienne Cantrelle,[28] with whom they had journeyed since leaving France, bade farewell to the swampy pit of New Orleans, and once again boarded a pirogue for their new promised land.

---

[1] Powell, p. 21.

[2] *Ibid*, p. 41f.

[3] *Ibid*, p. 43.

[4] Joan B Garvey and Mary Lou Widmer, *Beautiful Crescent: A History of New Orleans*, Pelican Publishing, Gretna, 2013, p. 20.

[5] *Ibid*, p. 39.

[6] Powell, p. 45.

[7] *Ibid*, p. 57.

[8] *Sacramental Record of the Roman Catholic Church of the Archdiocese of New Orleans, Volume 1 - 1718-1750*, p. 247.

[9] Judy Riffel, *A History of Pointe Coupee Parish And Its Families,* Le Comité Des Archives De La Louisiane, Baton Rouge, 1983, p. 159; cf. *Marriage Book A, Cathedral of St. Louis King of France,* New Orleans.

[10] Giraud, p. 256f.

[11] *Ibid*, p. 257.

[12] Powell, p. 59.

[13] *Ibid*, p. 65.

[14] Giraud, p. 263f.

[15] Powell, p. 65.

[16] Pierre Mayeux served as a witness for his wedding in March, 1727.

[17] Mark R. Matrana, *Lost Plantation: The Rise And Fall Of Seven Oaks,* University Press of Mississippi, Jackson, 2011, p. 152.

[18] Powell, p. 66.
[19] Giraud, p. 210f.
[20] Ibid, p. 216.
[21] *Ibid*, p. 264.
[22] *Ibid*, p. 265.
[23] *Ibid*, p. 212.
[24] Powell, p. 67.
[25] *Ibid*, p. 69.
[26] Giraud, p. 271.
[27] *Ibid*, p. 271.
[28] Jacques Cantrelle is listed as a resident of Natchez in March, 1728; http://digitalcollections.uark.edu/cdm/compoundobject/collection/CAPA/id/305.

Chapter Seven
The Grand Village
1728

The old Indian sat across the room from Le Page du Pratz and complained about how things had changed. Du Pratz had stopped the old man as he walked along a trail near his house. "What has happened? We used to be friends, are we no longer? You used to come to my house but now you just walk by. Have you forgotten where I live, or is my house disagreeable to you? My heart is the same toward you, and toward all my friends. I am not capable of changing it. But why have you changed?"

At first the Indian, called the Tattooed Serpent, was embarrassed, but his disposition soon turned to anger and frustration as he described the situation. "I am ashamed to have gone so long without seeing you, but when the French went to war with us, you were part of them."

"You are wrong to think that way," du Platz told the old man, "Monsieur de Bienville is our War Chief, and we are bound to obey him just like you are bound to obey your brother, the Great Sun Chief, and are obliged to kill or cause to be killed whoever he orders put to death."

Tattooed Serpent lamented the frustrations of recent times, "You know that I did not approve the war our people made on the French when we avenged the deaths of our relatives. I am the one who made them carry the peace pipe to the French - you know this well because you were the first one to smoke the pipe with us. Do the French have two hearts, a good one today and a bad one tomorrow? As for my brother and me, we have only one heart, one word. Tell me then if you are, as you say, my true friend, and what you think of all this. We don't know what to think of the French. They began the war, then granted peace and offered it of themselves, and then when we were living quietly and thought we were at peace, people come to kill us without saying a word!"

The old man, second only to the Great Sun in power and authority among the Natchez, continued, "Why did the French come into our country at all? We didn't go looking for them! They asked for land because their country was too little for all the men who were in it and we told them they could take land anywhere they pleased, that there was enough for them and for us, and that we would share with them our provisions and help them build and work in their fields. Haven't we done this? Why did we need the French? Before they came didn't we live better lives than we do now? We do without some of our corn, our game, our fish, because we share it with them. Why did we need them? Was it for their guns? The bows and arrows we used gave us a good life. Was it for their white, blue and red blankets? We can do well enough with buffalo skins, and they are warmer. Our women made feather blankets for the winter, and mulberry mantles for the summer. Maybe they weren't as beautiful as your blankets, but our women were harder workers then and less vain than they are now. In short, before the French arrived we lived like men who were satisfied with what they had, now we live like slaves who are not allowed to do as they please."[1]

The people dwelling in the half a dozen Indian villages along the east bank of the Mississippi River and collectively called by the French "the Natchez" were in fact not a homogenous group, but were rather a conglomeration of Natchez, Tiou and Griga tribes who had united themselves for the sake of commerce and protection. They were, in effect, refugees banding together to become a new people.[2]

The Natchez themselves were descendants of the Plaquemine culture which had thrived in the area since the 700's. At the height of its power between the 13th and 16th centuries the Plaquemine culture covered the Mississippi valley from central Arkansas to the Gulf of Mexico and built the massive Emerald Mound ceremonial site eleven miles northeast of Natchez, an eight acre mound that is the second largest mound in the United States. As their culture began to wane sometime before 1700 the Natchez abandoned the great Emerald Mound and built the Grand Village near present day Natchez, Mississippi where in five or six villages the confederate tribes hunted and planted crops along the bluffs of the river.

The Grand Village was the ceremonial center for the Natchez and the smaller refugee groups that had joined them, but few residents actually lived there. Composed of two mounds in the center of a flat grassy area, the village was surrounded by trees and bordered on one side by a creek. The northernmost mound was the Great Sun Chief's house made of vertical poles and a thatched roof and the southern mound was the temple and burial site. The temple building was sixty feet long and forty-two feet wide, and divided into a large room and a smaller one. There were five or more villages with a combined population of more than 3,500 in close proximity to Grand Village which served as home to the federation of tribes. The Flower village was closest, just across St. Catherine Creek from the Grand Village and populated by Natchezan people. The Tiou village was about three miles west of the Grand and the Griga village was a similar distance east. The Jenzenqaque village was near the Emerald Mound eleven miles northeast, and the largest of these neighborhoods, the White Apple Village, was a few miles north of the Grand Village.[3]

Because the cluster of villages were composed of different tribes, there was no single chief over them all. Instead, it was "an uneasy coalition of big-men"[4] working together under the general oversight of the Great Sun Chief. Neither were these groups united in allegiances. The two villages closest to the Mississippi River, the Flour and Tiou settlements, were pro-French, while the White Apple, Jenzenaque and Griga tended to favor the far off English along the eastern seaboard of Carolina who were attempting to make inroads into the Mississippi valley.[5]

These tall and proud Indians stirred up a mixture of awe and fear in the first French people to encounter them. The men were described as "very well formed" and the women as having, "well proportioned figures and are generally quite agreeable in appearance," who, "take very good care of their appearance and pride themselves on an extreme cleanliness."[6] The Natchez also practice head flattening and tattooing. The men shaved their heads except for the crown, which was grown long and braided, while the women wore their hair long and unadorned.[7]

Depending on the season, the Indians of the villages might be practically naked, with nothing more than a belt around the waist with a small cloth hanging in front or, when it was colder, the women wore dresses that extended from the neck to the feet while the men wore leather pants and jackets. When they began trading with the French they also incorporated some French clothing into their attire.[8]

The warriors had pierced ears, and some of them had huge holes in their earlobes "large enough to pass an egg through."[9] Among the warriors, tattoos were badges of bravery. Andre Pénicaut, who traveled with d'Iberville through Natchez country, wrote,

> "The greater part have fantastic marks imprinted on the face, the arms, the legs, and the thighs; so far as the body is concerned, this is a right which belongs only to the warriors, and one must be noted on account of the death of some enemy in order to merit this distinction. They imprint on the stomachs of their heroes an infinity of black, red, and blue lines; which is not done without pain...but the greatest ornament of all theses savages of both sexes consists in certain figures of suns, serpents, and other things, which they carry pictured on their bodies in the manner of the ancient Britons...The warriors, as well as the wives of the chiefs and the Honored men, have these figures pictured on the face, arms, shoulders, thighs, legs, but principally on the

belly and stomach. It is not for them only an ornament, but also a mark of honor and distinction, which is only acquired after many brave deeds."[10]

The warriors who had distinguished themselves in battle had tattoos of war clubs on their right shoulders, as well as symbols of their defeated foe.[11]

Although the first Frenchmen in Louisiana found the Natchez intriguing and attractive, they did not find them trustworthy. Fr. Jean-Francios Bisson de St. Cosme who served as a missionary among the Natchez for seven years beginning in 1699, told a friend of his that the Natchez "practice polygamy, steal, and are very vicious, the girls and women more than the men and boys." He wrote in another letter, "One is persuaded that they are all thieves and try only to do harm, and that if they had no fear they would kill a man in order to get his knife."[12] Not only were the girls given to thievery and viciousness, according to more than one account they were also particularly promiscuous. Pénicaut wrote in the account of his time among them that the women were "lustful and without restraint," and that the girls' "fathers and their mothers and their religion teach them that, when they leave this world, they have to cross over a narrow and difficult plank before they can enter their Grand Village, where they claim they go after death, and that in the Grand Village will be only those who will have made merry indeed with the boys." Pénicaut concluded, "They will pass easily across this plank."[13] The standing tradition among the Natchez, which was carried out with their French guests as much as with their fellow tribesmen, was for the father of a home, as an act of hospitality, to offer a visiting guest his daughter for the evening.[14]

There was, among the Natchez, a "third sex." Dumont related that while the women remained in the villages caring for the home and cultivating the soil, when the men went out hunting they took with them a man,

> "...who is useful to them when love arouses urges contrary to the craft of hunting. This Indian wears an alconand [skirt] like the women, has hair like theirs, has altogether the appearance of a woman, and in the village is looked upon as the chief of women. When he returns to his house, he is permitted, during the days of the full moon, to go see the wives of the men with whom he has had relations, so as to return at least some of what had been lent to him during the hunting trip and thus to relieve, in part, the jealousy that the women might have on his account. During the rest of the lunar cycle, he is regarded as female and works alongside the women."[15]

The temple at the Grand Village was the center of religious life for the Natchez, and contained a perpetual sacred fire guarded by several warriors who were also responsible for gathering wood to keep the flame alive. If the flame ever died, all the guardians along with their wives and children were put to death.[16] The Natchez believed in the "Great Chief," the creator who is "goodness itself, which cannot do evil," as well as a devil character who was "forever trying to injure them in their bodies and their possessions, whether in hunting or fishing, or even in war, and that because he is evil, it is to them they must pray, so that he does not do them any harm."[17] Du Pratz interviewed the guardian of the sacred fire in the temple and was told that the Natchez worshiped, "*Coyocop-Chill* or *Great Spirit*...the word *chill*, in their language, signifies the most superlative degree of perfection, and is added by them to the word which signifies fire, when they want to mention the Sun... therefore, by the word *Coyocop-Chill* they mean a spirit that surpasses other spirits as much as the sun does common fire." According to the Natchez, God

> "...was so great and powerful, that, in comparison to him, all other things were as nothing; he had made all that we see, all that we can see, and all that we cannot see; he was so good, that he could not do ill to any one, even if he had a mind to it. They believe that God had made all things by his will; that nevertheless the little spirits, who are his servants, might, by his orders, have made many excellent works in the universe, which we admire; but that God himself formed man with his own hands."[18]

When du Pratz asked the guardian exactly how God made man with his own hands, he was told,

> "that God had kneaded some clay, such as that which potters use, and had made it into a little man; and that after examining it, and finding it well formed, he blew upon his work, and forthwith that little man had life, grew, acted, walked, and found himself a man perfectly well shaped... the man was made first, and was the strongest and most courageous, because he was to be the head and support of the woman, who was made to be his companion."[19]

If the creation narrative of the Natchez sounds similar to the Jewish creation story, so does the ethics given by God to humanity. The temple guardian continued his conversation with du Pratz, telling him that many years ago a man and his wife appeared to the Natchez who had come down from the sun, both of whom shone with the brilliance of light. The man saw the sorry state in which the Natchez conducted themselves and had come down to instruct them in a better manner of life.

> "He moreover told us, that in order to live in peace among ourselves, and to please the supreme Spirit, we must indispensably observe the following points: we must never kill any one but in defense of our own lives; we must never know any other woman besides our own; we must never take any thing that belongs to another; we must never lie nor get drunk; we must not be avaricious, but must give liberally, and with joy, part of what we have to others who are in want, and generously share our subsistence with those who are in need of it."[20]

The temple was built at the command of this man from the sun and he instructed that a sacred fire should be kept, kindled with a flame which the man would bring down from the sun, and which should be eternally preserved, guarded by eight men day and night.

> "He likewise ordered another temple to be built in a distant part of our nation, which was then very populous, and the eternal fire to be kept there also, that in case it should be extinguished in the one it might be brought from the other; in which case, till it was again lighted, the nation would be afflicted with great mortality."

Unlike other nations, du Pratz recounted, "The Natchez have neither sacrifices, libations, or offerings: their whole worship consists in preserving the eternal fire."[21]

Later, when visited in his home by the Great Sun Chief, du Pratz told him that it was a simple thing to call down fire from the sun. He then brought out a magnifying glass and some tinder, spoke the Natchez word *caheuch*, that is, "come," and kindled a flame on a chip of wood. The chief was astonished and asked if any man could do the same, so du Pratz placed the glass in the chief's hands and told him to say *caheuch*. When the flame again appeared the chief was so confounded, "that he dropped both the chip on which it was laid and the glass out of his hands, crying out, 'Ah, what a miracle!'" When the chief offered to purchase the glass for any price, even to be paid by every family of the nation, du Pratz asked only for food. In return for the glass the chief gave him, "twenty barrels of maize, of 150 pounds each, twenty fowls, twenty turkeys, and told me that he would send me game and fish every time his warriors brought him any, and his promise was punctually fulfilled." The following day the chief gathered all his nobles and demonstrated his newfound ability to kindle fire from the sun.[22]

Like other Native American cultures, the Natchez believed that spirits dwelled in many of the animals and they prayed to lesser gods in the forms of snakes, crawfish and turtles.[23] But unlike the simple and peaceful Quapaw to the north, the Natchez had very elaborate rituals tied to their gods, the seasons of the year, and important events in the villages such as the declaration of war or the death of a chief.[24]

Dumont, who lived among the Natchez in the 1720's, was an eyewitness to the funeral of Natchez nobility, and his description shows both the pageantry and the brutality that was Natchez religious ceremony.

> "As soon as the Great Chief died, his corpse is dressed in his finest clothing, just as if he were alive, and he is laid out upon his bed. He continues to be given food to eat and a pipe to smoke, just as if he were alive and speaking, for nine days. While he is lying in state on his bed, women with young infants at the breast come to offer him their innocents, whom they suffocate and throw down before him as sacrificial victims."

All the wives and servants of the Chief join in the festivities, and show no sadness or dread, although they are fully aware that when the Chief is buried, they too will be killed to escort him and serve him in the afterlife.

> "At the temple, a large grave is prepared, deep and spacious enough to be able to hold, as if in one grand vessel, all the corpses that are destined to accompany their chief into the land of the dead. When the day of the ceremony has at last arrived, those who must die arrive in the village plaza at dawn, dressed in all their best finery...They bow toward the four corners of the earth as if to bid them a final farewell. Then the corpse of the chief is taken up on a litter, and four of the Indian leaders or honored men of the village carry it on their shoulders, though, rather than take it straight to the temple, they turn back and forth so as to take the longest possible route. Along this path, women continue to throw, at the feet of the pallbearers, their suckling infants, who are crushed...The other victims, at the sound of the drums, rattles, maracas, and jingle bells, and the cries and wails of the populace, march in step, jumping and striking a thousand different poses, some of them indecent, around the chief's litter."

When they finally arrived at the temple gravesite the wives and servants destined to be sacrificed were seated in a row facing the temple, their heads were covered with deerskin sacks tightened at the neck with a cord, and "the victims' relatives, fathers, mothers, and even their children...stand on either side and pull the cord." Finally, the servants were buried on the bottom of the grave, followed by the chief and his wife, and the infants placed on top.[25]

The social structure of the Natchez was two tiered, nobility and commoner. In marriage, all members of the nobility clan were required to take partners from among the common people, and the noble line of chiefdom was passed down through the matrilineal line, that is, through the mother.[26] Although each village had a "big man" chief, the two most powerful men among the Natchez were the Great Sun, the chief among chiefs who lived in the Grand Village, and the Tattooed Serpent, an office akin to a modern day secretary of state who was responsible for diplomacy and negotiations with other tribes and with the recently arrived Europeans.[27]

Handsomeness, bravery and promiscuity were not the only characteristics the Natchez were known for. They were also known for being brutal with their enemies. Dumont describes the brutality in his account of their handling of prisoners. He wrote that, "the prisoners are led into the plaza in front of the temples, and if they are not to be kept as slaves, a council is assembled in the home of the chief, and there they are condemned to be burned." The prisoners were stripped naked and paraded into the plaza and made to stand in front of wooden square frames where one of the women from the noble class had the option of buying the prisoner as a personal slave. If no buyer comes forward,

> "...they begin to remove the scalps from the victims' heads. Then their two arms are tied to each end of the top beam of the square, and their feet rest on the lower one without being tied to it, and then more than twenty or thirty Indians holding dried canes flaming at one end burn the victims, first on one side, then on the other, or perhaps first on an arm, then a buttock, all the while taunting them with a thousand insults and raillery. And if, during this barbecue, he should cry out or shed a tear...rather than continue the torture, it is halted so that the victim might be given something to eat to restore his strength, after which it will begin again in earnest."

Dumont describes personally witnessing the torture of a young Indian woman, no more than fifteen or sixteen years old, who endured the flames for more than four hours without ever shedding a tear or crying out. If the fire torture alone did not cause suitable suffering in the eyes of the Natchez warriors, they would cut the flesh off the victims and chew it before their very eyes.[28]

Considering the violent and duplicitous culture of the Natchez, it is perhaps something of a surprise that they initially had a relatively peaceful coexistence with the newly arrived French people in Louisiana, except for two "wars" which would be considered "conflicts" in today's parlance.

In 1710 Antoine de La Mothe, Sieur de Cadillac, who had founded Detroit nine years earlier, was appointed by the King of France as the new governor of Louisiana. Ignoring the king's orders to immediately take up residence in Mobile, Cadillac instead returned to France and didn't arrive in Louisiana until three years later. In 1715 he traveled up the Mississippi River where the pompous and arrogant governor insulted the Natchez by refusing to smoke the peace pipe with the chief. Bienville, at that time Cadillac's lieutenant, reported to France that as they traveled up the river, "he quarreled as he went up with all the nations that are along the river." In spite of the various tribes welcoming him and offering him gifts, "He made them no presents." On his return down the river Cadillac completely ignored the Indians. "That made a very bad impression," Bienville wrote, "all the nations are talking about it with very great scorn to the shame of the French to the extent of threatening to kill some of them."[29] To the Natchez, refusing to smoke the calumet or peace pipe was tantamount to a declaration of war.

About the same time as Cadillac made his rude display of condescension, a group of four French *voyageurs* or trappers hired four Natchez Indians to assist them in paddling upriver. Once upriver, the Indians murdered the trappers and took their canoes and supplies. When Bienville heard the report he was convinced this was an act brought on by Cadillac's arrogance and seeming declaration of war. It may, instead, have been brought on by any number of possible misunderstandings or treacheries between the trappers and the Indians. The Indians also looted the trading post of the La Loire brothers, the first French settlers among the Natchez. But whatever the cause of the conflict on the river between the French rivermen and the Indians, the consequence was a short conflict called by the French, "The First Natchez War."

Even before the Cadillac incident, Bienville had received orders from the King to establish a fort at Natchez in order to counter the threat of English encroachment into the territory.

These forts or outposts which were springing up along the Mississippi were actually seen as mutually beneficial by both the French and the Indians by whose villages the forts were always established. The French soldiers and settlers could depend on the Indians for supplying game, crops and skins, and the Indians were happy to trade for European cloth, metal pots and utensils, metal knives, guns, powder, and lead balls, all of which made life easier. A French fort among friendly Indians was a symbiotic relationship in which both groups prospered.

With a group of about fifty soldiers (there were only 150 in the entire Louisiana colony at the time), Bienville left from Mobile in eight canoes and made his way up the Mississippi to an island across from Natchez where he set up camp on April 24, 1716. Three days later a group of Natchez warriors appeared offering to smoke the calumet. Bienville refused, saying he would smoke only with the chiefs of the tribe. On April 8, a party of eight Natchez chiefs including the Great Sun and his brother the Tattooed Serpent arrived on the island to smoke with Bienville. Instead, he had his men arrest the chiefs and threw them into a makeshift jail. That night Bienville told the Great Sun and the Tattooed Serpent that in order to have peace, he wanted the heads of the murdering Indians, and the heads of the chiefs who had ordered or condoned the attack on the river men. One chief, the Little Sun, younger brother of the Great Sun, was released to return to the Indian village and carry out the deed. Less than a week later he returned carrying three heads, two belonging to the murderers, one belonging to a brother of a murderer who couldn't be found. Bienville was not satisfied, and returned Little Sun to the jail.

Still held captive, the Great Sun told Bienville that the troubles were the result of the pro-English groups within the villages.

Bienville had two of the pro-English chiefs in his jail and wanted the third, so he released the other chiefs on the condition that they deliver the head of the pro-English chief, Oleylape, restore the merchandize pillaged from the trading post, and supply labor for the planned fort to be built near their Grand Village. On June 7, Bienville smoked the calumet with the pro-French chiefs, and secretly had the two pro-English chiefs executed.[30]

The same day that Bienville smoked the calumet with the three chiefs, Barbazan de Pailloux returned to the island having been sent to scout a place for the fort, and reported that he "had seen the entire nation assembled; that it had shown great joy at what their chiefs had agreed with us; and that all these Indians were very much disposed to execute all that had been demanded of them." He also informed Bienville that he had "found near the river a hill situated very advantageously for the construction of our fort."[31] The next day Bienville sent four soldiers in a pirogue back across the river, loaded down with axes, spades, pickaxes, nails, and anything else necessary for building a fort.

Captain Chavange de Richelbourg, who kept a journal of the events, wrote that on the 25th and 26th of July Indians from neighboring villages began to arrive, 30 Yazoo, 30 Tunicas, and over 800 Natchez men and women, for a grand celebration during which the chiefs smoked the calumet with Bienville and told him that, "all these people were coming to dance at his gate in order to show him their joy at having Frenchmen established among them."[32] When Fort Rosalie, named after the wife of Louis Phélypeaux, Compte de Pontchartrain, the French secretary of the navy, was finished on August 3, 1716, it measured 150 feet by 90 feet, with wooden palisades, a guardhouse, barracks and two other storage buildings.[33]

With the safety provided by the fort and the friendly disposition of the Natchez toward the French, in 1718 workers newly arrived from France began to build homes around Fort Rosalie and to establish small farms. In 1719, John Law's Mississippi Company granted the establishment of two large concessions or plantations in Natchez near the Indian villages, the St. Catherine Concession located upstream and on the same side as the Grand Village, and the Terre Blanche Concession, located downstream and across the creek from the Grand Village. Viewed from above, the scene would have been one of a mottled patchwork of French and Indian homes and farms, all peacefully coexisting under the watchful eye of Fort Rosalie. And so it remained until 1722 and the conflict which came to be known as "The Second Natchez War."

The population of Natchez continued to grow as new French farmers and workers moved into the area. Every new arrival who was unfamiliar with Indian ways was a potential threat to the peaceful if fragile coexistence between the Indians and the settlers in Natchez. On October 21, 1722, just three or four months after Pierre and Marie Mayeux and the Arkansas bound workers had passed by on their way to the post, a heated dispute arose over a debt of corn owed by an Indian to sergeant La Fontaine of Fort Rosalie. In Natchez, more than in any other place in all of Louisiana, the intermingling of the French and the Indians was intimate. Indians worked for the French. Some Natchez women were housemaids for the French women. There was constant borrowing and loaning, with the French pledging repayment when the next supply ship arrived from New Orleans, or the Indians promising to make good on the loans as soon as the harvest came in or after a good hunting trip. The argument over the payment of corn escalated, and as more soldiers joined the side of the sergeant and more Indians joined the side of their fellow villager, things got out of control and became violent. The result was several Indians were wounded and one was killed.

When the sergeant was only reprimanded and not punished, the Indians were infuriated.[34] Du Pratz, who was living in Natchez at the time, wrote, "Revenge is the predominant passion of the people of America: so that we ought not be surprised, if the death of this old warrior raised his whole village against the French. The rest of the nation took no part at first in the quarrel."[35] The Indians went on a rampage, killing two men, then attacking both concessions. The commandant of Fort Rosalie sent du Pratz to the Tattooed Serpent to beg his help in calming the situation. As a result of the Tattooed Serpent's help, the leaders from the village came to du Pratz with the calumet, smoked it with him, and then went to the fort and smoked it with the commandant. This "war," du Pratz wrote, "lasted only three or four days."[36]

A year later another misunderstanding took place between the French and the Indians, this one a dispute about land boundaries and the theft and killing of farm animals from the St. Catherine concession. For some unknown reason, when Bienville heard of this latest breach of peace he reacted with a kind of scorched earth policy. On September 29, 1723, he left New Orleans with four boat loads of soldiers, rendezvoused with Canadian river men, and Tunica, Choctaw and Yazoo Indians, and fell upon the White Apple village with a fury. On the first of November Bienville and his men, along with the Indians who had joined his campaign, set out from St. Catherine and attacked the village with over 700 men, killing and scalping men, capturing women, and torching cabins.

The next day Bienville attacked the pro-English Griga village, burning the homes and scattering the people there, and then continued to the Jenzenaque village near the Emerald Mound and razed it. The pro-French villages quickly reaffirmed peace with Bienville and once again an uneasy peace settled onto Natchez.

The following years saw a few misunderstandings and small skirmishes between the Natchez and the French, but overall there was a sense of calm and peace. In 1725, the French lost a close ally with the death of the pro-French Tattooed Serpent. Three years later his older brother, the Great Sun, along with the chief of the Flour village died. The new Great Sun was immature and inexperienced, and as a result the chief of the pro-English White Apple settlement became the real power among the villages.

Sometime in late 1727 or early 1728 Pierre and Marie Mayeux, along with Jacques and Francienne Cantrelle, relocated from New Orleans to Natchez with the hopes of carving out a prosperous life in the place that Fr. Paul du Poisson described as "the finest, the most fertile, and the most populous in all Louisiana."[37] They arrived just before things took a severe turn for the worse.

---

[1] Paraphrased from du Pratz, pp. 90-92.

[2] Barnett, p. 44.

[3] *Ibid*, pp. 41-43.

[4] *Ibid*, p. 44.

[5] *Ibid*, p 44.)

[6] Swanton, p. 48, quoting Dumont.

[7] *Ibid*, p. 51.
[8] *Ibid*, p. 52.
[9] *Ibid*, p. 56.
[10] *Ibid*, p. 56.
[11] *Ibid*, p. 57.
[12] *Ibid*, p. 51
[13] Barnett, p. 51f.
[14] Caillot, p. 122.
[15] Dumont, p. 257f.
[16] *Ibid*, p. 344.
[17] *Ibid*, p. 345.
[18] du Pratz, p. 378.
[19] du Ibid, p. 379.
[20] *Ibid*, p. 380.
[21] *Ibid*, p. 381.
[22] *Ibid*, p. 383f.
[23] Dumont, p. 345.
[24] For a detailed description of the religious life of the Natchez gathered from a variety of eyewitness sources, cf. Swanton, pp. 158-181.
[25] Dumont, pp. 358-361.
[26] Barnett, p. 53.
[27] *Ibid*, p. xv, 86, 95.
[28] Dumont, p. 353f.
[29] Barnett, p. 61f.
[30] *Ibid*, pp. 67-71.
[31] Jack D. Elliott, *The Fort of Natchez and the Colonial Origins of Mississippi*, Eastern National, Fort Washington, PA, 2013, p. 9.
[32] Elliott, p. 9.
[33] Barnett, p. 71.
[34] *Ibid*, p. 85.
[35] du Pratz, p. 84.
[36] *Ibid*, p 86.
[37] French, p. 141, footnote.

The mill at Maintenay, the hometown of Pierre and Marie Mayeux, was originally built in the 12th century and is still a local attraction today. It would have been a familiar sight for the couple before their departure for Louisiana (photo by the author).

Transport of Prostitutes to the Salpetriere by Etienne Jearat, 1755; Musée Carnavalet, Paris. Many were forced into marriage to convicts and shipped to Louisiana.

LE COMMERCE QUE LES INDIENS DU MEXIQUE FONT AVEC LES FRANÇOIS AU PORT DE MISSISIPI

Facing page: *Le Commerce que les Indiens du Mexique Font avec les François au Port de Missisipi* by François-Gérard Jollain, c. 1720; The Historic New Orleans Collection 1952.3. Used by permission.

The Company of the Indies, the financial company chartered under John Law, produced this poster ca. 1720 to encourage immigration to Louisiana. Distributed in France and several German states, such posters presented highly inaccurate depictions of Louisiana. New Orleans, shown as a solidly built, fortified town, was actually only a few small houses and a warehouse at the time. The mountainous terrain and depictions of indigenous animals are pure conjecture. A partial translation of the text at the bottom of the painting reads:

"The climate is very mild and temperate. A good air is breathed in it, and one feels a perpetual spring, which contributes much to the fertility of the country which abounds in all things. The meadows watered by the Mississippi make excellent pastures from which fatten the cows, oxen, sheep, and other animals useful to the inhabitants. We also find grasses needed for the Horses. Trees, without being grafted or cultivated, naturally bear fruits of an exquisite taste, and plants of all kinds, both vegetable and medicinal, are found in the grass. We have found a means of taming the birds, the poultry, from which we derive great utility. The land and the vineyards with simple cultivation return corn and wine in abundance. Above the Mississippi there are mountains full of gold, silver, copper, lead, and quicksilver, which favor commerce, for the savages have become so much acquainted with the French colonies that they trade in good faith without distrusting or fearing on either side. Ass gold and silver are very common, and the savages do not know the value of it, they exchange pieces of gold or silver for European goods like knives, iron pots, axes to cut wood, and often even for a small mirror, a little brandy or something similar to their taste. The French trade for Indian canvases, threads, hemps, skins, wools, and things in demand in Europe.

"The plan of a new town…has been drawn up. It will be the capital of Louisiana. It is now called New Orleans. There are already more than six hundred well built houses for the inhabitants, each of whom…receives a free allotment of one hundred and twenty acres of land, which they can cultivate to their advantage. As this town is situated on the bank of the Mississippi River and is not far from the sea, it will be the center of commerce. Its port is magnificent in extent and proportion, able to contain the vessels which approach it from all parts…

"…The Catholic religion makes great progress through the indefatigable zeal of the missionaries. The frequent instructions given to the catechumens, together with the good examples of new converts, attract the idolatrous Indians to the joy of Jesus Christ, who ask with emulation to receive baptism. Great care is taken in the education of children. Finally, good order reigns everywhere by the attention and care of the chiefs or principal officers of the Company."

A ship being careened in La Rochelle and prepared for voyage. Artist unknown.

The port of La Rochelle, from which Pierre and Marie departed France in 1720 (photo by the author).

An 18th century Flute ship, similar to *Le Profond*, on which the Mayeuxs sailed to Louisiana.

De Lautre part	3690 ll
Mathurin Reis	21
Etne chans Luseau	21
françois descasor	21
Jacques Canterelle	21
Joseph Morcaux	21
pierre dovideau	21
Jean delanclos	21
andre tesier	21
francois Bourdon	21
Isac Bien Venu	21
Jerome Marquant	21
pierre dalbert	21
Louis bromart	21
Simon abivain	21
Jean fourquade	21
Thomas Lardreaux	21
pierre Guillien	18
Nicolas Gastier	18
pierre Mailleux	21
Jean Coste	21
Jean Pesere	21
Claude pequan	18
Jacques Michel	18
	1161

Type to enter text

The ship's registry from *Le Profond*. Pierre Mayeux is listed fifth from the bottom. Note Pierre's friend Jacques Cantrelle listed in line 4.

View of the Camp of John Law's Concession in New Biloxi, Louisiana by Jean Baptiste Michel Le Bouteaux, 1720. This drawing was created a year before the Mayeuxs' arrived in Biloxi.

Depiction of Arkansas Post in 1689 by Annie Hatley, 1904; used by permission of Arkansas State Archives.

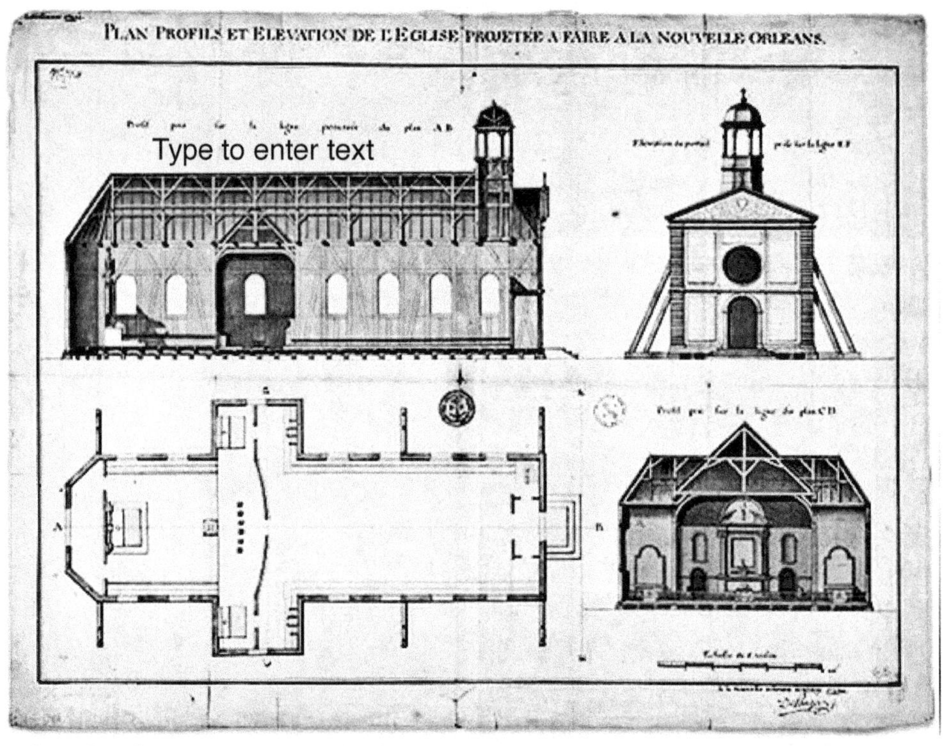

Plans for the St. Louis parish church in New Orleans by Adrien de Pauger, completed in 1727. There is circumstantial evidence that Pierre Mayeux worked as a carpenter on this building.

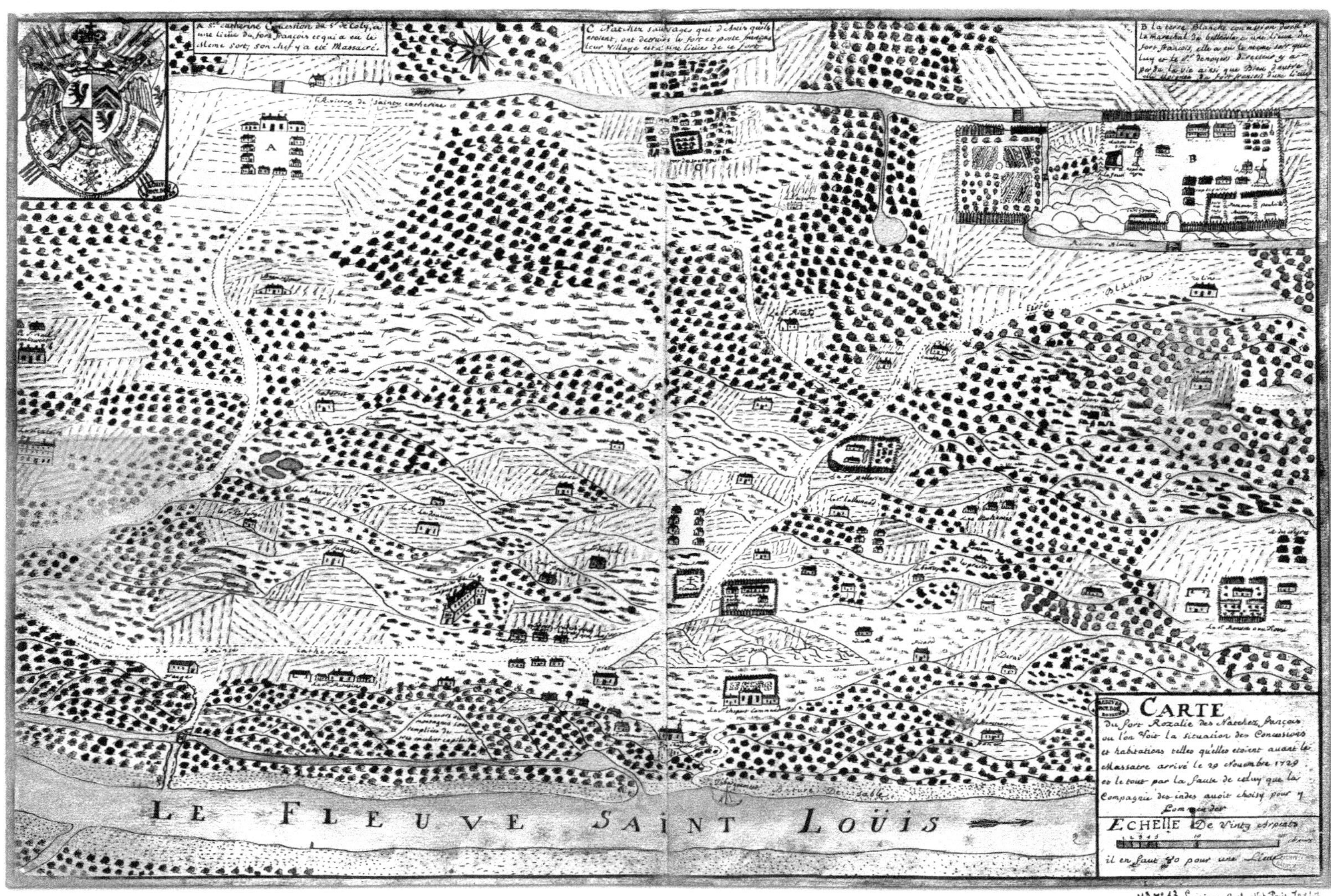

Map of 1729 Natchez by Dumont de Montigny, who lived in there shortly before the massacre. The Mayeux home was just south (left) of Fort Rosalie.

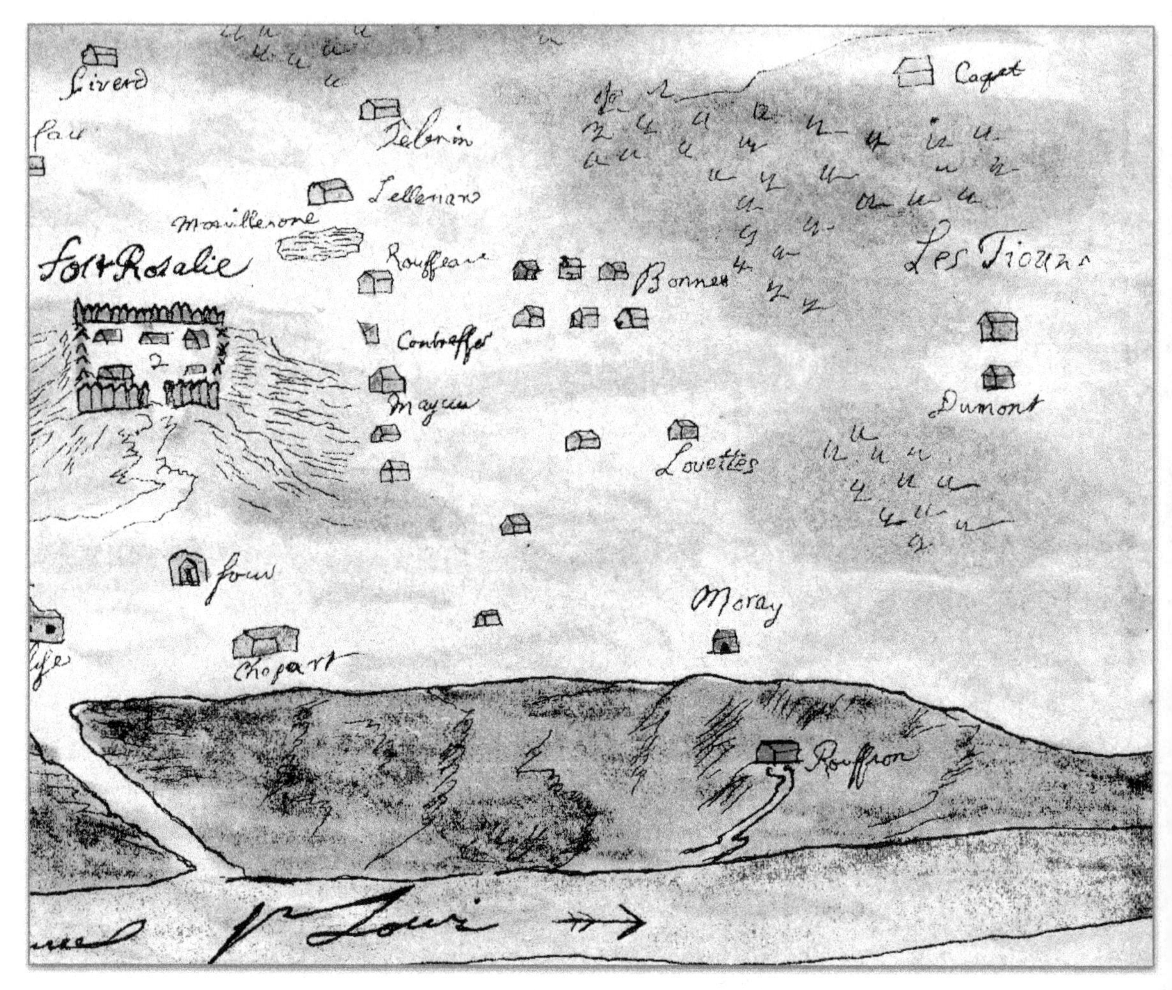

Tracing of circa 1730 map of Natchez by Dumont de Montigny. Note the Mayeux name is listed by the house just south (left) and downhill from Fort Rosalie. Note Dumont's own house on the far left. Courtesy of "Smokye" Joseph Frank, Natchez, MS.

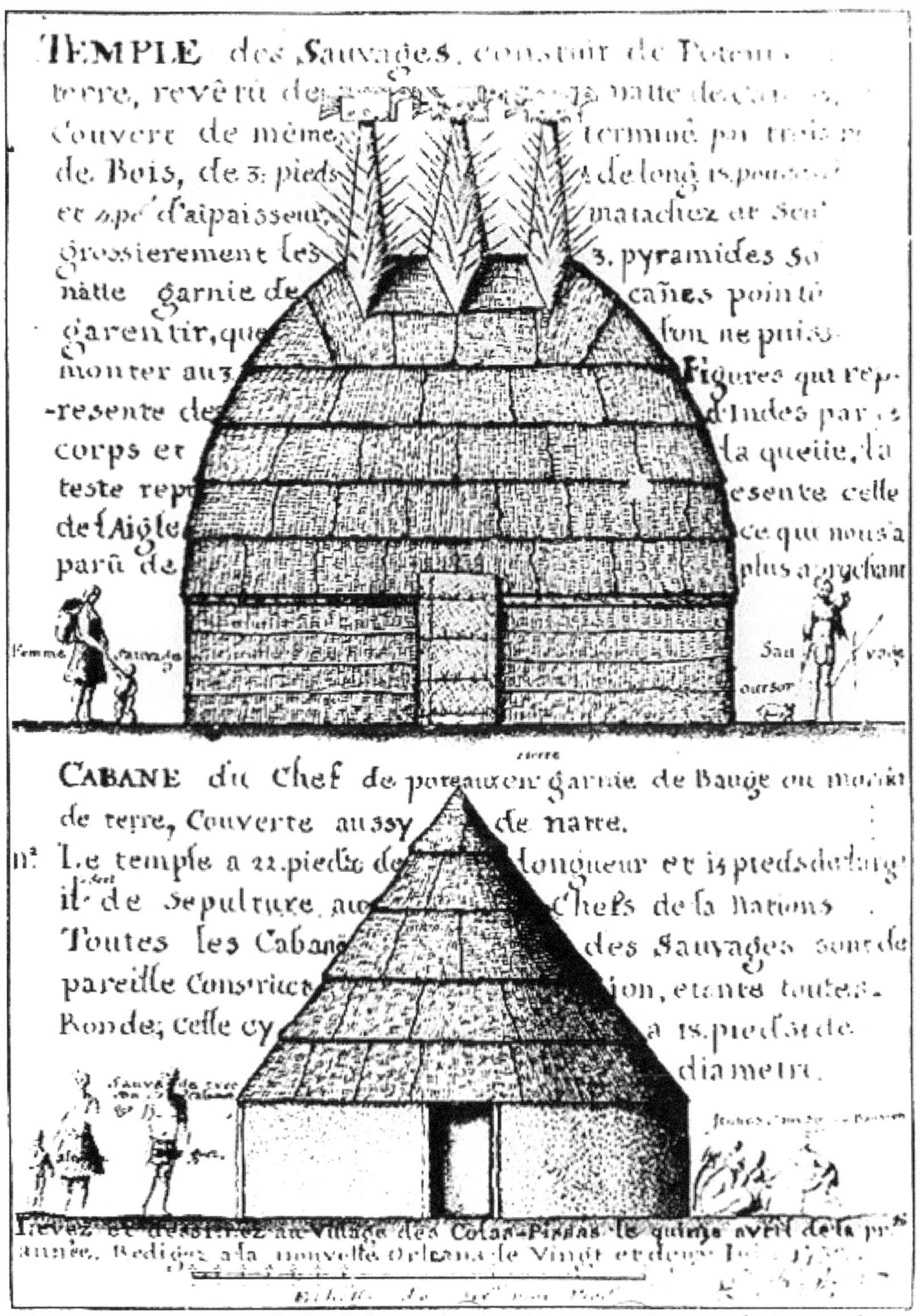

The Natchez Temple and Chief's house, by Antoine-Simon Le Page du Pratz, who lived in Natchez at the same time as the Mayeuxs. He relocated to New Orleans in 1728 and thus avoided the massacre.

Du Pratz depicts the Natchez warriors marching in procession with the calumet or peace pipe. A not uncommon occurrence, this march was part of the ruse before the massacre.

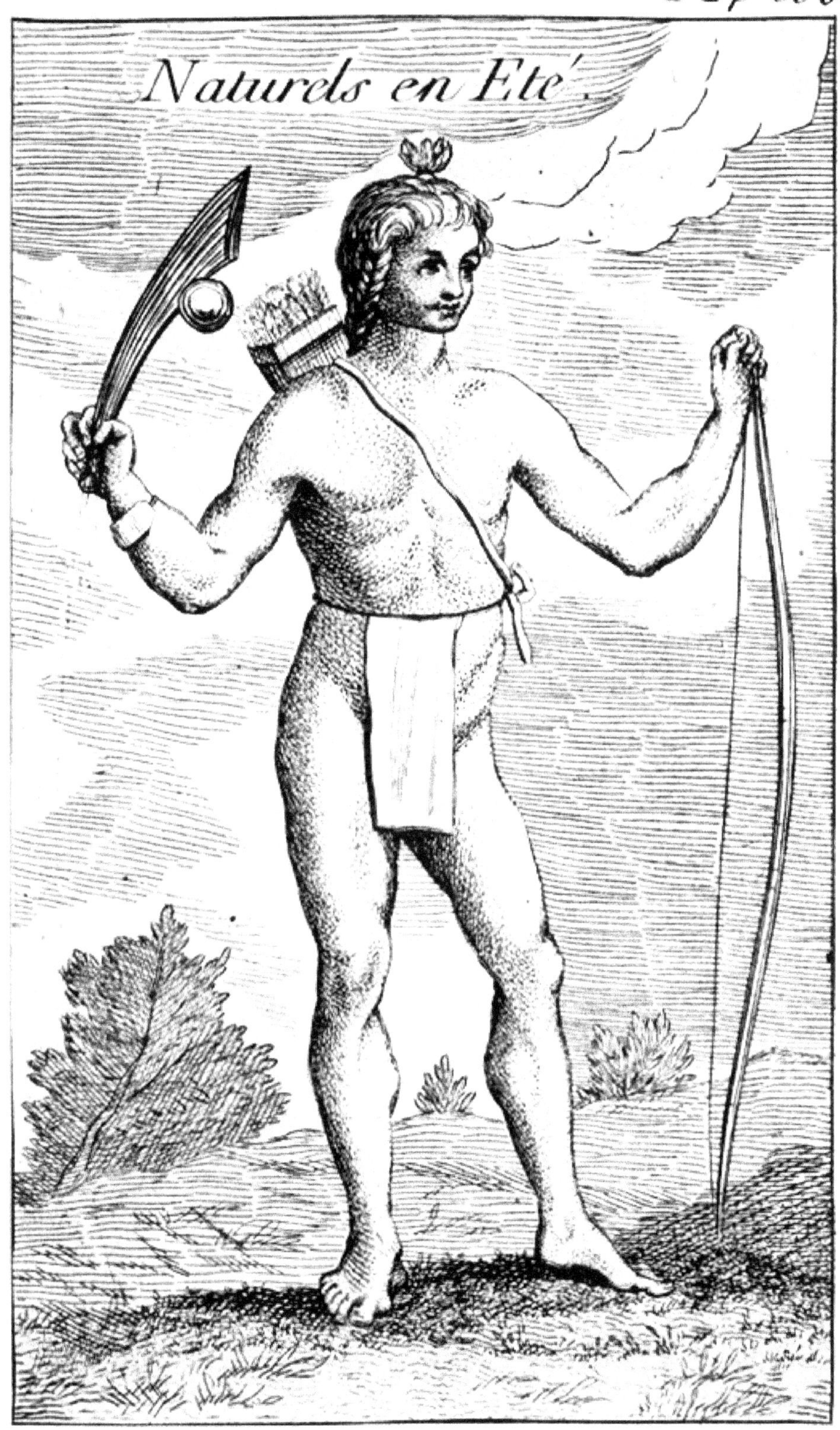

A Natchez warrior, by du Pratz.

Fort Rosalie; Extermination of the French in 1729; Grand Battle Scene by John J. Egan, c. 1850; The Saint Louis Art Museum, Eliza McMillan Trust 34:1953. Used by permission.

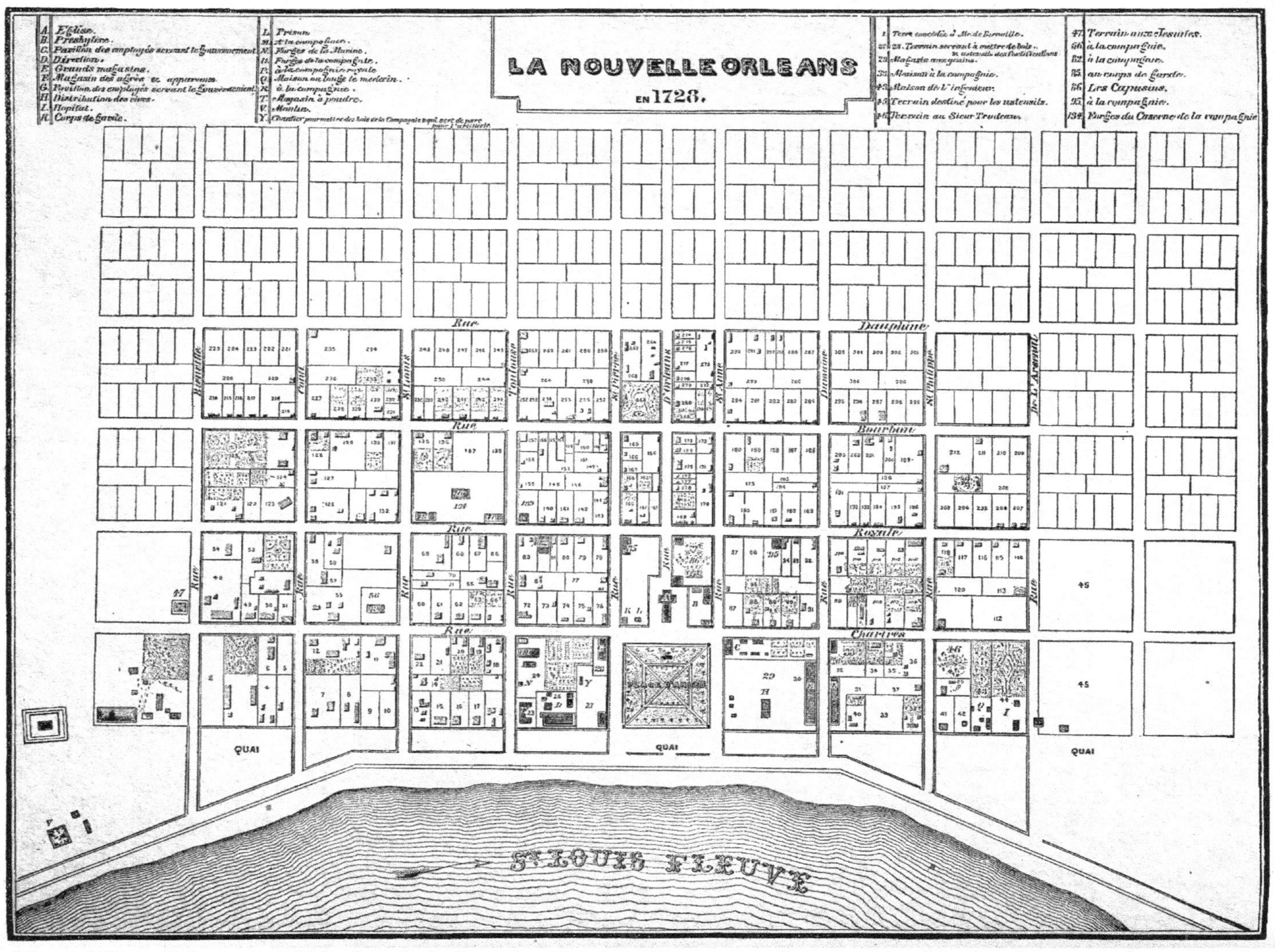

Map of New Orleans in 1728, shortly before the Natchez Massacre refugees arrived in the city to receive medical care and begin rebuilding their lives.

The Nicolas LaCour House in Pointe Coupee Parish, now owned by Dr. Jack and Pat Holden, is the oldest standing structure in Louisiana. It was originally part of the commandant's headquarters at Poste Pointe Coupee, and there exists a contract in which Pierre Mayeux was hired to work on repairs to the building.

Chapter Eight
Natchez
1729

Next to nothing is known about Captain Chepart, the new commandant of Fort Rosalie sent from New Orleans by Governor Périer in 1728. Even his name is uncertain: in various documents and histories he is called Chepart, Chepare, Chopart, Etcheparte, and Detcheparre, and his first name is completely lost to history. He came to Louisiana in 1719 aboard *Le Duc de Noailles* and was listed as a lieutenant of the infantry and served in the Arkansas territory in 1722, so he may have been known to the Mayeuxs and Cantrelles from Arkansas Post.

Four years later, in 1726, he was overseeing a crew of soldiers marking off the new streets of New Orleans according to Pauger's plans.[1] Everything else known about him comes from his one year at Natchez, and none of it is good. He was, in the words of historian Charles Gayarré, "rapacious, haughty, tyrannical, and by repeated acts of oppression and injustice, had made himself odious to those over whom he ruled."[2] In other words, he was an egotistical despot whose avarice brought about his own death and the massacre of his post.

Chepart wasn't the first bad commandant to oversee the most promising settlement in the whole of Louisiana. "There was never a single good commandant at that post," an officer named de Laye wrote in 1730, "we have seen nothing but drunkards, tyrants, and misers there."[3] It is something of a mystery why Natchez, which promised to be the largest and most important French settlement on the Mississippi, was never given the priority of quality leadership and oversight it deserved. Fort Rosalie, built by Bienville in 1716 with Indian labor after the first Natchez conflict, had fallen into disrepair and was in such poor condition by 1725 that a report to the Superior Council in New Orleans stated, "it is very necessary to have another fort built at the said place of Natchez because the one that is there is completely decayed."[4] It was, according to one visitor at the time, "an enclosure of poor piles, half rotten, that permit free entrance almost everywhere that can be called a fort."[5]

In response to the report, the Council sent the engineer Ignace-Francois Broutin to take command of the post and repair its condition. Broutin served as commandant for a little more than a year, worked at repairing the fort, and made several very accurate maps of the area before being recalled to New Orleans by the newly arrived Governor Périer who considered his services more valuable in the capital.[6] Broutin was followed by the Canadian Captain Dutinsé, who had already been serving as an officer at Rosalie for four years. Under his command, against the advice of others, Dutinsé assisted the Natchez in building their own French style palisaded fort with four bastions.[7] Dutinsé was charged with pedophilia with a German boy from an earlier time when he served in the Illinois country and, because of this and other charges, was deemed "no longer fit for command" after only two months of serving as commandant at Fort Rosalie.[8]

In October, 1727 Dutinsé was replaced by the Swiss Captain Louis Merveilleux who, according to Dumont, "protected the inhabitants of the post, by whom he was equally loved, and under whose government the French always lived in perfect harmony with the Indians."[9] However, he was also known as a brutal man. In a letter to a subordinate he directed that a rebellious Indian slave be bound to a post and receive, "twenty-five lashes sparing only his hands and neck, but to make sure that all the blows draw blood. If he does not mend his ways, whip him fifty times, and then a third round of 100 lashes and this will continue on if he disobeys you like that."[10] Like Dutinsé before him, Merveilleux's command lasted only a few months and in February 1728 he was replaced by Chepart, a Basque captain sent from New Orleans by the governor.[11] Chepart was, without question, the worst commandant the fort had seen. He was, Dumont wrote,

> "no sooner at his post, than, instead of seeking to secure the friendship of the people, whom he came to direct, thought only of tyrannizing, ill treating all whom he suspected of not being his friends, trampling on all justice and equity, always inclining the balance in favor of such as he wished to favor, despising even the royal ordinances, and neglecting the service to such a degree as to leave it in the hands of sergeants, who, seeing themselves no longer controlled by officers, abused the power given them."[12]

About the same time that the Mayeux and Cantrelle families arrived at Fort Rosalie and the surrounding village now known as Natchez, Chepart was already being recognized as an arrogant despot by the French settlers. Given to the abuse of alcohol, Chepart was a lax commander, and at the same time a brutal one when the whim struck him. Dumont, who had a contentious relationship with him, wrote that, "He had no sooner become the master here than the officers stopped doing their duty…there were no rules, no discipline; everyone did as he pleased. The officers just drew their salaries and thought only of their own plantations."[13] As a result of this lack of attention, the fort once again fell into disrepair, and under Chepart, "was porous on all sides. It was no more than a palisade of old and rotten logs, manned by a very small garrison of soldiers who scarcely went through the motion of performing their duties."[14]

Dumont describes several personal confrontations with Chepart, including an occasion when the commandant, "who believed that he, himself, was the master of all the habitants and that there was no one who would dare oppose his orders or desires," sent men to pick two baskets of green peas from a garden belonging to Dumont's landlord. When Chepart learned that the landlord had stopped the men and took their baskets, he became enraged at him and Dumont. In another incident, Chepart took forty two promissory notes totaling three thousand livres of personal debt and had them burned. Dumont and another resident traveled to New Orleans to make a case against him for this and other crimes, and were awarded a favorable verdict by Governor Périer. Upon their return to Natchez, Chepart summoned the resident to his home.

"When he arrived in the presence of Sr. Chepart, that officer said to him, 'So it's you, sir, who dares to lodge a complaint against me,' and immediately struck him with a cane. But the bourgeois, finding himself so abused, grabbed the commandant by the arm, who called out to the guard to take the bourgeois and put him in irons and declared his intention to have him flogged as if he were a soldier."

When Dumont complained, Chepart released the other man and had Dumont thrown into a guardroom and his feet shackled. Two days later he was informed that the only way he would be released is if he signed a letter admitting that he, not Chepart, had destroyed the promissory notes thinking them to be of no value. When Dumont refused he was kept in the irons for over two months, being released in December, 1728.[15]

In January, Dumont traveled to New Orleans to once again lodge complaints against Chepart and was joined a few days later by other residents from Natchez who confirmed his stories. Chepart was called to New Orleans and on February 12 both men stood before the governor who severely reprimanded Chepart but nevertheless returned him to his post. It was then that Dumont prophesied to Governor Périer and the Council, "If you send Chepart back to Natchez, Messieurs, there will be either a rebellion of the habitants or some other great catastrophe."[16]

Between 1719 and 1729 the French population of Natchez grew an astonishing tenfold, from less than fifty to approximately 400 French and over 200 African slaves who were brought in to work the concessions.[17] During this same time span the soldier population was halved, from sixty in 1720 to thirty in 1729.[18] Comparatively, the surrounding Indian villages held a population of more than 3,500, 700 of them warriors, with White Apple village alone having over eighty cabins.[19]

The growth of the French population was brought on by the successful concessions and farms, the fertile land, and the relatively peaceful relationship with the Natchez villages, but it also grew by the births of children to the residents. Francienne Cantrelle became a midwife to the French women in Natchez, and in 1729 Marie Mayeux, already with a young son and an infant daughter, gave birth to her third child, a girl named Cecile.

In 1729 two of the reorganized Mississippi Company's concessions were in full development at Natchez and were essentially each functioning as villages in their own right. The St. Catherine plantation, which was cultivating about 280 acres of land, was located on the west bank of the creek that took its name from the concession, about two miles upstream from the Grand Village of the Natchez. The smaller concession, Terra Blanche (White Earth) was located about four miles directly south of Fort Rosalie, about two miles downstream from the Grand Village, on the opposite side of St. Catherine's Creek, and just across the creek from the Tiou village which lay between Terra Blanche and the fort. Both concessions were growing wheat, indigo, tobacco and cotton, and in 1729 were the most successful of the company's concessions in all of Louisiana.[20]

While the larger concessions were located several miles away from the fort, most of the habitants built homes nearby and the village that sprung up surrounded the fort with log homes and small gardens carved out of the woodlands. Pierre Mayeux was a carpenter by trade, and had spent his entire time in Louisiana building houses. His house in Natchez was just downhill and to the south of Fort Rosalie at a distance of about a hundred yards. It is likely that he found employment constructing homes for the other settlers as well, and may have even worked on the fort itself. Whatever the case, he would have also spent time raising crops, hunting in the nearby woods, fishing in the river and interacting with the Natchez in their villages. Marie, on the other hand, would have had her hands full with three children under the age of six years, and likely had an Indian maid assisting her in some of her chores.

The French population explosion in Natchez was a boon for the Indians. They were eager to trade with the French for gunpowder, lead, guns, brandy and European cloth, and in return provided corn, animal skins and game meat. The Indians also found employment among the French, helping the villagers to clear timber for their farms, work their fields, and build their houses. Dumont wrote,

> "These Indian inhabitants called Natchez were friends to the French, hunting for them, trading each year some of their poultry, grain, and oil, and working for the French as willing servants (for pay, that is). It was these Indians who carried wood and water, cleared the lands, and even rowed like galley slaves in the boats up and down the river. They not only hunted for the French, as I have said, but also fished. They did all this of their own free will. The Indian women sold bread, corn meal, and pots and plates that they made with great skill, as well as hiring themselves out to make beds and unmake them."[21]

In addition, several of the Indian women were lovers with some of the French men, living with them and keeping house. The relationship between the French and the Indians was very much a symbiotic one, benefitting both groups, until the antics of Commandant Chepart changed everything.

If Chepart was brusque and overbearing with the French villagers, he was nothing short of a megalomaniacal dictator toward the Indians. With designs of personal gain, soon after his arrival Chepart began looking for land for his personal plantation. After overviewing the entire area, he decided that the most desirable land was attached to the White Apple village of the Natchez. Calling Chief Oldhair of the village to his quarters, and without any ceremony and speaking to him as if he were, "speaking to a slave, whom we may command in a tone of absolute authority,"[22] Chepart informed him that he had decided to farm the land, and that the Natchez must look for another place for their village. When Oldhair told Chepart that this was their ancestral land, that they had lived on it for more years than they could count, and that their fathers were buried there, so it was not wise for them to move, Chepart flew into a rage and told the chief that if he didn't move from the village in a few days he would regret it. The chief tried to reason with Chepart that there was plenty of land for everyone, both the Natchez and the French, but the commandant cut him off and told him the matter was settled. The chief told Chepart that he would call a meeting with the tribal elders and discuss the matter. Chepart had designs not only on White Apple, but also on the Grand Village, the holy site for the Natchez. When the Indians resisted his idea, Chepart threatened to burn their temple to the ground and drive them out.[23]

When Oldhair met with his elders at White Apple the council decided to attempt to reason with Chepart that the timing for such a move was not good. Their corn had just begun to spring from the ground and their chickens were laying eggs. If they were forced to relocate immediately, the harvest would be lost to both the Indians and the French. They proposed to Chepart that they be allowed to stay until early winter, when the corn would not only be harvested but dried, and that in lieu of not moving according to his schedule, the Indians would pay Chepart every month with a basket of corn and some fowl.[24] Chepart agreed to the delay, "but on the condition that they pay a large sum in poultry, grain, and pots of oil, as well as pelts, as interest for the delay that he was allowing them."[25] The Indians conceded and Chepart accepted the proposition, although he acted to the Indians as if he were showing them a great favor.

Chepart's demand for relocation was disastrous for the Natchez, and while they had bought some time with the argument of waiting until harvest, they had no intention of actually moving. In more council meetings the elders agreed that the French were encroaching more and more on them, and that, although the relationship in the past had been mutually beneficial, under Chepart they were being treated as not much more than slaves and had lost their freedom. The demand to relocate was more than they could bear, and their only alternative was to retaliate by attacking Chepart and those under his command. One of the old men spoke up in the council and said,

> "We have a long time been sensible that the neighborhood of the French is a greater prejudice than benefit to us: we, who are old men, see this; the young see it not. The wares of the French yield pleasure to the youth but in effect, to what purpose is all this, but to debauch the young women and taint the blood of the nation, and make them vain and idle? The young men are in the same case;

> and the married must work themselves to death to maintain their families, and please their children. Before the French came amongst us, we were men, content with what we had, and that was sufficient: we walked with boldness every road, because we were our own masters: but now we go groping, afraid of meeting thorns, we walk like slaves, which we shall soon be, since the French already treat us as if we were such. When they are sufficiently strong, they will no longer dissemble. For the least fault of our young people, they will tie them to a post, and whip them as they do their black slaves. Have they not already done so to one of our young men; and is not death preferable to slavery?"[26]

The Natchez at White Apple had never been as favorable toward the French as some of the other villages had, and since the deaths of the pro-French Great Sun and Tattooed Serpent, the other villages were prone to be influenced more by the chief of White Apple. The young new Great Sun, Saint Cosme, was inexperienced, and was easily convinced by the White Apple chief to join in a plan to save the Grand Village and White Apple from Chepart's designs. It was agreed that during the negotiated delay the Indians would prepare themselves for an attack to obliterate the French from Natchez. There has been significant debate as to whether they invited other tribes along the river to join with them, and some have suggested that there were plans for a pan-Indian attack upon all the French in Louisiana, a concerted effort to wipe out not only Natchez, but Fort Pierre on the Yazoo (now Vicksburg, Mississippi), Pointe Coupee, the concession at Baton Rouge, New Orleans and even Biloxi. This notion was described by both Dumont and du Pratz,[27] but most historians agree that there is little if any evidence that such a plan actually existed. It may have been concocted by the Natchez, but it clearly was never adopted by other native nations.[28]

For several months the Natchez paid their tribute to Chepart and continued life as normal among the French, trading with them, working for them, and some of the native women living with some of the French men. Commerce and conversation continued between the two groups until November, 1729. But all this while the Natchez were biding their time, planning their attack, and waiting for the perfect opportunity to spring their trap. Because of the close ties between some of the French and Natchez, especially between the Indian women who served as maids to the French households, word began to trickle out that danger was brewing. One of the French officers had been warned by his Natchez lover that her people were planning to attack.[29] Another had been warned by an old woman who was the female Sun of the Natchez, Tattooed Arm, who was the mother of Saint Cosme, the new Great Sun. According to du Pratz, Saint Cosme was the son of a French man, and it has been conjectured that his father was Jean-Francois Buisson de Saint-Cosme, the Canadian priest who established the first mission among the Natchez in 1699 and was murdered on the Mississippi River in 1706.[30]

On Friday, November 25th, two men went to Chepart to tell him of the rumors they had heard of an imminent attack. Far from heeding their warnings, Chepart, "flew into a rage, fulminating against these prophets, abusing them for disturbing the public peace, and calling them traitors and lazy cowards unworthy of protection."[31] Every man who came to Chepart with concerns was ridiculed and called a coward, and Chepart, "clapt seven of them in irons,"[32] including the officer who had been warned by Tattooed Arm. Seeing that her attempts to warn the French were falling on deaf ears, Tattooed Arm approached the sub-lieutenant Massé, but Chepart disregarded his warning as well.[33]

Perhaps the trigger for the attack was news that a large flat bottom supply boat was arriving at the end of November, carrying valuable cargo to Natchez from New Orleans. Aboard the boat were supplies for the garrison, foodstuff, goods for trading with the Indians, a large amount of brandy, and Jean-Daniel Kolly, the wealthy owner of the St. Catherine concession who was coming from France with his son to inspect his holdings. The boat would be emptied of its goods, then reloaded with a bumper crop of tobacco from Natchez to be shipped back to France from New Orleans.[34]

The boat arrived on Sunday, the 27th of November, and that evening Chepart, the fort judge Sr. Bailly, the storehouse manager Ricard, and one of the merchants who had come to Natchez to trade, had dinner together then made their way to the Grand Village loaded with brandy, wine and bread for an evening of partying. It was the custom of the Indians to share their daughters with visiting guests, and the French were quick to take advantage of this custom. In his journal, Fr. Charlevoix wrote, "We know no nation on this continent, where the female sex are more irregular, than in this. They are even forced by the Great Chief and his subalterns to prostitute themselves to all comers; and a woman, for being common, is not the less esteemed."[35] In this the Natchez were not unlike the nearby Chakchiuma tribe that Marc-Antoine Caillot visited when he worked for the Mississippi Company in New Orleans. Caillot wrote,

> "They are very jealous of their wives and do not wish for them to be touched. It is the opposite with their daughters,

> for, if you go see them and you drink with them, they offer you their daughters to take enjoyment of as long as you want to stay with them. This is the way of them, from the great chief to the least of his subjects, and, if you refuse, they regard that as a great insult that you have committed against them and their daughters, who are for the most part young and quite playful."[36]

Dumont records that Chepart and his friends, "were well received there by the Indians and by their chief and began to drink and smoke and trade boasts together, after which they chose Indian women with whom to spend the night in debaucheries, combining the worship of Bacchus with that of Venus. In a word, the night passed in pleasure and celebrations."

It wasn't until four o'clock on the morning of Monday, November 28th that Chepart made his way back to the fort to sleep off his hangover.[37]

Monday morning broke like any other autumn day in Natchez. Fr. Paul du Poisson, a Jesuit priest visiting from the Arkansas territory, had delayed his departure in order to say Mass at the church on Sunday because Fr. Philibert was away on business. He had made his way down the bluff onto the flat ground along the river to say morning Mass in the chapel and then to take the sacrament to some sick habitants before continuing upriver to the Arkansas. The storehouse director Pierre Ricard, who had spent the night carousing at Grand Village with Chepart and the others, was down at the river with a crew of men unloading the boats that had come from New Orleans. Others throughout the village were arising from sleep, having breakfast, and preparing for another day of work in the fields or plying their trades. Chepart was in the fort sound asleep.

At nine o'clock the Great Sun, leading an entourage of thirty men, marched in procession through the front gate of the fort, bearing their monthly payment to Chepart as well as gifts. The chief held aloft a calumet. Awakened by the beating drums of the Indians, Chepart came striding into the yard of the fort wearing only his sleeping shirt. Seeing the formal procession and the men carrying poultry, deerskins and baskets of corn, he ordered a soldier to go and free the men he had put in irons a few days before so he could prove to them once and for all that the Indians were friendly and that they both feared and respected him.[38] At the same time, other Indians made their way to the various homes in the village around the fort, bringing gifts to the Frenchmen they personally knew, some asking to borrow muskets, powder and balls for a great hunt, with the promise of returning with game meat and skins for the French.[39] Another group of Indians made its way down to the banks of the river where the chapel was located, and where the boats were being unloaded.[40]

As the Great Sun raised the calumet and offered it to Chepart, gunshots rang out from the river and resounded through the village. At this signal, Indians poured into the fort from the gaps and holes in the disrepaired walls and attacked the unsuspecting soldiers, some still asleep in their beds. Guns fired, arrows flew, and tomahawks were raised in every part of the village. Outside the chapel, Fr. du Poisson was tackled by an Indian who threw him to the ground, raised his tomahawk and dealt him a death blow. To the shock of those looking on, the Indian used his hatchet to sever the priest's head from his body. When Monsieur du

Codere drew his sword to defend the priest, he was instantly killed by a musket ball fired by another Indian.[41]

The men on the riverbank who were unloading the boats were assaulted by a large group of warriors firing their guns and charging with knives and tomahawks. The boat captain and all the men were killed. Pierre Ricard, the storehouse keeper, dove into the water and swam toward the middle of the river, musket balls splashing all around him. On reaching to a cypress swamp downriver, he stayed there until dark, then worked his way through the woods to the cabin of a local potter. At the cabin he found two Yazoo Indians who had come to Natchez with Fr. Poisson. These Yazoo men had heard nothing about the massacre, but fed Ricard, bandaged his wounds, and gave him their pirogue to make his way south. Not knowing the disposition of any of the natives along the way, Ricard did not stop until he reached New Orleans, the first of the survivors to tell his tale there.[42]

At the fort, Chepart was wounded but not killed because he was held in such contempt that the warriors thought it beneath themselves to kill him, and set him aside to be killed by a "stinkard," a lower class Natchez.[43] He was forced to watch helplessly as his men were slaughtered, scalped, and beheaded before his very eyes.[44] The scene was the same at every homestead in the village. The Indians who had been friendly only moments before suddenly unleashed their fury in an unimaginable bloodbath. Men were stabbed, tomahawked or shot, as the horrified women and children helplessly looked on. Women who fought back or tried to protect their husbands were brutally killed as well. Even pregnant women were not spared. The warriors, "ripped up the belly of every pregnant woman, and killed almost all those who were nursing their children, because they were disturbed by their cries and tears."[45]

Most of the men never had the chance to fight back. Two, called Jappio and Brisebois, "fought to defend themselves, holding off fifty Natchez whom they repelled with the loss of three men. They escaped by the skin of their teeth and stole a pirgogue from in front of a hundred and fifty of the savages, firing at them as they left."[46]

One habitant named Navarre escaped after attempting to bring warning to the French but found himself too late. An Indian girl, "with whom he was very much in love came to him early in the morning and warned him that the French were going to be killed by the Natchez; that he should escape promptly and that he had no time to lose." His lover gave him a pistol, some lead balls, and some powder, and he climbed onto his horse and rode swiftly toward the fort, only to find the slaughter already in progress and people fleeing. He hid himself in the woods and waited until dark when he snuck to the home of his Indian lover, deep in the nearby forest, where he was hidden for ten days before making his way to the French forces camped at the Tunica village downriver.[47]

The only soldier to escape hid himself in a large outdoor oven beneath the bluff along the river and waited until darkness fell, then made his way southward on foot through the woods to the Tunica village.[48]

When Jacques Cantrelle saw the massacre unfolding, he and Francienne fled from their home and hid in his grain barn. After nightfall they took what possessions they could and made their way through the woods toward the river. Along the way, Cantrelle remembered something important that he had left at his home and had Francienne hide in the woods while he went back to the house. When he returned Francienne was nowhere to be found, and after a fruitless search Jacques snuck through the woods to the river, found a pirogue, and escaped downstream alone.[49]

In less than an hour, the French village of Natchez had been completely destroyed. At the same time large groups of Indians attacked the St. Catherine and Terra Blanche concessions. Sr. De la Loire des Ursins, who lived at Terre Blanche with his Indian wife, heard the drumbeats and saddled his horse to ride to the fort and see what the commotion was about. "But what bloody spectacle was offered up for his eyes," Dumont wrote,

> "the soldiers killed, scalps stripped off their heads, and their naked bodies strewn about here and there. So he quickly turned his eyes and his horse back toward his farm to defend his life along with that of his son and his slaves and servants. But he had not gone thirty or forty paces when the Indians let loose a volley of gunshots, from which he received a deadly blow and fell from his horse, without life or feeling."[50]

Jean-Daniel Kolly and his son, who had traveled from France and arrived in Natchez the day before to inspect their holdings at the St. Catherine concession, rode to the fort early Monday morning to visit the commandant. Stepping down from their horses they saw a man named Baillif coming out to greet them, and before words could be exchanged he fell at their feet. They hurried back onto their horses and sped back to the concession only to see, "two hundred fifty or three hundred Indians…coming toward them carrying scalps at the end of many canes, all of them armed to the teeth." The father and son ran to hide but to no avail. Kolly had climbed into a big empty wine cask and was immediately killed by the Indians. His son, seeing what had happened to Kolly, drew his sword and attacked the Indians, managing to kill seven or eight of them before being captured. Badly wounded and bleeding profusely, he was tortured with fire until he died eight days later.

Commandant Chepart, whose arrogance and avarice had brought on this ghastly event, was kept alive until close to the end of the massacre. All the warriors regarded him as less than a dog and thought it beneath their dignity to kill him, and yet they determined that he should not remain alive. Finally, they found an old man from the commoner caste of the tribe, called "stinkards," gave him a wooden club, and looked on as he beat the commandant to death.[51]

By noon the whole thing was over. No more than about twenty of the French had escaped into the woods or the river.[52] Although it is impossible to accurately count the death toll, between 250 and 300 French men, women and children lay dead. The official casualty list was 145 men, 36 women, and 56 children.[53] According to the earliest accounts, about 80 women and 150 children were taken hostage by the Indians, along with an equal number of African slaves. Many of the slaves had been warned ahead of time about the attack, and while some fought and died along side their masters, others kept the attack secret and were complicit in the deaths of the French. Promised freedom by the Indians, they were in fact put to work loading wagons and moving goods from the French settlement to the Indian villages, and were going to be sold as slaves to the Chickasaw who in turn would sell them to the English in Carolina.

Only two French men were taken alive. One was a tailor named Le Beau that the Natchez set to work refitting the clothes they had taken off the dead French men and women. Le Beau was also used as a decoy by the Indians, to lure surviving Frenchmen to their deaths. The other was a carpenter and a wagon driver who was kept alive to transport goods from the French Village to the Natchez forts, and to help strengthen the forts for the inevitable French counterattack. His name was Pierre Mayeux, and somehow not only had he survived, but so had his wife, his six-year-old son Francois, his two-year-old daughter Genevieve, and his newborn baby, Cecile.[54] No records exist of another entire family surviving the massacre.

When the frenzy of the attack had waned, the Indians went through the village and finished killing any of the wounded, beheading them and stripping the bodies of their clothes. The heads of the victims were lined up in rows before the chief, and the decapitated bodies of Chepart and other notables were placed in a circle, each holding the hands of the ones next to him. The chief began to speak to them, preaching, haranguing, as if they were still alive. For over an hour he told them how they had brought this calamity on themselves, how their deaths were the result of tyranny and oppression and greed.[55]

With the killing done, the plundering began. The houses and other buildings were ransacked then burned, leaving both concessions, the fort, and the surrounding village as smoldering heaps of ashes. The clothing of the French people was piled onto wagons, along with food, guns, furniture, cooking pots and utensils, and anything else the Indians fancied to take with them. The surviving women and children were herded into houses that had yet to be burned and were guarded by a few warriors.

The supply ship that had arrived from New Orleans carried over 300,000 livres worth of food, clothing, hats, shoes, gunpowder, musket balls, brandy and flour.[56] The Indians began drinking the brandy before they finished emptying the ship and their drunkenness helped save at least one Frenchman's life. Two Frenchmen were outside the fort area when the slaughter began and hid in a canebrake until well after dark. Coming up on the main warehouse of the Company one of the men peeked through the keyhole and saw it filled with what he thought was French people. When he opened the door he discovered the room was actually filled with Indians who had dressed themselves in the clothing of their victims. They were drinking wine and brandy and offered him some. After he had drunk his fill, the Indians chopped off his head on the butcher's block.[57] When his companion saw what happened, he fled the scene and came upon a house from which he clearly heard French being spoken. When he opened the door he saw the room filled with women and children who shouted for him to run away, and that all of the men had been killed. He pulled his knife, stabbed the Indian guard in the stomach, and ran toward the bluff. Arriving at the river's edge, he saw the Indians on the boat celebrating and too drunk to pursue him, and so fled into the woods and to safety.[58]

Although the pan-Indian attack upon all the French settlements in Louisiana never materialized, the Natchez were able to threaten and deceive a few other villages to join in their melee. The day of the massacre, several of the French escaped only to meet death after a day or two of running. Four men went to the Tiou village just south of Natchez, hoping this tribe, though part of the Natchez federation, was not part of the massacre. They were welcomed and cared for, but after consulting with the Natchez at the Grand Village, Tiou warriors returned, killed the refugees, then crossed the Mississippi River and made their way up the Red River to the concession of the Marquise de Mezières and slaughtered eighteen people there. Another group of survivors made their way to a camp of traveling Yazoos who were returning north to the Yazoo River from a meeting they had had in the south with the Houma Indians. The Yazoos were quick to render aid to the Frenchmen, giving them clothing, food, and a pirogue. However, the next day they changed their minds and burned the Frenchmen to death. They had been told by the Natchez that the Choctaw had attacked New Orleans, and that there were no Frenchmen left alive in Louisiana. Believing this lie, and that it would be foolish to align themselves with the defeated French, they returned to the Yazoo River, near present day Vicksburg, and on December 11 attacked the tiny Fort Pierre and killed all the Frenchmen there.[59]

A few days after the massacre, a group of Natchez warriors heard a quiet voice in the woods calling for help. They sent the tailor Le Beau to offer the man promises of protection if he surrendered himself to the Natchez. Le Beau emerged from the woods with a severely wounded man named Le Hou, the storekeeper from Fort Pierre on the Yazoo who had been at Fort Rosalie at the time of the attack. The Indians washed the Le Hou, put brandy on his wounds, gave him plenty to drink, then beheaded him.[60] A few days later, Le Beau was used as a decoy to hail a passing pirogue holding five men. As the pirogue approached the bank of the river, the Indians shot and killed three, and captured one more. Dumont related that the Indians, "began by stripping him, blacking his body with coal-dust, bound his hands, and in this state made him run to the village, firing blank charges at him, with their muzzles touching his body." The prisoner was condemned to burning by the chief and,

> "The Indians immediately proceeded to prepare, in the square before the temple, a wooden frame...when bound, with his two arms extended on the frame, in the Indian fashion, he saw some French women, and called to them to pray to God for him...scarcely had he uttered these words, when the Indians, armed with bundles of lighted canes, began to burn him slowly, applying them to his sides, thighs, breasts, back, sides and face, so that he underwent a long and painful martyrdom."[61]

Pierre Mayeux, "was employed in carting to the Great Village all that had belonged to the French - provisions, furniture, effects, goods, even the cannon of the fort, with their carriages, as well as the powder, balls and bullets found there."[62] Whether he was allowed to be with his family or kept separate from them is not known. Neither is it known what depredations, ravages, or tortures they suffered. Most certainly they endured hardships and witnessed unimaginable horrors after the massacre. The massacre had been a fury of blood and gunsmoke that was over almost as soon as it had begun. The horrors witnessed in the weeks following were purposeful and methodical, cruel barbarisms played out before the eyes of the captives.

The women were used as slaves, some for various Indian families, but most for the Great Sun and his family. "The least miserable," Fr. Le Petit wrote, "were those who knew how to sew, because they kept them busy making shirts, dresses, etc. The others were employed in cutting and carrying wood for cooking, and in pounding corn of which they make their sagamité."[63] Many of the women were raped and treated "with every indignity,"[64] and many were tortured and killed because they had been married to notable Frenchmen, as in the case of the widow of the interpreter René Pepin, and Madame Massé, wife of the sub-lieutenant, who was shot through with arrows at close range.[65]

Every time a Natchez man died, a French woman was buried alive with him, and when an Indian child died, a French child was killed. Caillot was told by surviving women that the Natchez "would take the first child they happened upon and throw him into the air, and other Indians would catch him on pointed cane spears, and they would bury him like this, or else they would take them by their feet and strike their heads against the ground." Perhaps the most gruesome and barbaric incident among the captives was also recounted to Caillot.

> "They told us they had seen another atrocity even more terrible...upon the death of a young Indian woman, those vile brutes took a young German woman who was ready to give birth at any moment. They took her, cut off her nose, lips, and ears, which they put in her mouth, then they opened her belly with a knife, from which they pulled out the baby, cutting off his head and putting him back in the body of the hapless woman, who was making horrid cries. They sewed up her belly, then they all pissed in her mouth, and buried her alive in this state."[66]

The Indians continued in a drunken orgy of celebration for several days after the massacre, dancing, desecrating the bodies of their victims, and drinking and eating until the food and brandy were gone. It would be months before the captives found freedom, and when they did it was no freedom at all.

[1] Giraud, p. 396.

[2] Charles Gayarré, *Louisiana: Its Colonial History and Romance*, Harper and Sons, New York, 1851, p. 395.

[3] de Laye, p. 57; see Appendix 1.

[4] Galloway, p. 199.

[5] *Ibid*, p. 200.

[6] *Ibid*, p. 200.

[7] Dumont, p. 212f.

[8] George Edward Milne, *Natchez Country: Indians, Colonists, and the Landscapes of Race in French Louisiana*, University of Georgia Press, Atlanta, 2015, p. 148.

[9] French, *Historical Memoirs*, p. 61.

[10] Milne, p. 154.

[11] Dumont, p. 213.

[12] Benjamin Franklin French, *Historical Memoirs of Louisiana, from the First Settlement of the Colony to the Departure of Governor O'Reilly in 1770*, Nabu Press, 2011, originally published in 1853, p. 62.

[13] Dumont, p. 213.

[14] *Ibid*, p. 229.

[15] *Ibid*, p. 217f.

[16] *Ibid*, p. 224.

[17] Caillot, xxvii; Barnett, p. 99.

[18] Barnett, p. 78.

[19] *Ibid*, p. 102.

[20] *Ibid*, p. 84.

[21] Dumont, p. 228.

[22] du Pratz, p. 127.

[23] Dumont, p. 228, du Pratz, p. 127.

[24] du Pratz, p. 128.

[25] Dumont, p. 228.

[26] du Pratz, p. 129f.

[27] Dumont, p 229f; du Pratz, p. 130.

[28] Barnett, pp. 106-109; Dumont, p. 239.

[29] Barnett, p. 104.
[30] du Pratz, p. 133.
[31] Dumont, p. 231.
[32] du Pratz, p. 135.
[33] *Ibid*, p. 135; Dumont, p. 231.
[34] French, *Historic Memoirs*, p. 68.
[35] French, *Historical Collections*, p. 165.
[36] Caillot, p. 122.
[37] Dumont, p. 230f.
[38] *Ibid*, p. 232.
[39] Caillot, p. 126.
[40] Dumont, p. 232, Le Petit, p. 164.
[41] French, *Historical Collection*, p. 152.
[42] Milne, p. 177; cf. Dumont p. 238; French, *Memoirs*, p. 74.
[43] Du Pratz, p. 135.
[44] Dumont, p. 233.
[45] Le Petit, p. 166f.
[46] de Lay, p. 60.
[47] Swanton, p. 228.
[48] Dumont, p. 234.
[49] Swanton, p. 227; French, *Historical Memoirs*, p. 75f.
[50] Dumont, p. 234.
[51] *Ibid*, p. 233.
[52] Caillot, p. 125.
[53] Milne, p. 176.
[54] Dumont, p. 236, footnote
[55] Caillot, p. 126.
[56] *Ibid*, p. 127.
[57] Dumont, p. 236.
[58] *Ibid*, p. 237.
[59] de Laye, p. 6.
[60] French, *Historical Memoirs*, p. 77f.
[61] *Ibid*, p. 78f.
[62] *Ibid*, p. 77.
[63] Le Petit, p. 167; see Appendix 3.
[64] *Ibid*
[65] Milne, p. 178.
[66] Caillot, p. 142.

Chapter Nine
New Orleans
1730

The Natchez storehouse manager Pierre Ricard escaped the initial attack of the Indians at the boat landing by diving into the water and swimming for his life amid a hail of musket balls. He swam into the middle of the Mississippi River, no small feat in itself, floated downstream, hid out in a cypress swamp until nightfall, and then found his way to the cabin of a local potter. Two Yazoo Indians who were visiting Natchez were in the cabin, and when they heard Ricard's story they washed and bandaged him, fed him, and gave him a pirogue for his descent to New Orleans. Ricard did not stop along the way, and was the first to arrive in New Orleans with news of the massacre.[1] "All terror-stricken and in a wretched condition," the townspeople thought he had "lost his head," unable to imagine that what he described to them could be true.[2]

Any suspicions about Ricard's story were set aside the next day when another boatload of escapees arrived. Marc-Antoine Caillot was walking along the levee with a group of friends when they saw the boat approaching, being paddled vigorously even though it was going downstream, a sure indication that the passengers were in a hurry to reach their destination. "We were very surprised to see some of these people completely naked, others in their drawers, maimed," wrote Caillot. These naked and wounded survivors told the crowd that gathered around them that they were the only ones who escaped, that everyone else in Natchez was dead, and that, "everything was on fire and covered in blood."[3] The survivors were taken to the house of the governor, Ettiane Périer where they told him of the brutal attack, and how they themselves had fought their way to the river and escaped, "throwing themselves through a hail of musket balls into a little pirogue, where, when they were in the middle of the river, they bound their wounds. One had been hit in his arm and leg, and the other in the middle of his stomach."[4]

As word spread through New Orleans, a city that in 1729 had fewer than 800 inhabitants and was itself not much larger than Natchez,[5] panic set in among the townspeople. If such a destructive attack could be launched by the Natchez tribe at Fort Rosalie, there was nothing to keep the same thing from happening in New Orleans itself. Did the Natchez act alone? Were other tribes involved? Could any be trusted? Were the Indians who freely walked through their streets preparing to spring an attack on them next? Périer organized a militia of four companies to guard the city[6] and ordered the African slaves to begin digging defensive trenches around its perimeter.[7] The governor was newly arrived in Louisiana and had no experience in dealing with the

Indians. For all he knew this little pirogue full of people was all that was left of New Orlean's sister city to the north. At the same time that he was taking measures to protect the capital, he sent Captain Merveilleux with a small detachment of soldiers to warn all the inhabitants along the river of the imminent danger, and gave orders to the settlers to be on guard and to build defense works.[8] Périer then sent an envoy to call for two Choctaw chiefs to meet with him in New Orleans.[9]

Perhaps the first time any Frenchman heard word of a pan-Indian attack was the next day, on December 3, when a Choctaw man returning in a pirogue from the Illinois country arrived in New Orleans and asked to speak to the governor. The Indian told Périer that he had been told by some Chickasaw that, "all the Indians were to destroy all the French settlements, and massacre all the men." He was hesitant to believe that his own tribe, long friendly toward the French, were complicit in this conspiracy, and begged Périer permission to go to his people, "and immediately return to render a good report of what I have done there."[10]

As soon as the Choctaw man left, men from other tribes came to Périer warning him to not trust the Choctaw. This general confusion was complicated by the news arriving from Mobile that two Frenchmen had been murdered there, and although the killers had not been found, the word among the settlers was that the Choctaw were going to attack the fort and homes in Mobile. There were also rumors of a slavery revolt, and that the Africans and Indians were joining together to overthrow the French and obliterate them from the face of Louisiana. These whispers spread through New Orleans like wildfire and the entire population was set on edge, not knowing what calamity any day might hold. To add superstitious fuel to the fires of fear, between December 1729 and February 15, 1730 a comet hung in the sky above New Orleans and was seen by many as a portent of doom.[11]

On December 5, one of the Choctaw chiefs that Périer had sent for arrived in New Orleans and informed him that it was the smaller tribes who were not to be trusted, and that they were in league with the Natchez. Furthermore, the chief told him, he had sent messages to all of his tribe inviting, "all who were enemies of the Natchez to march against them."[12]

Four weeks after the arrival of the Natchez survivors, a wounded Fr. Stephan d'Outreleau arrived in New Orleans with his boatman, and his story added fuel to the fire of a pan-Indian conspiracy. Fr. d'Outreleau was a missionary to the Illinois territory who had traveled from there to Fort Pierre on the Yazoo near present day Vicksburg, Mississippi. Not reaching the fort in time, he stopped with his companions to say Mass at the mouth of the Yazoo River. As he was praying the *kyrie eleison,* Indians fired at him, wounding him in his right arm and killing one of his men. The priest knelt down "to receive in that posture the death blow," but when three more gunshots missed him, he ran for the pirogue which was already being paddled away by two of his men who thought he had been killed. Wading to the pirogue, the priest turned to see if he was being pursued and caught a blast of duck-shot in his face before climbing aboard. His two companions, one with a leg broken by a musket ball, rowed furiously to escape the Indians, who pursued them for more than an hour before giving up the chase.

The priest and his two men arrived in Natchez, hoping to find rest and medical care, but when they approached the landing they saw all the houses burned or demolished. Indians came to the riverbank showing signs of friendship and inviting them to land, but the Frenchmen passed as quickly as they could while the warriors fired guns toward them. When they arrived at the Tunica village they intended to pass it too, but were so weary that they were unable to outrow a pirogue coming from the village. Convinced they had finally met their end, they were thrilled to hear French being spoken from the pirogue and realized they had come upon a company of soldiers recently sent out by Périer. The company surgeon cared for the man with the broken leg, dressed the wounds of the priest, and sent them on to New Orleans.[13]

The inexperienced Périer was completely confused, had no idea which, if any, of the nations to trust, and had his hands full with trying to calm and protect the citizens of New Orleans and at the same time mount a campaign against the Natchez and any others who may have joined them in the massacre. In a hasty and ill conceived response to the rumors Périer made the worst decision of his career. The governor armed a group of African slaves and forced them to attack a group of peaceful Chaouacha Indians who lived in a small village of no more than thirty homes just south of New Orleans.[14] Whether this action was taken out of fear or confusion or was simply taking retribution on the nearest Indians, Périer may have actually had some method to his madness. If indeed there was a conspiracy involving both the Indians and the Africans, an attack by Africans on the innocent Chaouacha would serve as a wedge between these two groups of people and might well frustrate any attempts of an organized pan-Indian and African plan for unity.

No one trusted the Choctaw. They seemed to be favorable toward the French, dealings with them were always tempered by suspicions regarding their motives, as if perhaps they were working an angle or running a con game. Marc-Antoine Caillot wrote that the Choctaw were friendly enough from all outward appearances, "but it is only to get presents" from the Europeans. The French in New Orleans nicknamed them "Parisians" because of their reputation for cowardice, and consequently, Caillot wrote, "Of all the Indians, in general most of them are people whom you should never trust."[15] And yet, trustworthy or not, the Choctaw were the most populous nation in French Louisiana, sworn enemies of the pro-English Chickasaw, feared by other smaller nations, and, other than the small Tunica band, the closest Indian allies the French had. As one priest who had dealt with them wrote, "There had never yet been seen in all America Indians more insolent, more ferocious, more disgusting, more importune, more insatiable."[16] Périer had no other option than to enlist them in his campaign against the Natchez. To fight the Natchez alone was daunting enough, with their population of 3,500 including over 700 warriors. But to go to war with the Choctaw, who had more than 18,000 people in their tribe, would have been insanity and certain suicide. At the time, New Orleans had only 145 soldiers, less than sixty fit for battle, and the entire colony held less than 400 military men.[17]

If there actually had been a pan-Indian conspiracy, it unraveled quickly. The governor was assured by the Choctaw, truthfully or not, that they had nothing to do with such a plot, that they had heard of it and feigned to join in the scheme only to gain information on behalf of the French to whom they were loyal, and that in actuality they were sworn enemies of the Natchez and had sought to destroy them years before had the French not intervened and prevented it.[18] Later evidence suggests that the pan-Indian plot was one hatched by the pro-British Chickasaw who at first tried to woo the Choctaw into their scheme and when that failed enlisted the Natchez. Giraud explained, "In order to convince the other tribes more thoroughly and stimulate them to action, the Chickasaws spread the story that all the nations, even the Choctaws, were ready to rise. They had no success with the tribes already won for France...But they did succeed with the Natchez."[19]

On December 1, 1729, an officer at the post in Pointe Coupee, Jean Baptiste de Laye (also spelled de la Houssaye), who had previously served as the surgeon at a concession there,[20] learned of the attack on Natchez and left immediately for New Orleans to inform the governor and offer him his services. After dispatching Captian Merveilleux and his small band on their mission to warn the settlers, Périer directed de Laye to take whatever he needed from the storehouse in New Orleans and go back to Pointe Coupee to guard the settlement there. De Laye arrived at his post on December 11, with a few officers and a handful of Houma Indians only to find that Merveilleux was there with fifty men, and instead of continuing toward Natchez was harassing the residents of his post, stealing their brandy and threatening them with his sword. De Laye had no respect for Merveilleux and wrote in his journal,

> "He displayed such temerity, that when he took to the saddle, he had himself escorted by four armed men, and when he slept, he always had four soldiers guarding him, with bayonets on their guns. He showed such folly and such venality that it would take a stack of paper to record it all, and so I will pass over it in silence. There is no better comparison for the character of this man than to the soldier of the guard who acts brave in town but is a coward in the country."

When Périer was informed of the accusations against Merveilleux, he recalled him and put in his place a man named Louboey, "whose kindness and good manners earned him friendship from everyone."[21]

At Pointe Coupee de Laye convinced all the people to rally to their defenses and took 15 men with him to the Tunica village across and just upstream from the post which was to serve as the staging ground for an attack on the Natchez.

There they built two defensive forts and waited for a rendezvous with additional troops.[22] At the Tunica village the initial force was 90 soldiers, 110 volunteers from the various villages along the river, and 300 warriors from the "little nations."[23] The combined forces stayed at the Tunica village for almost a month, with Louboey uncertain in his plan of action and sending out only a few small spy parties to reconnoiter the Natchez.

On Monday, January 9, six pirogues arrived in New Orleans from the Tunica, carrying eight Natchez warriors who had been captured when they tried to come to the Tunica village to convince them to join against the French.[24]

On January 19, six weeks after the massacre, Monsieur Mesplat, a soldier from the Pointe Coupee troops volunteered to lead a party to Natchez in an attempt to kidnap a few women to gain information about the conditions of the Natchez and the locations of their forts. The volunteers prepared for their mission by getting drunk the night before.[25] According to officer de Laye, six days later one of the soldiers, named Lagrandeur, returned to the Tunica village, "completely naked, and overcome by fear and misery," and reported that the small party had been surrounded by 300 warriors who had killed four soldiers and wounded and took captive the others. The Natchez were offering to sue for peace and release the hostages and, "demanded at least one hundred thousand livres of merchandise in exchange." They also informed Loubouy that, "it was not they who had declared war on the French, but the commandant who had mistreated them, and who had made them work as slaves without pay." Their demands were clear, including that the peace settlement be arranged by sending only a small party from the French which should specifically include Ignace-Francois Broutin, the former commandant of Natchez, and the chief of the Tunicas.[26] Another report was more specific:

> "[The Natchez] sent back one of these prisoners the next day with a letter demanding as hostages Sieur Broutin, who had been in command, and the Chief of the Tunicas. Besides this, they demanded as ransom for the women, children, and slaves the following: 200 muskets, 200 casks of powder, 200 casks of balls, 2000 musket-flints, 200 knives, 200 axes, 200 mattocks, 20 casks of brandy, 20 barrels of wine, 20 casks of vermillion, 200 shirts, 20 bolts of limbourg, 20 bolts of linen, 20 coats with laced seams, 20 hats bordered with plumes, and a hundred ordinary coats."[27]

After waiting a week for an answer from the French, the Natchez chief grew impatient and called for Mesplet and his sole living companion, the others having either died from their wounds or having been killed by the Indians after their capture. Dumont recounted, "They were stripped of their clothes and left stark naked, their skin smeared all over with black. They were each given a switch to hold, and they became toys for the bannerets, that is, the children and youths, who made them run back and forth while periodically firing blank shots of powder at their bare flesh." After wearing them down, the two men were dragged to the ceremonial grounds and tied to wooden frames where the Indians, "began to burn them little by little, carefully, a bit on one side, a bit on the other, after removing their scalps."[28] This torture continued until both men were dead.

While the French forces lingered at the Tunica village with no clear plan, the poor captive women in Natchez were forced to serve the Indians and continued to suffer barbaric brutalities or witness their close friends suffer them. Dumont, who had lived in Natchez and whose landlady, whom he later married, was one of the widowed captives, wrote,

> "Each woman was at the home of her master, that is, the men who had captured them...The negro slaves became free, you might say, and the Frenchwomen, slaves. It was the latter who ground the corn, made the bread, heated the kettles, and had to go look for water and for corn in the fields. In a word, they were reduced to the utmost extremes of slavery. What's more, when an Indian master of the French woman happened to die, either from wounds or from illness, the French woman slave was strangled so as to go serve him in the afterlife."[29]

Still, many of the Natchez women did what they could to save the captives. Tattooed Arm, the mother of the Great Sun who had apparently conceived him from her union with a Jesuit priest, and had tried to warn the French of the massacre the day before it happened, was responsible for saving several women from being burned on the squares. Survivors told Caillot,

> "...that they had twice been attached to the frame to be roasted, with the wood all ready to be set on fire. But, luckily for them, they had had the ability, even though they were attached like that, to persuade the Indians that there was no point in killing them like that...They cut them free that time, but, since they were not so young, they reattached them a second time. Since they no longer had any hope of escaping, and were preparing themselves to die, the great chief's wife happened to pass by where they were, and, as they had already begun to set fire to their legs, she made them stop and untie them, to take them as slaves for herself."[30]

At the Tunica Village the combined forces of 500 soldiers, volunteers, and Tunica warriors waited for a promised force of 800 Choctaw warriors to join them. But, whether due to bad communication or the trickiness of the Choctaw, the large force of Choctaw warriors marched on its own to Natchez and launched a surprise attack on January 27, 1730. Charlevoix wrote, "they charged the enemy so fiercely that they killed eighty men, took sixteen women prisoners, delivered fifty-one French women and children, the two mechanics whom the Natchez had spared, and a hundred and fifty negroes and negresses." Charlevoix believed that the Choctaw offensive would have been complete, had it not been for some of the African slaves who had aligned with the Natchez taking up arms against the Choctaw.[31]

Dumont gives more detail. The Choctaw,

"divided into two groups, one going toward the main fort of the Natchez Indians and the other toward the house of the female chief, where my landlady was with her children and two other Frenchwomen, who, as soon as they saw the Choctaws around the house, cried out for them to come closer, telling them that there were no Indians there to guard them. Indeed, the Indians, with the female chief, had holed up in the fort of the Grand village and had left their slaves in the house, being pressed for time when they fled and not daring to risk going back to them."

As barbaric as the Natchez, the Choctaw, "found there an elderly Natchez woman, ripped off her scalp, laid her across a pile of old dry canes, and burned her."[32]

"The two mechanics whom the Natchez had spared," mentioned by Charlevoix is a reference to the tailor Le Beau and Pierre Mayeux. Whether Marie and her three children were among the fifty one women and children rescued is uncertain, but likely. On February 2, a week after assaulting the Natchez fort, seven Choctaw warriors arrived at the Tunica village bringing with them Pierre Mayeux. It was he who gave the French the report of what had happened to the unfortunate spy party of Mesplet, that, "as soon as the little Legrandeur departed, the Natchez had taken Mesplet and his companion and burned them, and that when they had asked for Broutin and the others to come talk peace it was to burn them too."[33]

By this stage in the game, Marie and her children were pawns, whether they were with the Natchez or the Choctaw, for the Choctaw refused to release the women and children they had freed from the Natchez until they were richly repaid for their efforts, and for missing their winter hunting season.[34] Dumont, whose future wife was among those rescued, wrote that these Frenchwomen, "thought themselves lucky to have fallen into the hands of those who came in the name of the French. But they were merely changing to a different nation, for they were, in fact, worse off among the Choctaws than they had been among the killers of their husbands."[35]

When the French learned that the Choctaw had attacked the fort rather than rendezvousing with them at the Tunica village they hurriedly headed north. The plan had been for a joint assault of the French, Tunica and Choctaw. That the Choctaw had acted prematurely and alone was troublesome to those in command of the French forces, and reinforced the French perceptions that the Choctaw were not trustworthy and had ulterior motives. A joint attack would have almost certainly led to the defeat of the Natchez, but may well have also led to the murdering of the captives.

On February 8, an astonishingly late ten days after the Choctaw surprise attack, French forces finally arrived in Natchez and made their camp at the St. Catherine concession near the Choctaw camp. Officer de Laye described the condition of the concession as,

> "completely ruined and abandoned. There was no remnant of the settlement - the Indians killed men, women, children, several slaves and even all the livestock, and burned all the houses..we saw only dead bodies on one side and the other, gnawed upon by dogs and other animals. In short this concession gave us the greatest possible horror, and should serve as inspiration for valor even among the

most timid men, to avenge the death of all these poor victims."[36]

The French seized the deserted temple mound in the Grand village, placed artillery on it, and in the age old convention of siege warfare, began digging trenches toward the Indian forts into which the Natchez has barricaded themselves after the Choctaw attack. These two forts lay on either side of the St. Catherine Creek about 500 yards downstream from the Grand Village[37], and unlike Fort Rosalie, were substantial. The walls were made of tree trunks six feet in circumference, driven five feet into the ground, with sharpened tops rising ten feet into the air.[38] As the Frenchmen dug their trenches in the evenings, they heard the Natchez singing their death songs, and occasionally hurling insults at the Choctaw and accusing them of betrayal.[39] While the French laid siege, the Natchez fired into them with their cannon which were manned by African slaves.

For the next several days there were small skirmishes initiated by both sides. On February 8 the Choctaw schemed to capture the Great Sun in a feigned parley, but their plans were frustrated when one of the Choctaw recognized in the Natchez party emerging from the fort a man who had killed one of his relatives and in a rage fired at him with his musket. Gunfire erupted from the fort and one Frenchman was killed. On the 11th a group of Choctaw went to negotiate with the Natchez but were unsuccessful, the Natchez only trying to convince them to turn against the French and join them. The Choctaw were successful, however, in recovering four more French women.[40]

On the 14th the French conducted a six hour barrage of cannon fire, but fearing for the captives in the fort the cannonballs fell short and never dislodged a single palisade.[41] On the 15th the French sent a soldier with a flag to call for the surrender of the Natchez, but they opened fire on him and he fled, leaving the flag in the field. A brave solder ran forward to recover the flag. He was met with a hail of gunfire, Dumont says more than 400 shots were fired at him, but he successfully retrieved the flag and returned safely to the French trenches, where he was applauded by the troops and given a field promotion to the rank of sergeant for his bravery. During the confusion of this episode several French women escaped, leaving their children behind in the fort. The Natchez retaliated by quickly torturing and killing their children and hanging their bodies on the wall of the fort. That same day a group of Indians snuck out of the fort and made an attempt to take the temple mound and the French cannon, but were repelled.[42]

Skirmishes between the Natchez and the united French and Choctaw forces continued for another week, until February 23, when the Natchez sent one of the French captives, Angelique Desnoyers, to propose a peace settlement. Madame Desnoyers who, being the widow of a major and manager of one of the concessions and fluent in the Natchez language, was considered by the Natchez as a woman of high rank and something of an advisor to them in regard to dealing with the French forces. While de Laye and Dumont describe her as emerging from the Natchez fortress under a flag raised by the Natchez[43], Caillot recounts a different story that he heard from Madame Desnoyer herself when she arrived in New Orleans after the battle. It may be that she was a messenger on several occasions, returning to the Natchez with replies from the French, but,

> "Then one day the Indians, having asked for peace, and capitulating to us, had her brought to their Fort de la

Valeur…in order to negotiate terms with the interpreter of our army. Turning around to see if there were any Indians behind her, she saw only one, who was listening. She approached him, and, under the pretext of wanting to whisper in his ear, stabbed him with her knife. Being near the fort's entrance, she escaped by coming out and throwing herself into the army. However, she had one bitter regret, and that was leaving behind her twelve-year-old daughter, who was as beautiful as she could be."[44]

Angelique's daughter survived the massacre, but her three and a half month old son was killed by the Indians.[45] According to Caillot, the Natchez offered to release all the other women if Desnoyers was returned to them.[46]

The battle finally began to die by attrition. Inside the forts the Natchez were weary, many of them were sick, and food and supplies were becoming scarce. Outside the fort some of the Choctaw were frustrated and threatening to withdraw and return home, and the French were beginning to run out of ammunition.[47] The day after Madame Desnoyer ran to the French the Choctaw chief Alibamon Mingo went to the fort and shouted to the Natchez that their cause was hopeless and that they would, "die of hunger, until you have surrendered the women, children, and negroes who belong to the French, since we have resolved to sow here our fields and to make a village there, until you have executed what we demand of you."[48] In response, a Natchez warrior named Etté-Actal, who had served as a hunter for Bienville and spoke French, came out from the fort with a proposition: if the French would withdraw their cannon and troops three miles to the Mississippi River the Natchez would release the prisoners, and if not they would burn them alive.[49] Commander Louboey agreed to the peace and on February 25 he withdrew. Seeing the French complying with their demands, the Natchez released one small group at a time, the women, children and slaves emerging from the Natchez fort, "naked as the day they were born."[50] The prisoners, however, were not released to the French, but to the Choctaw who moved them to their campground at the ruins of the St. Catherine concession.[51]

Commander Louboey had every intention, now that the hostages were safe, of destroying the Natchez fort and the people inside. Apparently his intentions were assumed by the Natchez as well, so with the French withdrawn, the hostages released and the Choctaw camping at the concession, in the middle of the night the Natchez quietly abandoned their forts and disappeared.[52] "Thus," Charlevoix wrote, "the sole fruit of this expedition was the rescue of the prisoners, who had next to be ransomed from the Choctaws."[53]

The Choctaw were reluctant to release the captives, and in fact kept some of them for several months,[54] but with the help of a Tunica chief the French negotiated the release of most of the captives the same day they were freed from the Natchez in exchange for a partial payment of the ransom the Choctaw demanded, which was, in the words of du Pratz, "greater than they would have ever asked of sworn enemies."[55] It would be two more years before the negotiations for full repayment concluded between the French and the Choctaw.[56]

The French burned the empty Indian forts and prepared to return to their homes and farms, and, Dumont writes, "The French women with their children, and even the tailor and the carter, who now found themselves free, were loaded into a large boat to return to the capital, where, upon arrival, they were lodged in the hospital."[57]

In New Orleans, each of the survivors was given 60 livres to buy clothes and other necessities, but even this was a loan from the Company and had to be repaid.[58] When they arrived in New Orleans, Caillot wrote that they, "assuredly would have made even those with the most hardened hearts shed tears, to hear how those poor creatures were crying out. The air was filled with the sounds of people lamenting their deplorable fate; you would have to have been there to comprehend the sorrow that overwhelmed everyone[59]." "In New Orleans," Dumont wrote, "our altars were all adorned in black, and we saw nothing but smoke of the censors burning for peace for those poor victims' souls."[60]

Seeing the condition of the survivors and hearing their stories set the entire city on high alert for fear of a similar attack on New Orleans.There were repeated false alarms. The sound of hunters in the woods morphed into news of Indians attacking at Bayou St. John. A random and innocent gunshot translated into an imminent attack on the city. Caillot described the panic that set in: "It was a touching thing to see even the sick people, who had not even been able to move either hand or foot, find the strength to flee."[61]

A general distrust of all Indians, and a particular fear and hatred for the Natchez, left the French to vent their wrath in barbaric ways not far removed from the Natchez's own actions. In March, just days after the massacre survivors had arrived in New Orleans, a group of Tunica Indians came to the city with fifteen scalps, two Natchez women, one of whom was the female chief of the Flour Village, and three youth they had captured. During their questioning several of the French hostage women identified the female chief as the one who had ordered their heads to be broken near the end of the siege because there was no time to burn them. Périer ordered their execution to be carried out with the same torture the Natchez had used on the French and turned them back over to the Tunica. Dumont records,

> "A frame was raised on an elevated spot near the river, between the city and the government house, and here the poor wretch was tied and burnt with their ceremonies, before the whole city, who flocked to witness the spectacle. She was burnt first on one side, then the other, all down the body, but during that long and cruel torture never shed a tear. On the contrary, she seemed to deride the unskillfulness of her tormentors, insulting them, and threatening that her death would soon be avenged by her tribe."[62]

Caillot, who witnessed the execution, gave more descriptive detail. One Indian, a Natchez himself who had fled his people before the massacre,

> "began by burning the hair of her [vagina], then one breast, then her buttocks, then back to her left breast…She began, then, to jerk about a little, blood flowing everywhere…When they decided that they had burned her enough on all parts of her body, the Tunica chief's worthy took his tomahawk and cut a ring around her head where her hair was, and then he scalped her and threw her scalp into the air…As they were going to kill her, the Frenchwomen who had found themselves in the hands of the Natchez each took a pointed piece of cane and ran her

through repeatedly. Then she became like an enraged beast, and expired two or three minutes later."

This woman, according to Caillot, "was with the Indians who threw the children in the air and caught them on the tips of pointed cane spears. Afterwards, she put these innocent children on a spit and forced the mothers to turn them."[63]

In 1727, when the Ursuline nuns first arrived in New Orleans, the entire population of the Louisiana territory was 2,228 French settlers, excluding soldiers.[64] Having heard horror stories from people who had returned to France from Louisiana, none of the other orders in France were willing to establish convents or ministries in the region, but a small group of sisters from Rouen agreed to come to New Orleans primarily as teachers, and in the summer of 1727 Mother Marie Tranchepain and eleven sisters arrived, found temporary housing, and set to work establishing a school. The nuns were pressed into providing medical care, a thing they were neither called to nor prepared for. After seeing the local hospital Mother Marie complained in a letter back home that, "There is neither stable nor cattleshed that does not present more agreeable and commodious lodging…They say that there is very little sickness that would force one to this miserable shelter."[65] In 1729, when the Natchez massacre occurred, the community of nuns had dwindled from twelve to eight.

When the survivors of the massacre arrived in February, 1730, the nuns were overwhelmed by the sheer number of people needing attention. The survivors had suffered malnutrition, multiple rapes, and wounds from torture, not to mention the emotional trauma of enduring three months of captivity, and seeing their husbands and children brutally murdered. In addition to the widowed women needing medical attention, there were thirty orphans who had to be provided homes. As a result of this unexpected influx, classes at the tiny school were postponed and rooms were filled with beds for the orphans. The Company allotted a payment to the nuns of 150 livre for the care of each orphan.[66]

The Natchez tribe, in the meanwhile, had made a retreat across the Mississippi River and into the dense wilderness northwest of Natchez. The French forces hastily rebuilt Fort Rosalie and began searching out the location of the Natchez with the intention of completely eliminating the tribe from the face of the earth. The Indians gave away their general location by a few harassing raids on French settlements and attacks on boats going up and down the Mississippi River. In July a group of 100 warriors attacked French workers and soldiers cutting cypress shingles about five miles from Fort Rosalie.[67] In November, they attacked a boat and killed or wounded 16 Frenchmen.[68]

In December, 1730 three groups totaling over 500 volunteers and soldiers including Fresh troops from France, led by Governor Périer himself, left New Orleans and made their way up the Mississippi River, crossed over to the Red River, and then up the Black and Ouatchita Rivers in search of the new Natchez village.[69] Joined by a band of Tunica warriors and military detachments from the new Fort Rosalie at Natchez and Fort Jean-Baptiste at Natchitoches, they discovered the new Natchez fort on January 20, 1731, set up camp less than 400 yards away, and began the digging trenches for a siege.[70]

In Périer's report to his superiors in France, he wrote that he brought forward a wooden mortar and, "fired some heavy shells which fell into their huts and started fires." For two days the shelling continued, and the French could hear the screams and cries of the Natchez women and children. At seven in the morning on January 24, the Natchez flew a white flag of surrender. After several rounds of negotiations 450 women and children and 46 warriors came out of the fort and submitted to the French. An unexpected rain set in, preventing further shelling on the fort, and in the middle of the night the rest of the warriors, perhaps as many as a hundred, escaped into the darkness.[71]

The warriors who escaped continued sporadic harassments including an attack by a large group of Natchez on Fort Jean-Baptiste in Natchitoches in October, 1731 when they laid siege to it for several days.[72] But without their women they were unable to ever recover as a nation or people. Some made their way to the Chickasaw nation and some to the Cherokees, where they maintained their unique identities for a while but were eventually absorbed into those nations, adopting their languages and traditions. The Natchez who surrendered, including the Great Sun and the female chief Tattooed Arm, who had done so much to try to save the French captives, were put on boats and sent to New Orleans. A few were sold into slavery to the plantations along the Mississippi, but most of them were sent to the Caribbean island of St. Domingue where they lived out their lives as slaves in the sugar cane fields.[73] As du Pratz wrote in his memoirs, "And thus that nation, the most conspicuous in the Colony, and the most useful to the French, was destroyed."[74]

How long the Mayeux family stayed in New Orleans is unknown. They may have remained for several weeks or months, just long enough to recover from their ordeal, or they may have stayed as much as a year. What is known is that most of the widows and widowers remarried soon after recovering in New Orleans, and by the following year, 1731, Pierre, Marie, and many other survivors, including newlywed couples, had relocated up the river to the place called Pointe Coupee.

---

[1] Swanton, p. 228.
[2] French, *Historical Memoirs*, p. 84.
[3] Caillot, p. 124.
[4] *Ibid*, p. 125.
[5] Giraud, p. 201.
[6] Milne, p. 182.
[7] Barnett, p. 109.
[8] Charlevoix, p. 89.
[9] *Ibid*, p. 89.
[10] *Ibid*, p. 89.
[11] Caillot, p. 128.
[12] Charlevoix, p. 90.
[13] *Ibid*, p. 86-89.
[14] Barnett, p. 109.
[15] Caillot, p. 107f.
[16] Charlevoix, p. 107.
[17] Giraud, p. 403f.
[18] Charlevoix, p. 92.
[19] Giraud, p. 402.
[20] Brian J. Costello, *A History of Pointe Coupee Parish, Louisiana*, Margaret Media, Donaldville, LA, 2010, p. 21.
[21] de Laye, p. 9.
[22] *Ibid*, pp. 9-10.
[23] Giraud, p. 409.
[24] Caillot, p. 127.
[25] Dumont, p. 242, footnote 22.
[26] de Laye, p. 21.
[27] Barnett, p. 113.
[28] Dumont, p. 243.
[29] *Ibid*, p. 240.

[30] Caillot, p. 143.
[31] Charlevoix, p. 96.
[32] Dumont, p. 244.
[33] de Laye, p. 27.
[34] Milne, p. 196.
[35] Dumont, p. 244.
[36] de Laye, p. 29.
[37] Barnett, p. 111.
[38] *Ibid*, p. 112.
[39] Le Petit, p. 190f.
[40] de Laye, p. 29.
[41] Swanton, p. 239.
[42] *Ibid*, p. 239.
[43] de Laye, p. 34, Dumont, p. 246.
[44] Caillot, p. 142.
[45] Her daughter, Marie Louise Desnoyer, is listed as the wife of Pierre Ricard in the 1745 Pointe Coupee census. Her son was found dead after the siege, Milne, p. 194.
[46] Caillot, p. 143.
[47] Swanton, p. 240.
[48] Milne, p. 194.
[49] Charlevoix, p. 99.
[50] Caillot, p. 143.
[51] Charlevoix, p. 100.
[52] Barnett, p. 116,
[53] Charlevoix, p. 100.
[54] Milne, p. 185f.
[55] Barnett, p. 117.
[56] Milne, p. 196.
[57] Dumont, p. 247.
[58] *Ibid*, p. 247.
[59] Caillot, p. 143.
[60] Dumont, p. 249.
[61] Caillot, p. 145.
[62] French, *Historical Memoirs*, p. 96.
[63] Caillot, p. 148.
[64] Emily Clark, *Masterless Mistresses: The New Orleans Ursulines and the Development of a New World Society, 1727-1834*, University of North Carolina Press, Chapel Hill, 2007, p. 38.
[65] Clark, p. 55.
[66] Giraud, p. 309.
[67] *Ibid*, p. 418.

[68] Charlevoix, p. 108.
[69] *Ibid*, p. 107.
[70] Barnett, p. 120.
[71] Milne, p. 201f.
[72] Gould, p. 13.
[73] Barnett, p. 125.
[74] du Pratz, p. 140.

Chapter Ten
Pointe Coupee
1731

Arkansas Post, founded by Henri de Tonti in 1686, was the first French fort west of the Mississippi River. Natchitoches, founded along the banks of the Red River as Fort Jean Baptiste by Louis Jucherea de St. Denis in 1714, lays claim to being the oldest permanent settlement in what is now the state of Louisiana. But the town of Pointe Coupee has an equal claim to antiquity.

Located about thirty river miles upriver from Baton Rouge, and near the halfway point between New Orleans and Natchez, the Pointe Coupee area was home to several small Indian tribes before the arrival of the French in the early 18th century, most notably the Tunica who had their primary village on the east side of the river with several small satellite villages in the surrounding area.[1] When the French arrived they found the Tunica to be friendly, and the relationship endured throughout the entire time of French control in Louisiana. The French, however, were not the first Europeans in Pointe Coupee.

According to local tradition and some historical evidence, the Spanish explorer Hernando de Soto visited Pointe Coupee and died there in 1542.[2] The explorer worked at convincing the Indians that he was a deity with supernatural powers. In his book *Knights of Spain, Warriors of the Sun,* Charles Hudson wrote,

> "In their presence, he would hold up a mirror of himself, which the Indians had never seen before. He would tell them that the face in the mirror was his spiritual double, who told him about all that they were thinking and planning. In this way he hoped to dissuade them from attempting any covert action against him. But now that he had set himself up as such an extraordinary being, his death might make the people of Guachoya think the Spaniards were vulnerable, tempting them to attack."[3]

To cover his death, his body was hidden away for three days then secretly buried. The Spaniards told the Indians that he had gone to the sky, as he frequently did, and would not return for a long time. Fearing that the grave might be discovered, dug up, and desecrated, the Spaniards exhumed his body, wrapped it in cloth weighted with sand, and dropped it into the middle of the Mississippi River.[4]

In 1682, 140 years after de Soto, La Salle passed through the Pointe Coupee area on his way to discovering the mouth of the Mississippi River, but it wasn't until Iberville's expedition in 1699 that Pointe Coupee clearly entered into recorded history. As it is prone to do, the Mississippi River was recutting its path at the time, and traveling upriver on March 19, Iverville's party discovered a six foot wide creek running from the river which if taken, his Indian guides told him, would save a hard day of rowing.[5] This *pointe coupee,* or cut point soon after became the main channel of the river, leaving behind a 22 mile oxbow lake known as *Fausse Riviere* or False River. Andre Penicaut, a member of Iberville's expedition, recorded in his journal in 1723, "For some time the river current has been undermining this neck of land, so that the full stream now passes across it. This is why that neck of land now bears the name Pointe Coupée."[6]

In 1699, the same year as Iberville's expedition, two missionaries from Quebec, Fathers Davion and Montigny, met an English trader in the Tunica village who took them to the Chickasaw nation in what is now Tennessee where they learned of a strong trade between the English and the Chickasaw. A few years later, when the Tunica allied with the French, they became enemies of the Chickasaw and were in constant danger of attacks from the stronger and larger tribe.[7] Trappers and traders from Canada who came downriver in 1708 are thought to be the first French settlers in the Pointe Coupee area where they built primitive houses among the Tunica and took Tunica women as wives.[8]

Established as a settlement on the west bank of the Mississippi River in 1717, by 1722 John Law's Mississippi Company had established two plantations in the area, the Terre Blanche concession and the St. Reyne concession (owned by Jean-Daniel Kolly, who died in Natchez), and the census from that year records a total of 28 men, 11 women, and two children at the concessions, along with ten men, seven women and one child living at the Tunica village. Many of these first settlers came from France in 1720 aboard the ship *La Loire,* known as, "The Mayflower of Louisiana." Four years later, the population of Pointe Coupee had shrunk to a total population of only 21 people, although the French population at the Tunica village had grown to 52.[9]

It was not until after the massacre at Natchez that Pointe Coupee began to grow. Many survivors from Fort Rosalie, after recovering in New Orleans, made Pointe Coupee their home, including Nicolas and Perrine LaCour, who lost a child in the massacre; the widow Marguerite Ducro who married Jean Baptist Rabalais, and her daughter Catherine; Pierre and Marie Mayeux with their three children; and the storehouse overseer Pierre Ricard who married Marie Louise Desnoyer, 21 years his junior and the daughter of the notable widow Angelique Desnoyer who interpreted for the Natchez, escaped, and made her way to New Orleans not knowing if her daughter was still alive.[10]

Among the massacre survivors who did not settle in Pointe Coupee was the longtime friend of the Mayeuxs, Jacques Cantrelle, whose wife Francienne was murdered by the Natchez. Cantrelle, whose journey mirrored that of Pierre Mayeux from France aboard *Le Profond,* to Biloxi, to Arkansas Post, to New Orleans, and then to Natchez, remarried to Marie Larmasiau, a Natchez widow, and kept a residence in New Orleans until 1763 where he served as a notary for the Superior Council. Frustrated by the violence in the city, Cantrelle, a man now in his sixties, relocated along the German Coast upriver from New Orleans and founded a plantation he named Cabonocey, Choctaw for "mallard's roost." He served as the commandant for the post there, built the settlement's first church, and helped many Acadians settle in the area, which became known as the first "Cajun" settlement in

Louisiana. After his death in 1778, the parish in which he settled was given his baptismal name, Saint James Parish. There is no record that Pierre Mayeux and Jacques Cantrelle ever met again after they parted ways in New Orleans following the massacre, but commerce between the two communities remained strong for decades to come.[11]

With the destruction of Natchez, Pointe Coupee not only became a refuge for many of its survivors, but also became, "the front line of defense against the Natchez and the Chickasaw."[12] It also became an important agricultural center, growing tobacco and indigo, and later cotton and sugar cane.[13] When Pierre and Marie relocated to Pointe Coupee in 1730, they chose to settle across the river from the fort and town, near the Tunica village. The 1731 census records them as living on the, "left bank descending of the Mississippi River; 1 woman, 3 children, 1 male capable of bearing arms, 1 Negro slave."

That same year a remnant of the Natchez tribe under the pretense of making peace with the Tunica led an attack on their village and the surrounding French farms. Four Natchez warriors arrived at the Tunica village asking Chief Cahura-Joligo to serve as a liaison between them and the French. The chief traveled to New Orleans and brought the news to Governor Périer. Charlevoix details the story: "Perrier replied that he consented to their settling two leagues from his village, but not nearer, to avoid all occasions of quarrel between the two nations; but that above all things, he exacted that they should come unarmed." Returning to his home, the chief welcomed thirty Natchez warriors, requiring them to put aside their arms. A few days later, on June 13th, over 100 warriors as well as women and children arrived at the Tunica village, "having concealed fifty Chickasaws and Corrois in the canebrake around the village." When the chief instructed them to lay aside their weapons, the agreed to, but asked to keep them for a little longer lest their women think they were prisoners. That night the Tunica gave their guests food and there was a celebration dance until after midnight. The Tunica retired to their huts and slept until an hour before sunrise when the Natchez attacked and killed many in their sleep. Chief Cahura-Joligo fought back, killing four Natchez before being killed himself, along with 12 warriors. The fighting continued for five days until the Tunica finally vanquished the Natchez and drove them away. The Tunica lost 20 men in the battle, killed 33 Natchez, and took three prisoners, whom they later burned.[14] From there the Natchez retreated once again into the swamps and woods of Louisiana and in October attacked Fort Jean Baptiste in Natchitoches, where they were again defeated.

Pierre and Marie Mayeux and the other French settlers living on the east bank of the river immediately relocated across the river and settled in Pointe Coupee.[15] The Tunica, in turn, relocated their village a few miles away, in what is present day Tunica, Louisiana.

Whether the slave listed as belonging to Pierre Mayeux had been with him since Natchez is uncertain, but is very much a possibility. In any case, by now Pierre was a slaveholder. The Natchez, always seeking to destroy the French and gain as many allies as they could, made league not only with the Chickasaw, but also some of the slaves from the Bambara tribe who had come from Senegal in west Africa. The Natchez sent a Bambara slave, probably one who had escaped from one of the concessions at Natchez and sided with them in the war, to New Orleans where word spread among all the Bambara people that on June 24, only weeks after Pierre and Marie had relocated to Pointe Coupee, a massive slave uprising was planned to be launched. All the French from Pointe Coupee to the gulf were to be killed. In return for their cooperation, the Natchez promised the Bambara slaves that they could live in freedom and enjoy a life of ease by trading with the English. The other Africans would remain as slaves to the Natchez and Bambara.[16]

When the attack was delayed for a week for additional preparation, the plot came to light. A slave woman told a friend that she herself would soon be named Madame Périer.[17] Questioning one slave woman, the governor learned that the plan was to attack while the French were at Mass on Sunday, killing them in the St. Louis church, and setting the city on fire so the rest could be killed as they fled.[18] When the plot was discovered and aborted, one woman was hanged in the presence of the conspirators and eight slave men were tortured to death "on the wheel," their bodies tied to a large wagon wheel and their torso and limbs severely beaten with clubs, breaking at the open spaces between the spokes.[19]

The foiled slave uprising set all the French on edge. Now they not only had to guard against hostile Indians, but even the slaves in their midst presented a significant threat, and in 1731 there were twice as many Africans in Louisiana as there were French.[20] And if Indian attacks and slave uprisings were not enough to deal with, the weather in south Louisiana presented a third danger. During the first growing season after the Mayeuxs crossed the river, in August, 1732, another devastating hurricane hit Louisiana leveling homes and destroying crops. Were it not for the distribution of rice from the royal storehouse, many settlers would have died of starvation.[21]

The survivors of the Natchez massacre may have thought Pointe Coupee would offer a new and safe place to recover from their losses, but they were wrong. "Between the Natchez uprising of 1729 and the end of the Chickasaw Wars in 1741," Gwendolyn Midlo Hall writes in her *Africans in Colonial Louisiana*, "Pointe Coupee was constantly exposed to Indian raids."[22] In October, 1731, Indians ambushed three Frenchmen and two women in a cypress swamp and hacked them to death. In February, 1732, a group of about 50 Natchez and Chickasaw Indians attacked the large farm of Nicolas Paillart on the east side of the Mississippi burning the houses, stealing the goods, and either kidnapping or freeing nine slaves. In response, Governor Périer increased the military presence in Pointe Coupee from two soldiers to 17. In May, four Ofougaoula Indians, allies with the French, reported that they had encountered ten pirogues of Natchez who told them of plans to attack the Tunica, Pointe Coupee, the German Coast, and then New Orleans where they intended to capture the governor and turn him over to the English. On June 4, a group of Natchez again attacked a farm near Pointe Coupee and made off with a haul of cattle and several slaves. Ten days later they built an entrenched camp near Pointe Coupee and left two tomahawks as a declaration of war. In July a slave woman who had escaped the Natchez reported that a group of 200 warriors were planning an imminent attack on the town. Subsequently, the villagers built two forts, one at each end of the town, and Périer doubled the number of soldiers to 35.[23]

The attacks continued for at least another decade. In 1741 seven Chickasaw warriors camped out on the land of Pierre Ricard near the center of the Pointe Coupee settlement and kidnapped three black girls and a French boy. They sold the girls to the English as slaves and killed the boy.[24]

In 1732, with a population of 95 French men, women, and children, 70 African men, women, and children, and in regular commerce with the friendly Tunica, the three groups found themselves relying on one another for defense against enemy tribes and consequently shared an intimate relationship unique in Louisiana. Hall writes, "Clearly, the primary concern of whites, blacks, and friendly Indians was mutual protection. The common danger they faced cemented ties among them."[25] Although the French owned the Africans as slaves, they also stood as godparents for their baptisms, and French, black, and Christian Indians worshiped together at the St. Francis Church which was built in 1738.[26] Cultures mixed at Pointe Coupee perhaps more readily than in any other place in Louisiana, or in the world, for that matter. Languages melded, customs meshed, and families blended with interracial marriages being not infrequent. Hall notes that even, "the most prominent men of Pointe Coupee chose women of African descent" as their wives, and not because of a shortage of French women.[27]

In 1733, two years after relocating to Pointe Coupee, Marie gave birth to her fourth child, Magdalaine, and in 1735 another daughter, Marguerite. As the family grew, so did its wealth and the village of Pointe Coupee. In spite of all the hardships they had endured, Pierre and Marie could consider themselves fortunate compared to others they had known. Jacques Cantrelle had lost his wife in Natchez. Nicolas LaCour lost a child. Marguerite Ducro lost her husband. Marie Louse Desnoyer lost her father. And yet, having survived so many misfortunes since leaving France, the Mayeux family was intact with five healthy children.

Intact, perhaps, but not unscathed. The physical and emotional stress of such a life must have caused a great deal of sorrow and weariness for the couple, perhaps breaking down their stamina prematurely. On January 29, 1739, Marie Mayeux passed from this world at the age of 38 and was buried in the St. Francis cemetery in Pointe Coupee. By now the Mayeux family was prosperous enough that her death required succession papers, with the distribution of her goods to various family members. The cause of her death is unknown, but three weeks earlier another resident of Pointe Coupee, Laurent David, met with an untimely death.

On January 8, David passed away leaving behind a widow, Marie Francoise Manne. David, who had come from France aboard *La Gironde* six months before the Mayeuxs sailed on *Le Profond*, began his life in Louisiana as an indentured servant on the Chapitoulas (or Tchoupitoulas) concession in what is now Metarie, just a few miles west of New Orleans. Laurent's first wife, Jeanne Francoise Dauphin died in October, 1732, less than a year after their marriage. Four months later, in February, 1733, he married the 26 year old Marie Manne in New Orleans and moved to Pointe Coupee.

Epidemics were not uncommon in Louisiana at the time, and it may be that both Marie Mayeux and Laurent David died from illness. Whatever the case, a month later, on February 27, 1739, Pierre Mayeux and Marie Manne were married at the St. Francis church in Pointe Coupee. The Superior Court records show that, "the future bride brings a dowry of 2,000 livres plus a house in the city consisting of household furniture, clothing, etc."[28]

Genevieve, the daughter born in New Orleans after Pierre and Marie had abandoned Arkansas Post, married in Pointe Coupee on November 5, 1743 at the age of 16. Her husband, Jean Francois DeCuir, was 33 years old. Together they had twelve children, two of whom died in childhood, and became progenitors of a large and important family line in Pointe Coupee.

By 1745, Pierre had become one of the wealthiest landowners in Pointe Coupee. The census from that year listed Pierre as 48 years old, his wife Marie Manne as 38, Cecile 16, and Magdalaine 12. The census continued:

- 6 black men
- 6 black women
- 4 black boys
- 6 black girls
- Horses: 1
- Cattle: 36
- Hogs: 8
- Muskets: 4
- Pistols: 1
- Powder: 10
- Lead and Balls: 4
- Corn: 150
- Beans: 40
- Tobacco: 15
- Land cultivated: 80 arpents[29]

Before the census was taken, in February of the same year, Pierre's only son Francois Pierre, married Nicole Prevost, a sixteen year old native of Natchitoches who had moved to Pointe Coupee with her parents. Being an only son, Francois became the sole carrier of the Mayeux name and a successful plantation owner and civic leader himself. His son, Jean Baptiste Mayeux, moved to Avoyelles Post and became a respected alcalde, or mayor, there under the Spanish government.

Cecile, the daughter born in Natchez, married Jean Louis Homard on April 18, 1747, when she was 18 and he was 20. The Homard family had come from France aboard *Le Profond* with Pierre and Marie, and had lived with them and the Cantrelles in Arkansas Post before settling in Pointe Coupee. The newlywed couple's life together was cut sadly short when the groom died two months later on June 28. The cause of death is not recorded, but he may have died from a measles epidemic that swept through the area in 1747.[30] Because of vaccines, measles is thought of as a short-lived childhood disease today, but in the past it was a deadly disease that ravaged entire cities and left a wide path of death in its wake. An airborne disease which is considered the most contagious disease in the world, it is spread through sneezing, coughing or simply breathing the same air, and in colonial times spread to 90% of the people who were in close contact with those infected. In the 16th century half of the population of Honduras and two thirds of the population of Cuba died when measles epidemics swept through those countries.[31] Before the advent of a vaccine in 1963 it is estimated that measles killed over 8 million people annually worldwide.[32]

The reason it is suggested that Cecile's husband Jean Louis may have died of measles during the epidemic of 1747 is because that same year, on December 16, Pierre Mayeux himself died at the age of 50, and eleven days later his daughter, the newly widowed 18 year old Cecile died. In less than a year, three members of the family died.

On April 15, 1749, Magdalene married at the age of 16. Her husband, the 23 year old Joseph Prevost, was the older brother to Francois Mayeux's wife Nicole, and like her, was born in Natchitoches before his family moved to Pointe Coupee. The Mayeux and Prevost families were thus doubly joined, something which though uncommon elsewhere was a very common occurrence among families in Pointe Coupee and neighboring Avoyelles, where, because of the insular nature of the geography and culture and small original population, family genealogies tangle quickly and often. Anyone today with deep roots in Pointe Coupee is almost certainly related to anyone else with deep roots in Pointe Coupee. Magdalene had five children and died at the age of 25 in 1758, two weeks after the birth of her fifth child.

Marguerite, the youngest of the Mayeux children, married Antoine Patin on June 2, 1749, when she was 14 years old and he was 26. Together they had seven children and Marguerite was the only member of her family to live into old age, dying in 1812 at the age of 77. She lived to see Louisiana pass from French to Spanish rule in 1762, back to French in 1800, and ultimately become part of the United States with the Louisiana Purchase of 1803.

Pierre Mayeux, who began his days in the poverty and famine-stricken France of Louis XIV, and spent his entire adult life trying to survive a chain of dangerous and tragic events that were simply life in Louisiana at the time, died at the age of 50, a respected and relatively wealthy husband, father and grandfather. His five decades of harrowing experiences were enough to fill many lifetimes. The fact that he survived at all is itself a testimony to his tenacity and resilience. But his story is not unique. Similar tales could be told of the thousands of the early settlers in Louisiana. These brave and hardy men and women laid hold of their lives of *tristes débris* - sorrowful wreckage - and like an alchemist who turns lead into gold, transformed them into a foundation of family, faith, and unique culture on which Louisiana was built.

---

[1] Costello, p. 6.

[2] While historians are inclined to opt for the Arkansas option, there is continuing dispute as to whether Pointe Coupee or the Arkansas River area was de Soto's death site.

[3] Hall, p. 350.

[4] *Ibid*, p. 350.

[5] Costello, p. 12.

[6] *Ibid*, p. 14.

[7] Hall, p. 242f.

[8] Costello, p. 17.

[9] Hall, p. 243.

[10] Caillot, p. 143.

[11] Bourgeois, p. 6-9.

[12] Hall, p. 244.

[13] Costello, p. 25.

[14] Charlevoix, p. 117.

[15] Giraud, p. 381.

[16] Hall, p. 106.

[17] *Ibid*, p. 107.

[18] *Ibid*, p. 106.

[19] *Ibid*, p. 110.

[20] *Ibid*, p. 10.

[21] Surrey, p. 173.

[22] Hall, p. 245.

[23] *Ibid*, p. 245f.

[24] *Ibid*, p. 249.

[25] *Ibid*, p. 247, 249.

[26] Costello, p. 24.

[27] Hall, p. 257.

[28] Copy of original document is in the author's personal collection.

[29] Records in author's personal collection.

[30] Paul Keddy, *Water, Earth, Fire: Louisiana's Natural Heritage*, Xlibris Corporation, Bloomington, 2008, p. 109.

[31] Byrne, Joseph Patrick, *Encyclopedia of Pestilence, Pandemics, and Plagues: A-M*, Santa Barbara, Greenwood, 2008; cited on https://en.wikipedia.org/wiki/Measles, accessed 10/7/15.

[32] Ludlow M, McQuaid S, Milner D, de Swart RL, Duprex WP (January 2015). "Pathological consequences of systemic measles virus infection". *The Journal of pathology* 235 (2): 253–65. doi:10.1002/path.4457.PMID 25294240. https://en.wikipedia.org/wiki/Measles, accessed 10/7/15.

Appendices

Appendix One
Relations Of The Massacre Of The French At Natchez

by Officer Delaye

Translated from French Manuscripts by Dave Cottrell, 2016

Note: The archaic punctuation of the original has been kept intact. It is awkward reading it in English, but it accurately reflects the original document.

Account of the massacre of the French at Natchez – 1729

June 1st, 1730

[1] The first of December 1729, Mr. Bunel, employed by the Company, and the appointed captain, La Pierre, arrived with an escort at four o'clock in the morning and told me that the Natchez had struck the French on the 28th of November, and they believed the French had been completely defeated, because no resident was on guard for the attack, even though they had all been warned two days before the massacre; such was the name that must be given in this case.

The Indian women of the Colly [*Kolly*] concession were warned by other Indian women of their nation, who regretted the impending death of the French; they alerted their masters, and Mr. de Longrais; Mr. de Colly went immediately to the field at the fort to give his report to Mr. de Chepare [Chépart, also known as Etcheparre and Chopart], the Commandant of the post, who said he was delusional and treated his warning with ridicule, regarding it as a product of fear. Other settlers also went to the fort to give notice of the rumor to Mr. de Chepare, who became so angry at them that he called them cowards and traitors, and also threatened them with prison, or some other harsh treatment. It was on the 25th or 26th of November that this rumor began to spread there.

On the 27th, which was a Sunday, Mr. de Colly spoke to Mr. de Chepare as he came out of Mass of the talk among the settlers of the Natchez plan, of which he was fully informed.
Mr. de Longrais insisted that they refer the matter to the Commandant, in the presence of all the habitants, who made up jokes about the news; they made Mrs. des Noyers Queen of the Indians and made several princesses. In the end, the morning passed in laughter. Everyone acted as if he was not afraid, and was

safe in his home. But Mr. de la Loire, knowing the savages well, believed the rumors, and took weapons from the store.

[2] The evening of the same day, seven or eight settlers again went to the Commandant's house. They told him that the Natchez were set upon murdering all the French, and that it was time to assemble all the settlers and put them in a state of defense. This salutary advice ought to have made him take all necessary precautions to secure his post against all such threats, and duty should have compelled him to further pursue this matter by spreading notice of all the warnings. Instead, he regarded these men as seditious, mutineers and cowards, and he had them put in irons.

A moment later the chief of that nation, perceiving something in the movement that he had seen among the French, brought fifty chickens to the commandant to remove any suspicion. He received this warmly, and looking at it as a sign of his friendship, let it be known to all that he was the master of the Indians, who would never dare undertake anything against the French, so much was he feared and loved. The barbarian, more subtle than he was, had distracted him with the present, and by knowing well his mentality and greed, had found the way to dazzle him.

Mr. Massée, as garrison officer, also warned him and was immediately arrested. He set up a guard more as a joke and a whim, than for security, and in the meantime put Nicolas de la Cour and Nicolas le Blond, who also knew about it, in irons.

About ten o'clock at night, Mr. Cailly, Ricard, Bourbeaux, and du Coder, and the interpreter went to the village to ask the savages if perhaps they wanted to kill us as was said, but they protested that no, they did not. However they did want [3] to arrest and kill them, but changed their resolution on the advice of some of the more experienced ones who said that if they killed these men then, they would miss their shot, they left them alone and received them as usual, they asked the Indian women if they would do a little dancing that night to which the women replied that the really beautiful dance would be tomorrow night. It seems that these gentlemen had no other desire than to go play with these savage women who they never thought would rebel against the French, it was necessary for these men to be completely bereft of common sense to make such a request to the savages; thinking they would have told them something when they were held under fear and pain of death; passion blinded them, and had these infamous pleasures thought to shorten their lives by one night, it would have been a good thing for the post because in perishing, they would have prevented the total loss of the settlement; it must also be that they were really blind not to sense something in the speech of these Indian women, especially in such a situation with all the rumors that were spreading around.

The savages did not begin anything that night, because they had seen some movements among our men. When daybreak came and having perceived that the post was very quiet, they gave order to everyone to attack at the same hour, and that the first gunshot would serve as a signal to all. At the crack of dawn, Mr. de Chepare had all the settlers who were in irons set free. He said to them that if anyone else came to him with such talk, he would seize them, and he taunted several men for all that had been said on the subject.

At seven o'clock in the morning a resident named Navarre came to the post in a great hurry to warn the commandant that all the Natchez were gathering to attack the French. When he found two men who told him that they had just been released from irons, on account of making similar warnings, he was forced to reverse his [4] steps and find a way to save himself, in apprehension of being subject to the same punishment as the others and to be killed while in irons.

At nine o'clock in the morning, the commandant saw a large number of savages coming, loaded with presents, the grand chief at their head, holding the peace pipe; a less presumptuous officer would have had some suspicion of this maneuver, especially after all the rumors that had been spreading, and would have fired a cannon to assemble everybody, which would have disrupted the plot that was in progress. This peace pipe he carried had two goals, the first was the hope of a bigger surprise, because the savages do not carry the peace pipe as a symbol of peace and alliance, the second was in case they implement their plan, the peace pipe and the presents might alleviate all suspicion that anyone might have of their activities; by this you can see that the barbarians had more tricks than one might imagine, the blind interest of this officer made him wait for them with a sense of trust, hoping this ceremony would bring him a large profit, he saw a large number of savages disembark at the water's edge, others go to all the homes of neighboring settlers of the fort, all with something, whether ducks, fish, etc; and when each was in position the first gunshot that was fired by the water was the signal, they attacked the fort, the galley, and all the settlers at the same time, they killed the commandant with a blow to the head at the moment when he was examining the presents that they had just brought him; these barbarians have recounted to our women that after having received the first blow, he told them that if they would spare his life, he [5] would give them all the merchandise that was in the store, they had no need for him to give them the goods, because they were already the masters, they seized the open galley which had no guards, nor sentries, but only the chef, and they cut his throat, they also seized the store killing those inside except for Mr. Ricard, the store keeper, who had time to save himself, they cut Mr. Bailley's throat in his bed, finally the two concessions, and all the settlers suffered the same fate at the same time, with the exception of thirty people, workers and settlers, whom the soldiers and voyageurs have found there.

These barbarians after having massacred all the soldiers and all the settlers, which they accomplished in less than a quarter of an hour, took possession of all the goods of both the Company and individuals, after they took all our wives, children and negroes, they exercised the greatest possible cruelty imaginable upon our women, they violated some, killed, massacred, and impaled others, they did all that the spirit of vengeance might dictate to more cruelly satisfy their rage and to assuage the brutality of their passion; it was the savages of the Pomme [White Apple] village who distinguished themselves in committing most of the crimes, and doing the most evil, the other villages treated them with less inhumanity and cruelty, here in brief is what happened at Natchez the 28th of November last year.

The fugitives who were saved, went across the water on a piece of wood, and others traveled by land, making their way to the Tioux who had seemed to be loyal to us. In the beginning they received these unfortunates quite well, saying that they wanted to avenge the [6] death of the French; after these signs of friendship one would never have imagined that they had declared themselves opposed to us, especially since the Natchez are not their friends, they had held a council among themselves, and had sent some deputies to the Natchez to see what was happening and to choose a side; the latter had received them well, and had given them presents, and they promised to attack us; they kept their promises, for no sooner had they returned to their village than they killed four poor unfortunates who had fled to their village in the hope of finding some relief, from there they went to the Tunicas to kill the settlers of that place, and to engage that nation in their plot; they did not find support in that village, where the greater part declared themselves in our favor and had saved all the settlers there, which forced the Tioux to return home.

These barbarians, seeing that they could do nothing on that side of the river went to the Black River where they took a concession belonging to Madame La Marquise de Mezieres, and killed eighteen people who had settled in that township; after which they went back to Natchez to collect payment for their scalps; it must be observed that the savages never kill men without also cutting off their scalps, this is the proof of their heroic deed.

The day of the massacre, fourteen of the Yazoos found themselves at Natchez; they were returning from the Houmas, carrying a peace pipe, they appeared at the beginning to be very zealous for the French, seeming to sympathize with our misfortune, those who escaped from the hands of the enemy [7] were clothed, given food and a canoe to save themselves, the next day it was a completely different story, because they turned, they burned the Frenchmen who were so unfortunate as to fall into their hands, they had been engaged to do this by the other barbarians who had persuaded them that the Choctaw had descended the Mississippi and that there were no more French alive, maybe they persuaded them with threats; it was believed after some discussion that this conspiracy was widespread instead of the contrary were it not for the inexpressible efforts of Mr. Perrier who found a quick remedy in assurances from the Choctaws. The Yazoos, after having received their presents, returned home and slaughtered the troops and settlers of the post.

Informed only of the destruction of the post at Natchez, I left on the first of December from Ecors ["the Bluffs," possibly Bayou des Ecores across the Mississippi River from Pointe Coupée Post] for New Orleans to alert Mr. Perrier of this disaster, and also to get weapons and munitions to arm the settlers in my district; I arrived at the city on the third at eleven o'clock in the morning, this same day news came of the arrival of a vessel from France; I offered my services to Mr. Perrier, I begged him for the authority to be involved with him in this affair; I laid out for him the necessity of arming all the settlers, above all those on my side of the river who were most exposed, he told me that this was his intention, he immediately dispatched the captain, Mr. Merveilleux, into the field to go the Tunicas so as to prevent an enemy uprising; and also to warn all the settlers on both sides of the river to be on their guard and to fortify themselves.

On the 4th Mr. Perrier told me to take anything I might need from the store and to promptly go up [8] to guard my district; he gave me orders of which a copy is attached here.

Mr. de Laye will take charge to assemble as many French in his district as he can for the purpose of going upstream, and if he foresees that there is too great a risk in guarding his district, he will come down with the French or with our savage friends, so as to join with the bulk of what I will bring up, he will also take charge, if he foresees too much to fear from the savages in the upper colony, to bring down as much grain as he can to New Orleans, he will put much attention and care to learn the latest news, and to inform me at New Orleans, this fourth day of December 1729 Perrier

I left the same day with only my men. I made it to the Houmas in three days, where I took seven savages to go faster, and thereby with great diligence I arrived at Pointe Coupée the eleventh of the same month, and I found all the settlers very upset with Mr. Merveilleux, one complained that he had taken brandy from him and then had resold the same brandy to him at a very high price, and for payment he had written an i.o.u. from the Company, so that he might be reimbursed, another complained of having received a blow from a saber, and a third of having to run the gauntlet, finally, so many settlers were making so many complaints that rather than encouraging his men, Merveilleux was alarming them, so that they jumped at the slightest noise, he had under him some fifty men with whom he could undertake some action, such as destroying the Tioux, who were few in number, he knew where they were and could go lay in wait to attack them as they passed, he could have gone to retake the galley that was at Natchez, neither honor nor his [9] duty concerned him so much as his own interest, he was known for a sordid avarice, and as an example, that teaches us that it is rare to find a man with this character who is brave, because he occupies a position he so loves, he avoids the danger where he might acquire real glory, we have seen this in the case of this officer, because he employed all his men only to protect himself, he displayed such fear, that when he took to the saddle, he took an escort of four armed soldiers, and when he slept, he always had four armed soldiers guarding him, with bayonets on their muskets, he showed such folly and baseness that it would take a hand full of paper to record it all, and so I will pass over it in silence, there is no better comparison for the character of this man than that of the soldier of the guard who acts brave in town but is a big coward in the country; Mr. Perrier, when informed of all these vexations recalled him and commissioned Mr. de Louboys [de Louboëy] in his place, whose kindness and good manners earned him friendship from everyone.

The army was to rendezvous at Tunica, and all the volunteers and all of our savage allies were also to assemble in this place.

Due to the sad situation of the colony, and its need for people of strong will, I looked for a way to be useful, and to distinguish myself, for this purpose, I took half of my men, and I urged all the settlers of Pointe Coupée and the surrounding area to follow me, explaining to them that the Company would recognize their service, that they could could rest assured that the only way they could protect their settlement after the destruction by these barbarians, was for each to contribute, especially the settlers, who have be full in heart and honor, most of the people there showed me much good will and promised to come with me [10] after being assured by me, I took a fortnight to go to the Tunicas, so as to know if it was true that they wanted to switch sides, as rumor had it, I left on the sixteenth from Pointe Coupée and I arrived at Tunica on the seventeenth; to better know what was happening among the savages, I took with me a young man who had been educated among them, and acted as though I was returning him to them, having forbidden him to speak to me or to any of my men, and ordered him to come to me every night around midnight when the savages were sleeping, to tell me what he had learned, I stayed in this place for five days to learn their secrets, and like their friends, I pulled in whoever I could whose words were consistent with what I was told every day by the man I had placed in their village, they confessed to me that there were among them some who had a badly made heart, this was the term they used, who had done what they could to engage us, but they did not recognize these people as Tunicas, what they felt was that the Tunica nation had a French heart, they would die in this state before they would betray them, that those who are worthless were gone with the Tioux, and they said they could would kill them all with their hands if they could catch them, they told me we should not be surprised about that, because in all nations, even in the most loyal, there are knaves everywhere, they gave me more harangues about their loyalties, saying the Natchez had offered their merchandise to kill us, they answered that merchandise can spoil, not the French, their neighbors and kinsmen tried to get them to declare themselves our enemies, they did not [11] want to, and as they were not strong enough to attack them, they were content to stay neutral until we arrived, they had sheltered all the French who were among them, and this was the best they were able to do in such conditions. Satisfied with the sincerity of their discourse, I wrote of this to Mr. Perrier who was in another area and was taking all possible steps, and who was with the Choctaws taking all necessary measures to destroy all these perfidious traitors.

Our people had built two forts among the Tunicas, one on an elevation commanding the entire village, and the other at the water's edge, the first was very useless, its location appeared to make it impregnable, but was in fact a veritable slaughter, and one would die of hunger and thirst, because of the difficulty of running from there, if it became necessary to retreat, the retreat would be very difficult and dangerous, due to the difficulty of passing through a bayou where men could only pass in single file on a log, exposing the detachment to being massacred before getting to the river without being able to defend themselves, there was no reason for giving approval to build this fort, why waste time looking at it when we could avoid this, the one on the bank of the river was very well located, both for the security of the wagons, and the goods as for that of the detachment and for the advantage of having water in spite of an invasion by the enemy, who could not harm this place in any way.

As I had a desire to descend to Pointe Coupée to see what was happening there, and because I was worried that my volunteers might change their resolve, I left them with the Tunicas, promising them to come and rejoin them in a few days; what made me make this decision is that there were several men who were [12] already discontented, and who could have soured the others whom I had brought with me. I went down on the 23rd with my men only, and arrived at Pointe Coupée the same day, I found everything very quiet there, and I stayed two days, during which I made a plan, purposing to go up the river as far as Arkansas to encourage all the voyageurs; I engaged twenty-five men to come with me and left Pointe Coupée on the evening of the 25th, I marched all night, I arrived at Tunica at noon on the 26th.

Barely had I arrived than I described my plan to Mr. de Louboys, which he approved right there on the field, and praised me for my zeal, promising to arrange for my prompt departure. This action caused a great deal of jealousy among the officers, who maintained that I was an idiot to go without them, each came forth to register his opposition to my journey, especially Mr. Broutin who asked for a lieutenant and forty soldiers, another made a similar demand, while Mr Dartaguiette and Mr. Coustilhas both kept completely silent and allowed the others to speak, they all knew well that there was plenty to keep everyone busy, yet they grumbled so much that they held the decision of the commandant in suspense, and they prevented me from departing despite my continued insistence that I was not at all weakening their troops since I was not taking any soldiers with me, and I found it very strange that they would oppose my expedition which inclined only toward the good of the service, since the men I had with me were volunteers who wanted nothing but to be under my orders, and whom I had recruited on, this condition, that only in this land would anyone oppose the good will of these people; finally after many speeches from both [13] sides I felt like going back had it not been for a letter I had received from Mr. Perrier who noted that he had written to Mr. deLouboys to provide me the opportunities to distinguish myself, according to the order from Mr. Perrier who continuously promised to send me; and would supply me with all I needed for my voyage and when finally ready, I asked the commandant to give me the orders. He told me to wait for a while, to which I replied that an expedition of this importance should not be delayed, because the barbarians were slaughtering our people every day who came down the river with great confidence, who know nothing about what's going on, who if I didn't leave, and no one else did, the upper colony ran the risk of suffering the same fate as this one, here, I again told him that he should not get in the way of the orders from Mr. Perrier who was sending a detachment from New Orleans for this purpose, or to have me take the same number from among his own troops, he always appeared ready to acquiesce to my way of thinking, but was being harassed by so many people that he could not make up his mind, and who diverted him constantly when he was taking on a cause for the good of the service, always coming up with new difficulties.

We rested in this state of inactivity from the 26th of December until the fourth of January of this year, when the Very Reverend Father Dutrelaud [Doutreleau], a Jesuit, arrived with a wound in his arm, he told us how as he was saying Mass on a sand bar near the Yazoo, he had been attacked by a party of the nation who had killed one of his men, broke the thigh of another, and had wounded him in his left arm, all in a single volley of gunfire. This news seemed to suddenly arouse the valor of these officers, each of whom seemed to want to go out against the enemy; [14] ultimately this goodwill was nothing but words, because rather than insisting on going there, they proved they have no pride, and they prevented me from leaving - I don't know what their purpose was, I have no idea other than that they concluded that I might earn the glory that they believed was reserved for the military. Our commandant made me a thousand promises and told me that he was reserving me for a better opportunity where I would be more useful; this did not stop me from carrying my complaints to Mr. Perrier about the opposition being made against my expedition, they found a means of justifying their conduct by sending some men named Voussant and Beneris to Arkansas by the Natchitoches Trace, I strongly decried this action, I said that it was a mere diversion, that these people would certainly never get there, and that it was pointless to go through the Natchitoches for two reasons - first because our enemies were hiding there, and they had received presents from the Natchez, and secondly because they were sworn enemies of the Arkansas for a very long time, and in consequence they could not serve as guides for the French, furthermore even if these two men had the good luck to arrive at the Arkansas, their trip would not guarantee the lives of all those who were on the river between the Arkansas and

commendable, the outcome convinced us that it wasn't the savages they wanted to kill, but it was the horses at the Avoveils that they wanted to get, because eight days after they left they came back with thirty, I perceived that during this time the greater part of these officers traded in poultry, in bear oil, and in corn, and that this was all they did, a pleasant means for acquiring glory, however, Mr. Perrier [18] expressly defended them.

These Tioux I have just spoken of could have been destroyed, if they had not taken a stand on trifles we could have gone to lay in wait for them at the entrance of the bayou of the Natchez, if they wanted, I offered to go there several times, and if Mr. Merveilleux had wanted to go or to send others in pursuit at the beginning, he could have easily defeated them even before they had massacred all the settlers of the Ouachitas, he had other projects in mind that were less dangerous, it was pillaging with which he could enrich himself.

Mr. Mesplet upon his return from the Avoveils proposed going to the Natchez to carry away some Indian women, and take prisoners, Mr. Louboys happily approved immediately to his proposal, and gave him seven select men, I could not hold myself back from telling him that he was not thinking of what he was doing, that he was sending seven men off to the slaughter, that if we wanted to go against the enemy we could not do it with less than fifty men, we would risk nothing with that number and we would risk all with such a small detachment, that such a plan was outrageous, a folly, and that the outcome would be deplorable, I explained that these small expeditions would only weaken our troops, and would serve no purpose; that the two men sent off to Arkansas by land were two men as good as lost, that if they survived they would endure great hardship, and they would have the displeasure of coming back without accomplishing anything, because that business was better suited to savages, and in this situation a troop of Frenchmen selected [19] for going by water, and able to oppose the enemy, whereas the second type of detachment was very weak and was lost, because it was a fool who commanded them, whose only form of bravery was in his own mind, and a vile presumption, all this talk served no purpose, he left on the nineteenth, before his departure he came to consult with me, I told him that I could give no advice to a fool, a pigheaded and self-serving man, because if all he wanted was to capture only one man, he could do it without risking his troops, but that out of his desire to capture him he would perish with his men, he implored me to tell him how he could go about it, I advised him that once he reached eight leagues above Tunica to travel only at night, to disembark below the little bluffs and to hide his boat there, then to go make an ambush along the path to the Natchez village, by which they came every day scouting, however after making sure of a line of retreat to take in case they were discovered, and forced out are sure to be able to capture one or two men, because there won't be any more warriors in a scouting parties, if he made it to this point, he should not lose any time returning, and that if, by chance, he took two men alive, he could leave one with his troops, after setting them up in a safe place, and then take the other to the savages, from whom he could obtain several French women in return, examine their forts, how they were constructed, how many savages were in them, and how we might attack them; this was the advice that I gave him before his departure, strongly recommending not to leave the water's edge, except [20] to make his ambush, and not to go inland, if he let such folly arise from that from a spirit of self interest, he would surely fall into the hands of the enemy warriors who would not grant him any mercy, he told me this was good advice, but that it was impossible for him to follow it because he was too quick tempered, that his impression was quite different from my own, that he wanted to go seize Indian women within a musket-shot of their fort, and that in a week he would return with several captives; I could not help saying that if he did not change his way of thinking, he would suffer the cruelty of these barbarians, because I was certain he would fall into their hands; I advised him to put his affairs in order before he left, he laughed at everything I said, and set off with great confidence.

On the twenty-first Itté Mastabé, a man of the Choctaw nation, in whom Mr. Perier had confidence, and who had been at the Tunicas since the beginning of the rendezvous there, formed a plan to go to Natchez a second time to take several scalps, he had not achieved anything the first time, and had returned very ashamed, which he blames on the Tunicas whom he described as fearful, he left on that day and returned on the twenty-fourth with a scalp, it is difficult to describe the pride with which he arrived, and which he has maintained ever since this feat, he says that he is the first of his nation to kill a Natchez in this war, that this is the action of a true warrior, and that it merits immensely.

The twenty-fifth a soldier named Lagrandeur [La Grandeur, Mesplet's drummer] a soldier of Mr. Mesplet's detachment, returned from the Natchez; he told us that Mr. Mesplet had arrived at the Natchez in broad daylight and had penetrated [21] into their lands to capture prisoners, and had been surrounded by a party of some three hundred savages, who killed four of his men in the first volley of gunfire and wounded the others, excepting himself, that they had taken them all prisoners to their village, well bound and trussed; as soon as they arrived in the village the barbarians painted them all black as a mark of their slavery, and they were soon to be burned on the field; however, after having talked among themselves for a long time, they agreed to send this young Lagrandeur to ask for peace on assurances given them from Mesplet that it would be granted, they asked for at least one hundred thousand pounds of merchandise in to seal it, by the message that they sent to Mr. deLouboys, they said that it was not they who had declared war on the French, but the commandant who had mistreated them, and who had made them work like slaves without pay; finally they told them many other reasons to soften and assuage their crimes; they demanded that Mr. Broutin come to conclude the peace, and the Chief of the Tunicas, stipulating that these two people come with only a small entourage, and unarmed; they untied our men, and told Mesplet to order some limbourg cloth to pay to the surgeon who had bandaged the wounds; they washed the prisoners, and left them free, though under a strong guard, and gave them food, the next day they took this soldier as far as the edge of the river with an escort, who arrived here completely naked, and overcome with misery.

Mr. de Louboys was distressed at the loss of this detachment, of which I had warned the assembled the officers, to see what action he might take in this sad conjuncture; Mr. Broutin offered to go to New Orleans to inform Mr. Perrier of the wishes of the barbarians, and also to find out what credit he believes [22] he has on them, because of their demands, he left immediately with an inconceivable ardor, I don't know how he will be received by Mr.Perrier with such outrageous propositions, coming downstream at a time when we are on the brink of heading upstream, this is no way to come against the enemy, nor to acquire glory.

From the beginning of this war Mr. de Louboys has not failed to send out detachments every day to build a road two leagues from the village, so as to stretch out the enemy and to make his post secure.

On the twenty-sixth the officers decided to send young Lagrandeur back with a letter to Mr. Mesplet telling the savages that we had written to New Orleans to find out the intentions of the Big Chief, and to take good care of Mesplet, I told these officers that the barbarians were much more clever than they thought, that the proposals were outrageous, that they had no other goal than to burn the people whom they asked to for a peace treaty, that it was not appropriate for us to listen to any proposal that would be ignominious in the nation, that if they regretted the massacre that they had committed, that they had to come to us to make extraordinary supplications, to ask for pardon and surrender at the discretion of the French, otherwise we should not listen to them, that all those who felt differently were men without heart, without honor, and without reason, several objected that it was not right to allow a man to perish who had sacrificed himself so courageously for his country, and that it was necessary to get them at whatever price. I told them that the sacrifice of a fool did not merit any attention at present, when even if he had done the most beautiful things in the world, he must be resolved to suffer the same [23] fate as those who were with him, that such time as we might, that we would rescue by settlement or by force of our arms, our women, our children, and all that belonged to us, we would take care not to forget him, if he should be alive, and that we should always recognize his good faith, but I believed that at that hour he was reduced to ashes unless he has been washed of his slavery; everyone says that when a French or other person who has fallen into the hands of the enemy savages, if he is washed will surely be allowed to live; it is true that he can have his life if it is redeemed by some old women, who have no men, this is the privilege of a woman, particularly if she has lost her husband in war; otherwise he should expect no salvation, I have studied the conduct of that nation, I have seen that it is filled with betrayal, and with trickery, if it requests Mr. Broutin it is in order to place him in the ranks of the other wretches, if requests the chief of the Tunicas, it is to burn him, for he is their sworn enemy, it sacrificed part of their village in order to get the head of that man; therefore all their requests tend only to increase their massacre, and to continue their cruelties, as was plain to see we were compelled to be on our guard, to be in a constant state of distrust, that is the speech I delivered to those gentlemen, who finally did change their minds, for they did not send send that soldier back.

On the twenty-eighth Mr. Girardo, an officer, arrived at the Tunicas with ten Frenchmen, and ten negroes, he had orders to go up to the Illinois to warn the post, and also all the travelers he encountered. Those gentlemen could now see that if they had let me go, they would not have prevented the intentions of Mr. Perrier who believed I was already [24] at the Arkansas, because I had written to him that I was counting on going up there, he did not think my trip had been interrupted, that my detachment had been held up in spite of the orders he had given to carry out with great diligence, and to not stop anywhere, until February 2nd when a party of Choctaws arrived; the reason for this delay was apprehension that the Natchez would perceive the boat going up with nothing but resentment, and worry, and would bring nothing but an evil end to Mesplet, I told them that we must act, as if Mesplet was no more, that continuing with the same attitude would mean never doing anything, and that the bests interests of the public must prevail over that of any one person: all these reasons were futile.

The party of Choctaw arrived with a letter from Mr. Le Sueur who informed Mr. de Louboys that the number of Choctaws had reached eight hundred, that they had attacked the Natchez on the twenty-eighth of last month, killing sixty-three, carrying off fifty of our women or children, and a hundred negroes along with twenty Indian women; this wasn't much in the world they were in, and surprising, for if they had the courage, they could have doubtless destroyed all the Natchez and could have seized the two forts, because there was nobody in them at the time they had attacked.

This attack had spoiled all the measures taken by Mr. Perrier, he had planned, he had given the order that when the Choctaws had come within a certain distance of the Natchez to alert our army at the Tunicas for half to come joined by land to join the Choctaws, and the other half by water, to all get there at the same time; if they had executed this plan, the [25] defeat of these barbarians would have been certain, because we would have seized both forts at the site, and as soon as the enemy came to try to enter them, we would kill them, or at least drive them away with our gunfire, and our savages would chase them into the forest, if they tried to flee there; that's how we would have succeeded, nevertheless our allies thought to win all the munitions, they grabbed that without the negroes who took the side of the Natchez, and who fought well in their defense, this inconvenience would not have come about if there had been any Frenchmen there.

The ambition of Mr. Le Sueur caused considerable harm to the colony, which could have been completely delivered of the enemies in one blow; nobody doubts this; there were no more effective actions that could have been taken, the Natchez do not doubt it and were not expecting us to come by land, they were all spread out at least ten arpents [about 2000 feet] from their forts, which we might have seized before they noticed us; our women, our children, and our slaves would have all been thrown into our arms, and would not have been able to flee with our enemies like they did out of fear of falling into the hands of the Choctaws whom they did not know, and whom they feared more than the Natchez; that is the sad result of the ambition of an ignoramous who imagined that his presence alone, was capable with our allies of decisively destroying our enemies, even if he had achieved that happy outcome, he would still be culpable because he contravened the orders of the general, he said by way of explanation that to alert us of his actions he had sent two savages, who were unable to find the village of the Tunicas, that is certainly false, because all the savages know [26] that place.

This party of Choctaws is composed of seven warriors, they brought a resident of Natchez named Mayeux whom the Natchez had saved to help build houses and repair their forts; they also saved a tailor named Dubos; these two men were saved by the Choctaws during the attack; this Mayeux reported that as soon as young Lagrandeur left the Natchez had taken Mesplet, and his companion and burned them, and that when they had asked for Mr. Broutin and others to come it was to burn them too; I knew this all along, which is why I warned these gentlemen who did not want to believe it. This Mayeux told us that they had sent back this soldier because he had not fired on them at the time they had attacked the party led by Mesplet, and had thrown his musket to the ground rather than defend himself; this had obliged them to grant him mercy as to a woman, and to send him back under a pretext of peace in the hope that he might bring back with him the men whom they requested; this seems very likely; this soldier did not give us an accurate account of the expedition of Mesplet, who had defended himself well and had killed, or wounded five savages according to their report, and to what our men had seen; and he says that no one fired, that as soon as they saw themselves surrounded, they surrendered; this is false, because if Mesplet had not put up any resistance, he would not have lost four men in a single volley.

Mr. Le Sueur requested powder and bullets with authority, which obliged M. de Louboys to quickly send Mr. Girard out to the yard to get some. The same day Mr. Chambellan, an officer, arrived, and he told us that Mr. Baron [27] was following him close behind.

Mr. de Louboys made all his garrison come to the water's edge to load the boats with all the supplies suitable for this kind of business; you will never see an officer of his age more active, nor more vigilant, he was second only to Mr. Dartaguiette for vitality, and for zeal these two are incomparable, I for worked for my part to get my boat ready, and I prepared my men for departure.

When everything was ready Mr. de Louboys sent out the 4th of February a detachment of fifty men under the orders of Mr. Dartaguiette, I followed them with my men, when we were two days from the Tunicas, we found a savage who had a letter from Mr. de Louboys who mandated to Mr. Dartaguiette to wait there, and informed him that Mr. Baron was to arrive, we waited there until the sixth when they arrived with Mr. Baron, and Mr. Chambellan, and the rest of the army composed in all of ninety men from the troops and one hundred ten settlers or volunteers, the smaller nations followed, numbering three hundred savages.

The next day we departed for the Natchez, where we arrived on the ninth, we endured a lot of rain on our trip, during which I noticed a little subordination among the officers, who made so much noise in our camps in spite of the constant warnings of the commandant and the principal officers; this was a matter of the greatest consequence, because it exposed us to being ambushed at the worst possible time; under the cover provided by this noise the enemy approached and identified each of the officers who was coming up; we found his canoe some two leagues above the old post, [28] we set it adrift, there would not have been two hours since he had set foot to earth to return to his village.

When we were within sight of the Natchez, we hesitated to disembark at the old fort, we waited for a while on the opposite side of the river, from which Mr. de Louboys sent word to the Choctaws. This precaution was useless and served no purpose, we had come up with the sole purpose of going there, and it was best to go there immediately without alerting anybody, this mistrust which was noticed by the Choctaws made a very bad impression, it testified to our resentment of them, and our actions were seen as those of men who were timid and fearful who feared them; their chiefs told us that they had come with their men to avenge the deaths of the Frenchmen, and not to be insulted by us, and that they were our friends, they gave us a thousand other signs of their friendship, they made numerous diatribes to our commandant which were very lengthy, that expressed their sufferings, and their poverty; Mr. de Louboys promised that he would take care of them, and that he would make sure they were rewarded by Mr. Perrier who saw them as his children.

It would have been best if had we gone straight to the old fort without alerting the Choctaw, because in alerting them we exposed ourselves to being slaughtered, if they had had malicious intent, made a little trench to make us safe from any attack, after which we could have alerted our allies and make talk with them, and to see their efforts, after that go lay out a suitable place to camp, and which was suitable for making a siege, this was the business of Mr. Broutin, who was to become well-known in this land [29] and who was appointed as engineer.

That same day we left to go to the camp of the Choctaws, where we arrived a half-hour before sunset, we passed a very awful night there because of the continuous rain that came upon us, we went from one extreme to another, from hesitating to cross the river because we were afraid of a Choctaws, to the next moment lying down with him.

On the tenth we made camp within a musket-shot from the Choctaws camp on the Saint Catherine's concession; this colony was completely abandoned, and ruined, there was no remnant of the establishment, the savages killed men, women, children, several negroes and even all the livestock, and they burned all the houses, it was not the only one that had suffered the cruelties of these barbarians, all the colonies had suffered likewise, having all been burned, above all those which had fallen into the hands of the men from Pomme village, who had spared neither women nor children in spite of their tears, and their wails; the savages from other villages treated them with less inhumanity, and spared the women, and the children who fell into their hands, we saw only dead bodies on one side and the other, eaten by dogs, and by other animals; in short, this post offered the greatest possible horror, and should offer inspiration, and valor even to the most timid men, for avenging the death of all these poor victims.

On the eleventh the Choctaws went to a rendezvous that had been set up by the Natchez to talk about peace, they could not settle anything because of numerous difficulties raised by one of the nations, however our allies brought back four women to us; it appeared that the Natchez had no other [30] end in view but to recruit the Choctaw into their force, so as to massacre us all, there were four Chicachats [Chickasaws] with the Natchez who came to the site of the rendezvous, they said to the Choctaws in the presence of Mr. Le Sueur that they had lost the desire to kill the Natchez, who were red men like them, and that it was better to all join up together to kill all the French, who wanted to reduce all the savages to slavery, they told them several other reasons which our allies rejected, they chose a place, and an hour talk the next day, they also promised to bring Mrs. Desnoyers, whom the Choctaws had asked for in exchange for whom they were obliged to give them two of their women.

Given that all these meetings with the Natchez tended only to weaken and win over the Choctaws, who in the end might well turn tail, I proposed to seize all the Natchez chiefs who might come to talk, by which if we could have them, we would get all our women, our children and our negroes without firing a shot; this plan was of infinite consequence to ensure the Choctaws, which were still wary of the Natchez for their treason, which I quickly proposed my thoughts to Mr. de Louboys, and all these gentlemen, who discussed it with the grand chief of the Choctaws, who strongly approved of the plan, he offered to go with the two Indian women who he had promised to the enemy, so as to erase any of their suspicions, he requested fifteen Frenchmen to support him, Mr. Dartaguiette offered to go, I offered to go with him as a volunteer, our allies went to create an [31] ambush to the right and to the left, we followed them, and in the time while we were making our way, were many gunshots, we did not know it was us they were shooting at, we saw nothing except a large number of Choctaws who had assembled at a musket-shot's distance from the fort of the Natchez; I realized at that time that we were betrayed, I asked them what it was they were firing at, that we were coming to remove the Natchez and not to fire into the air, despite my discourse, they set themselves behind trees telling us to go go forward, which we did upon orders from Mr. Dartaguiette, who wanted to make them see that we were as brave as they; At last we got within a pistol-shot of their fort, in the cover of a few trees, we were poorly situated, exposed to the fire of the Choctaws behind us and that of our enemies who were in front of us; we feared the latter less than the former, these two volleys were very violent, especially that of our allies whose smoke blinded us, who fired without restraint; this musketry served no purpose but to bring upon us that of the enemy who was closed up in their fort; for we could do not more than shoot at the pilings, seeing the uselessness of that maneuver I said to the Choctaws that they should cease firing, that they were using powder in vain, that should be used to fire on the enemy, and not on the wood. I also said to Mr. Dartaguiette that since the blow we had planned to strike was lost, it was best to retreat, he was of the same sentiment, but he could not assemble his troops who were dispersed from one side to the other, and he also felt he could only retreat after [32] the Choctaws; meanwhile the enemies made such a big volley that they killed a soldier next to me, lightly wounding Mr. Villainville in the chest as well as Mr. Izet, a cadet, who was beside Mr. Dartaguiette, at last our allies fell back, we followed them, and made our retreat in fairly good order.

It could be said in praise of Mr. Dartaguiette that he is brave, and full of courage, he has done the duty of a true officer;

Mr. Villainville also distinguished himself there, the latter was accused of cowardice because he came back without his clothes, he took them off not to keep from being recognized, as some claimed, because the enemy fired at the officers, rather than the soldiers, but because they were not suited for war, and the heat in them was excessive, and because he left them way behind him, the Choctaws stole them during the chaos, there are some who say that he did not dare go look for them because of enemy fire; these are people who weren't there who talk like this.

We went to join Mr. de Louboys who had come with the rest of his troops, at a shot, he was camped near the temple; after having given him an account of our adventure we all returned as a group into our camp, quite unhappy at having accomplished nothing, what made us miss our shot according to the report of several Choctaw chiefs, was that during our approach one of their men, upon recognizing a Natchez who had killed one of his relatives, could not prevent from firing; that the enemy seeing what was coming at them when they weren't expecting it, holed up in their fort, and responded in the same manner, this is the reason they gave to [33] Mr. de Louboys, who believed them in good faith; for me, ever since that day I have been suspicious of them, I have observed them not acting as our true friends; the Natchez were informed of our plan, they wanted to do the same to us, the musket shot fired by that Choctaw was a signal to them to retreat, for it is impossible that that Choctaw recognized the Natchez, who was six hundred paces away from him, I was a witness of this maneuver and I was very surprised by it, that was what made me understand, and for all our troops, the fire from the Choctaws at the time of this battle, I brought this to Mr. de Louboys.

We stayed in camp from the eleventh until the morning of the fourteenth when we left to advance our army toward that of the enemy; the reason for our stay was our ammunition, and while we were waiting some gentlemen took advantage of the opportunity to satisfy their avarice, they were totally occupied with visiting the Choctaws, for the purpose of trading with them, and they made very good gains in silver; the poor miserable slaves, I'm speaking about our women, that did not inspire compassion in anyone, especially those who might have sought to distinguish themselves by setting aside some of their wealth and their possessions, it was then that I observed for the second time that we had come more for gain than to make war.

All the goods and effects that were in the hands of the Choctaws had to be repurchased with merchandise from the Company to be distributed to the poor victims, who would be able to return these advances later, when they were able, this was the intention of Mr. Perrier who had [34] strongly recommended that we keep in mind the interests of the women who had lost their husbands, their families, and their wealth, I believe that Mr. deLouboys and Mr. Dartaguiette distinguished themselves with several generous gifts that they made from their own effects.

We camped that day ten arpents from the enemy on a small rise overlooking the fort of the Natchez; those barbarians sent one of our women to Mr. de Louboys, she brought a letter from Mrs. Desnoyers, wife of a manager of the d'Asfel concession, and adjutant major at the post, they asked for peace, and wanting to proceed, wanted to send this woman back, but I told these gentlemen that it was not advantageous to do so, that we should keep her, since they had sent her back, and that it would be better to keep them in suspense until we were camped, and had chosen our best method for laying a siege, they agreed with this thought, Mr. de Louboys made response to Mrs. Desnoyers, and sent it with the interpreter du Parc, who passed it along to a savage that he signaled to come out with our flag, because it rained hard all day, he decided to go camp in the temple, which is the place in which their idol is, I do not know who gave this advice that could come only from Mr. Broutin, as it was not what Mr. Louboys and Mr. Dartaguiette were thinking, that place is a veritable death trap, located on the banks of a small river, and surrounded by canes and brush, from which the enemy could ambush at any moment at their convenience. We made a small trench there.

The fifteenth we took control of a small mound of earth [35] connecting the prairie with the fort, we had made a trench for protection from enemy fire. This same day Mr. de Louboys had two cannons drawn up to the temple, where he could stand and strike both enemy forts at the same time, and before commencing the cannon fire, he resolved to try to find a way to obtain our women, and to do this he sent the interpreter to talk, who by presenting his flag caused the enemy to come out of his fort, also presenting his, our interpreter advanced and when he was at a certain distance, he stopped to wait for the enemy to advance, the latter feigned an advance but did not come close at all, his only goal was to cause our man to approach near enough that they could kill him, he was accompanied by some twenty other men who all had their muskets with them, and when they were ready they fired but the twenty shots did not hit anyone; this sudden discharge was not expected and forced our interpreter to abandon his flag and flee the field, the soldier named Parisien from Dartaguiette's company went out to find the flag, he brought it back to the Commandant who gave him the halberd as a reward, what obliged the Natchez to shoot at the interpreter was because they saw that he was misleading them, and that our actions did not correspond to what he was saying, when he went to speak with them, he was thinking only of getting silver, he said whatever he wanted, and not what we had ordered him to say, the savages, wiser than he was, perceived his deceit and wanted to take revenge by firing at him, there is no other reason that inspired them to insult us in this manner, to go to this extreme, for it is true that this interpreter never dealt with [36] the Natchez without coming away with spoons, forks, or goblets of silver. His self-interests have to warrant the loss of his life, and he deserved not simply to die at the hands of the Natchez, but to be hanged at a trial by the army.

Mr. de Louboys, irritated by the insolence of the enemy fired fifty cannon rounds at the two forts that day, it had no effect because of the distance, for it was at least two hundred toises [a quarter mile] away, the enemy came close to the mound that night, where they very seriously wounded one of my men with a gun shot.

On the sixteenth Mr. de Louboys, seeing great confusion in our army, too little order, and very little subordination in spite of all the worry, asked me to take charge as commandant of the militia, he said that it was only just that they serve under my orders since I had recruited the majority of them, I did not hesitate at this offer, on the contrary I was delighted and hoped to find an opportunity to distinguish myself, all the more so since I saw nothing but a great indolence among the soldiers serving under our officers, I appointed Mr. Soileau lieutenant, Mr. Guihaut sub-lieutenant, and Ricard as ensign, we were assigned to guard the mound, a dangerously exposed place, harassed day and night by the muskets of the enemy, I improved the trenches and built a small field kitchen, to protect my men from the constant fire, I doubled the number of nighttime guards and told them to fire at the slightest sound of danger, this precaution caused no grumbling even among the hot headed troops, I am surprised that the troops did not offer any opposition when [37] I was given a position to guard, it was on the front lines, it was their place, and not the militia, I did not try to remind them of their rights, nor their privileges, they seemed to ignore them. We put two cannons on the mound.

The night of the sixteenth to seventeenth I heard some noise in the bushes that were very close to my trench, I had prohibited my guards from crying out because the enemy fires at the sound of a voice, and thinking that it was the Natchez, I ordered the cannon, loaded with grapeshot, to be fired at that spot which killed several members of the party, and forced the others to flee, in this manner I protected my position.

The seventeenth at daybreak I saw three women near the fort seeking to save themselves coming to our side, pursued by a dozen savages, thinking that these were our women, I sent out a detachment of six men, who grabbed one, the other two were still too close to the fort, they were led away by the Natchez before my men could join them; the one was a Houma savage who saved herself in fear of dying, understanding that if we conquered the enemy she would be caught in the ruin of the others, the Natchez would have retaken her, the same as the other two, had I not sent to the front. When they saw that they could not capture her they fired more than twenty musket shots, none of which touched her, I presented her to M. de Louboys who interrogated her, she told us that the heart of the Natchez was still evil, that they killed some of our women from time to time, that many among them were ill, that their women and their children cried constantly, that they reproached their men for killing the French, and that they [38] referred to us as women, as capons, and gave us other such qualities.

Everyone remained in inaction, which enraged Mr. de Louboys, Mr. Dartaguiette, and Mr. Baron, the latter proposed making siege in formation, as the only means of reducing the enemy, everyone agreed with the idea, gabions were made to defend the trenches and mantlets to keep our workers safe from enemy fire, he asked me to provide men for this work, I gave them to him immediately.

Every day without ceasing we fired the cannon very ineffectively, for they passed more than forty feet over the fort, it was impossible for the cannoneer to properly adjust because of the distance, the enemy gathered up the balls, and sent them back at us with much more skill, they had a cannon that they had taken from one of the two concessions; this was a maneuver which I hated, and that M. de Louboys often could not stop for a considerable spell, it made the enemy more arrogant and more insolent, and brought on us the contempt of our allies. The Natchez feared nothing but the cannon, they would have given us everything we wanted and would have made peace with all the conditions we desired if only we had not fired it; this Choctaw impatient to see a breach became insolent, because when we began firing, many ignoramuses began to tell him that within two hours there would be a breach big enough for a row of thirty men to march through, it wasn't from the desire they had for [39] mounting the assault that made him so eager but because he expected we would chase the enemy out of their fort and that we would abandon it for plundering, this was the only reason he stayed with us.

When all the gabions were made, we opened the trench the night of the seventeenth to the eighteenth, it was the settlers who opened the trench, supported by thirty soldiers commanded by Mr. Dartaguiette who had for officers Mr. Coustilhas and Mr. Chambellan, both filled with good will, and an incomparable love for the service, we did not find any sappers among the troops, except for a sergeant named Brinville, and if I had not furnished him laborers, all the work would have stopped there; Mr. Baron led the workers, he filled the role of engineer with inexpressible zeal, and was more useful to us than Mr. Broutin. The enemy did not fire on us that night, and did not behold our work until the day. This trench was opened in a bad place, it was a meadow leading to below the fort, that we planned to attack first, my opinion was not to make it there, nor to attack that fort, because it was commanded by the other fort, which was on a very high eminence; it must be considered that the enemy had two forts located on the banks of the small river that passed in between the two, the smaller which is the stronger, is located on this elevation, and the larger in the meadow facing the other, they are both well-placed for security, and each flanked with four bastions; it is the lower one that we attacked very badly, against to all reason and rules of warfare. There was a [40] much better position for attacking the upper fort, it was not considered fitting mainly to Mr. Broutin, because he found it dangerous, I asked for a reason that could prevent an attack from that side, he objected that we would draw continuous enemy fire from the cane that the enemy would ambush us from; I told him they could not harm us in any way, that when we camped two arpents from the upper fort above the cane, we would have only the fire from the fort to weather, and we could protect ourselves from that for a least a quarter hour by using a small entrenchment, that the enemy would not come to attack us from behind for fear of being surrounded by our savages who would approach us, as we approached the enemy, and that the cane they found so detrimental was on the contrary an advantage because it would cover our advance, it was impossible for the enemy to make any ambush in that place, because it was a narrow border of canes of fifty to sixty feet in width that could be cleared in less than two hours. All these reasons were useless, this wasn't the opinion of Mr. Broutin, he who promised to perform miracles, saying he knew the territory better than the savage; my opinion was so different from his, and from those who thought the same way, that I said that if they wanted to attack the lower fort, it should not be done from the meadow, where we would have to weather the fire from both forts, and that from two other locations, that would serve the enemy as ambushes, that it should rather be attacked from the rear [41] where we had been with Mr. Dartaguiette, that we could approach very closely without a lot of risk, and without any work, explaining to him that we would have nothing but the fire from this fort to weather, this was essentially the opinion of the officers, but not of that engineer whose most notable quality was that spirit of caution so common in engineers; no one knew this place, Mr. de Louboys was forced to defer to the opinion of this man who had been there so long.

On the nineteenth eight negroes of good will went to find a favorable position to lay in wait for the enemy, they were under the orders of Simon a mulatto, they set up an ambush at the edge of the canes on the side toward the upper fort, which was called Flour, they quickly set to work on a small trench; the enemy was worried about their activity, they made it their business to drive them out, they vigorously repelled them with the loss of three men, one of the negroes came to warn Mr. de Louboys and to ask him for help telling him that their position was very suitable for overcoming the enemy as they left their fort, and also for setting up a battery of cannons. Mr. de Louboys quickly released twenty men with Mr. Broutin, who apparently pretended to reconnoiter the place, from where he returned after a time, he said that the spot was suitable for nothing but getting the troops slaughtered, this obliged Mr. deLouboys to send Mr. Bessantan officer with a detachment to bring back the negroes, I was curious to examine this place, on the way I found that officer hiding in the canes, from which he had sent a soldier named Legrandeur to tell these negroes to return; since it was necessary to pass through a small, very narrow meadow, from where we easily spotted the enemy, who had the [42] same advantage over us, and who fired continually, I moved very quickly, to try to spoil their shot, the soldier named Villemin who followed me did not take this precaution and he received a musket shot low in his stomach, I examined the setting of their fort, that of the trench of our negroes, which was well suited for skirmishes with the enemy, who were forced to let us work quietly on the trench, it is in that place from which they made their attack, and from where they fired continually, it was easy to see the essential value of the position by the prompt loss that the enemy caused, which heightened the ardor and the effort of these negroes, whom we had a lot of trouble making return, one of them was slightly wounded. I said to M. de Louboys that that position was of infinite consequence, and that we must hold it to drive out the enemy, in case they had the audacity to make any campaigns against us, he did not share this opinion, he was just trying to defer to that of Mr. Broutin in preference to any other.

We still continued the work on the trench day and night that pushed up to within sixty yards of the fort despite the enemy fire, this distance is where these gentlemen have resolved to place their gun batteries, we have lost three resident sappers, and Sergeant Brinville during the time of this work which lasted from the seventeenth until the twenty-second, I'm astonished that we have not lost more people because of the poor disposition of this trench that the Natchez have harassed on all sides with continuous firing.

The Natchez, worried of what would follow our approach, resolved to make a sortie in the hope of [43] chasing us out, or killing us, they did it the twenty-second of the current month, they chose the moment that the sun was opposite us, hiding their movements, and we could perceive little, they succeeded, in that they made it very close to the trench before those guarding it spotted them; it was the sentinel from my position who gave the alarm, the soldiers instead of taking a defensive position fled into enemy territory to whom they abandoned their cover, and their weapons for better running, the seven resident sappers, after having fired their shots saw no support from the troops, and fell back on me without warning me; the Natchez after having won the trench threw down the mantlets that had been put up to protect the workers they sheltered, and lodged themselves in the third horseshoe the distance of a pistol shot from my trench, from which they fired a frightful volley, and which was so violent that I was unable to see where they were, since I did not know that our men had abandoned the trench, I only fired to the right, and to the left to favor them, and dislodge the enemy, then when I saw Mr. de la Tour, who was in my position, who told me that the troops had passed right over his body, and that the enemies were in the trench, I made my men cease their fire for a while to better see the enemy's movements, I saw that there were at least two hundred warriors to the right and to left of my position, not more than fifty or sixty paces away, and that they were slowly approaching with their heads down; they were counting on the element of surprise due to the musketry from the trench where their men were, which excessive fire had distracted me and drawn my fire on them; seeing their advance [44] and guessing their thoughts, I ordered my men to fire no more than a foot above the ground in the meadow, I ordered a cannon loaded with grapeshot fired into the trench, which had a marvelous effect. The enemy was forced to abandon the ground that they had won, and to desist in their plans to make a second massacre, so would come to an end without difficulty, and all those who have knowledge of this case are very convinced that if I had not stood firm throughout the army would have been defeated; all the savages waited in suspense to see who would gain the upper hand, including the Tunicas that pursued the enemy when they saw them withdraw.

This temple where the officers were was also attacked, but the enemy had barely emerged from the canes, the warriors did not bother with that position, which they could have taken, when they wanted to be able to take over my position, which was essential because all the artillery was there, we can see from the conduct of these barbarians that they are men of pride, and resolved, and not women as some believe.

There is no doubt that the Choctaw were waiting for the moment of our defeat to turn on us, they had promised the Natchez to do so. Since I distrusted these barbarians, I arranged my position from the beginning of the attack, as if I had all the nations to fight, and if the Choctaw had approached at that time I would have fired, as at the Natchez, I had given this order, I was resolved to go to this extreme rather than to be vulnerable to any such betrayals, always more fatal than a straightforward attack by the enemy.

The Choctaw dreaded my position, he saw the continual distrust [45] that I maintained, I did not suffer them to come in at night, and very little during the day, and when they came in under the pretext of shooting at the Natchez, I advised my men to be on guard, and I expressly forbid them from firing in case the savages were waiting for that moment to massacre us, finally, seeing that they could not gain anything that way, they stirred up the Natchez to make an attack, counting on this bringing our rout, and profiting from this time in defeating us, this was their goal. The Natchez reproached them that same evening; it was unknown the number of men they had lost, they hid them from the eyes of our women, they had had at least forty men wounded, we learned after our retreat, we did not lose a single man, I had two slightly wounded, as I was on an elevation, and as the enemy was very close, the warriors could barely catch the edges of our hats because of the small entrenchment that I had, this is what misled them, and this is why they killed none of us, it's that my negro put several shirts to dry on some bushes on which the enemy fired many times, thinking that they were snipers, they saw this whiteness, they could not distinguish what it was due to the smoke of our musketry, there was not one shirt that received less than ten shots.

The firing ceased on one side and the other, and the enemy retreating into their fort, Mr. de Louboys visited all the positions to see what state they were in, he found Mr. de la Tour at mine and he asked him what made him come there, he replied that his men had abandoned him, and had passed right above [46] his body, and that he had come to this place to replace his musket which had been folded in two, and also to wait until the situation had been decided for one side or the other. Mr. Dartaguiette, who accompanied Mr. de Louboys, hearing the indignant stories of the cowardice of the troops took with him five or six volunteers and went into the trench to take the place of Mr. Villainville who was in command that day, this latter has been accused of cowardice, and all the blame has been placed on him, and especially his comrades, who have no idea what happened nor how it went, he was near the sappers at the head of the trench with thirty men, Sergeant Avignon was at the head of this advanced guard, Mr. Delatour, ensign, made the rear guard at the head of ten men, the sentinel gave no warning, he deserves death, the sergeant instead of encouraging his troops, was the first to save himself, he brought the entire detachment with him right over the body of Mr. Delatour who followed the fugitives. Mr. Villainville proceeded to retain his troops with bayonette in hand, the sappers reported that if he had not fallen he would have killed one soldier, at last he alone remained in the trench, what could he do, having been abandoned by everyone before he even knew it; if anyone is really guilty after the sentinel, it is the sergeant, and also those who made up the rear guard. Has anyone ever seen an officer allow his own men to run right over his body, having weapons in his hand, it is he who [47] should have restrained the fugitives, and prevented their rout. I don't pretend to condone the conduct of the Mr. Villainville, far from it; his actions were culpable, they came more from an ignorance of his duty than from cowardice, because when he saw that his men were abandoning him, he should have immediately alerted the commandant to get others to retake his position, not remain inactive, and after the action, he should have asked for a council of war to punish the guilty, this is what he should have done to make his own conduct above reproach. It is commonly seen that misfortunes never come on a man by themselves; that same day at nine o'clock in the morning the enemy began firing nonstop at that trench, our men responded with enough enthusiasm, until this officer ordered them to cease in fear that they might harm the sappers, and that they would draw the fire of the enemy who used this time to better adjust their aim, with the result that they killed one volunteer, he has been blamed with this for stopping his men from firing, considering that the sole reason for his troops being in the trench, was to support the workers. The commandant was on the verge of relieving him, that would have given him hope, because then the other case would not have happened to him; that's how it was that the enemy seized the trench without difficulty, and which I was personally forced to reconquer by my continual musketry, I had started with only twenty men, the rest being in the detachment, I was reinforced by fifteen of the runaways from the trench. Mr. Gueret, Mr. Guilhaut and Mr. Soileau distinguished themselves.

[48] This action does not honor the nation's wars. There were two cannons in the trench, neither one had been loaded, even if they had been, it would have served no purpose, because the enemy was firing on us, they could easily have continued as long as they wanted, this was the only occasion where we could have distinguished ourselves, there was not a man guarding the fort we were attacking, we could have gotten in with what little there was of us if there had been some sense of courage and of order in our army; on that evening the Natchez talked to us, they told us that all the savages had killed the French, that they were not the only ones involved.

The twenty-third they asked for peace, Mr. de Louboys told them to return all our women, and our slaves, he would only talk after that, they promised to do so, nonetheless Mr. Broutin continued to work on our battery which he finished preparing that night.

On the twenty-fourth Mr. de Louboys, seeing that the enemies were not making any effort to bring us our women, and that our slaves were getting impatient, ordered the cannoneer to fire, the enemy responded with volleys from two hundred muskets that they fired all at once directly at the battery, which on the seventh shot, wounded our cannoneer, and also two of my men, we could not find any soldier to operate the cannon, the officers were extremely embarrassed, the ignorance of the engineer was the cause. They did not know how to adapt this [49] battery, because of the continuous fire from the enemy; one spoke of setting up a log, another offered another measure that could not succeed, it was impossible to repair it with wood due to the danger, I proposed mattresses, we brought and placed them there, which was wonderfully effective.

As these gentlemen claimed they could make a breach in less than twenty cannon shots, Mr. de Louboys arranged the assault, Mr. de Louboys went up to the head of thirty men from the troops, he had Mr. Chambellan and Mr. Coustilhas as officers, I was to follow at the head of ten volunteers, we were assigned such a small number of men for this operation, because there was a much larger force ready to support us. The battery was repaired by means of our mattresses, we resumed the cannon fire, the enemy responded with enough enthusiasm, but without success, calculating that they had troops hiding, I recommended to the cannoneer that the fire into the subsurface, so as to cause more injuries, because the ball smashing into the ground would cause more damage than the advantage afforded by trying to make a breach for an assault, however, after thirty cannon shots, we did not see any breach. The balls simply made a hole, or fell beside the piles, we did however kill three people.

As we had no more powder of war [gun powder] , even less balls, and the Choctaw were asking for ammunition from us with an outrageous insolence, Mr. de Louboys assembled his council, he resolved to lift the siege; several men suggested that before going to this extreme to fire from time to time on the [50] fort, so as to distract the enemy, and then to attack them at Flour that night with grenades, who were in no way defeated, and who still had their flag flying during our cannonade, he would have gone with this idea, had he been confident of the bravery of his men, it was always on his mind since their previous cowardice, he could not resolve to do basically the same thing, for fear of losing the few brave men he had, and being left with the most cowardly, which would have put the colony at bay, it would have been exposed to continuous contempt and insults from all the nations, especially those who were beginning to despise us because of the minor effect of our cannon, he very wisely, at four in the afternoon presented our flag, the enemies put theirs outside, they promised to bring to us all our women, our children, and our slaves the next morning, on the condition that we withdraw our cannon.

The twenty-fifth at eight o'clock in the morning the one named Tactale came with many women, children, and negroes whom he returned to Mr. de Louboys, he made several trips that morning from his village to our camp, during which he brought all our women and our slaves, he had a great deal of difficulty in delivering some of the negroes, who were very much attached to them, and who had fired at us, they served them as cannoneers, and were bolder than them.

This Tactale is of the Natchez nation, he was formerly in the service of Mr. de Bienville, into whose arms he threw himself to save his life, the men of his village wanted to kill him, because he was the husband of the female chief, who died at that time, it is a custom among them to strangle the husband, and all the people [51] in her entourage to accompany the female chief into the other world, how as he did not in the least wish to be a part of this religious custom, he saved himself among the French, and attached himself to Mr. de Bienville, who reconciled him with his nation, every time that he came into our camp our interpreter took care to ask him for silver, and they also followed his example, especially Mr. Broutin who obtained many silver spoons and forks, such is the character of most of the officers of Louisiana.

When we had all that belonged to us, I told these gentlemen that it would be best to fortify our position, to see about food, which abounds at the riverside, and to sit tight until Mr. Perrier sent us help, that we would shortly receive ammunition, that we had enough for the short term until the arrival of the first convoy which would not be long, that if we abandoned this place, the enemy would leave their fort to cross the river, and retreat on the Black River so as to ensure a route safe from the Choctaws, that we were strong enough with the smaller tribes to destroy them, that I was fully persuaded that when Mr. Perrier knew of our situation, he would not fail to send us a party of the militia from below, by means of which we could easily overcome these barbarians.

That the Choctaw were embarrassing us too much, we had to give them all the goods we had to get rid of them, and send them back to their village, Mr. de Louboys and Mr. Dartaguiette were basically in agreement, but they saw their troops, and the settlers were very tired, and were very disgusted, and could not be counted [52] on. The officer had none of the ambition that was needed, he thought of nothing but his wife, or of his home, the value of which he extolled, he seemed to hate his job that restrained him so much, the soldier had the same sentiments as the officer and asked who would nurse him if he got wounded, in a word, it was difficult to find a good soldier when the officer is worthless, this inconvenience obliged Mr. de Louboys to make a retreat to the riverbank; all these gentlemen said that the enemy would never leave their village, because they believed themselves indomitable, this was never my sentiment, they would be poisoned by staying in this place because of the stench of their cadavers they buried in their forts, furthermore a nation never stays in the place where it was destroyed.

This same day M. de Louboys retreated to the banks of the water, I accompanied him with my men, I brought the greater part of the artillery with me, Mr. Dartaguiette who followed me, was insulted by the grand chief of the Choctaws, who wanted to have all the powder he had, he did not want to give him any without a specific order from Mr. de Louboys, this so irritated the chief who in a rage threw his hat to the ground, and walking on it, he said that when dead Frenchmen are found, it might have to be said that it was the Choctaws, and not Natchez, from there he went to his camp, as it was already very late; Mr. Dartaguiette was forced to make camp in place with his detachment, he was not, however, attacked, then he went to the river's edge the next day the twenty-sixth, that evening the chief came to see us looking at us with disdain, and we reproached him for his bad conduct, and his bad spirit, he told us he had just as much right to be angry as the French, that the [53] words were nothing, that they passed like the wind. Mr. de Louboys ordered that he be given two hundred pounds of gunpowder, which was half of what we had, this same day we tied up three mutinous negroes who were recognized by our women as having fired upon us, and for having tried to persuade the Natchez to burn them, one of them who felt guilty threw himself into the river with a knife in his mouth, as he reached the edge of the escarpment in a place where we could not get him, I shot and killed him.

We lost four soldiers throughout this war, and nine volunteers from among those I had brought, we had a dozen wounded, none of these wounds caused any problems later.

Mr. de Louboys had done all that a brave officer could do. I would rather he had made his retreat in a situation where a glorious victory could have been recorded, he had forced the enemy to return our women, our children, and our slaves, which was all he could do. Mr. Dartaguiette distinguished himself with ample proof of his valor, and Mr. Coustilhas, Mr. Chambellan, Mr. Saint Therèse, and Mr. Villainville all served well enough, and with enough good will.

On the twenty-seventh everyone was assembled on the river's edge, my men told me that it was necessary for them to go home to work on their property, that during the three months they had been absent, that they had none or few negroes, that if they did not go down promptly to prepare their land, they would not have a harvest, which would cause them a considerable loss; I told them to build a small provisional fort to put the troops in to shelter them from all affronts that Mr. de Louboys would not ask them for more than that, after which [54] we would leave, from the time they started working, they created a fortification sufficient to shelter all the troops from all affronts in four days, if they didn't have a home, I engaged them to stay there to cross three or four leagues above the Natchez, to prevent them from crossing the river, which was always their idea.

While we waited on the riverbank, the Choctaws continued their affronts, they stole with impunity here, abused our men there, there was one who broke the arm of one of our soldiers with a musket shot, they fired on Mr. Reytel the chief surgeon, they also fired on our dead, finally they were looking for a pretext to attack us, as they left they burned the buildings of the d'Asfeld concession. Mr. de Louboys got rid of them on the strength of goods he gave them and those they have stolen.

The subject of their dissatisfaction comes from the grand promises made to them by Mr. Sueur that they would find everything they desired at the Natchez, they counted on this, the plundering, and on the too great familiarity of our men, which made us contemptible, the escape of several negroes they stole especially from Mr. Broutin, it is true they were taken from him, he did not have to take them without payment, the savage was counting on the above to get merchandise, he saw with frustration at this time the bad faith of the Frenchman, this shocked him, therein is the cause of the affronts the Choctaws made against us in the end, because in the beginning, they were very zealous, at least appearing to be so, it could be seen by this that the Frenchman's avarice is always the author of his troubles.

[55] When the Choctaws were gone, and the main work was finished, I left from the Natchez with my men on the fourth of March for Point Coupée where I arrived on the fifth, I found a letter from Mr. Perrier there, which I have inserted into this account to give it weight.

I am very pleased sir with the distinction with which you served at the siege of the Natchez, I beg you engage your men to stay as they can help our men to prepare the fort at Rousseau's landing, when it will be in a state of defense, I would also be very pleased to speak with you in the meantime to let us know exactly, and without pretending to anything of the negroes, which I know some individuals have surreptitiously taken, either by trading them to the savages, or having seduced them from their allegiance, this is a thing of consequence for the good order of the service and for the good order, being neither just, nor natural that these poor individuals who have nothing to mortgage but their negroes lose them due to embezzlement by other individuals, I would add this service that you are doing for me on this occasion to the others you have rendered to the colony by your valor and good will that I will correspond to the Crown and with the Company, - I hope they will be recognized, it is the desire of my heart since I am here in the service of good subjects, I am charmed that you are of that number for whom I assure you that I am truly, sir, your very humble and obeisant servant, Perrier.

It can be seen by this letter that neither the cares, nor the worries which come with the duty of our commandant, nor the difficulty in which he is found in this conjuncture prevents him from having in sight the well-being of the unfortunate [56] who perished in this massacre, to ensure the property to his heirs, he thinks only of the interests the company has to the individual in how they see it; he encouraged by his example zealous persons to continue their services by giving them the hope of a reward, and he looked for ways to discover the embezzlers to punish them, finally in spite of all his sorrows, he has seen his company fail to bring the return that was nearly certain, and in these cases where there is overhead, it was to ensure security of person, and the safety of each, and the colony.

When the Natchez saw us leave, they all moved to the riverbank, or went home for a fortnight, until they had build canoes, during which time the chief of the Tunicas had taken or killed five women and three men, when their boats were built, they crossed the river, and made their way to the Tensas Bayou onto the Black River.

The one called Tactale fooled these gentlemen to the end, he came to see them several times, he told them that thirty Natchez had left to bring oil for the French, that he wanted to give a hundred pots of it to the commandant, and thirty to each of the other officers, they put credence in the words of this rascal who was more cunning than they thought, he was saying this to cover the march of his men, he brought a pewter dish to the commandant on behalf of the female chief who had sent it to him as a present, he came several times, and always with something to distract them, then he would suddenly disappear, and joined his troops, one can see that these savages are sharp, and crafty, they know the weakness of most Frenchmen, it is enough they have the secret to reach the end, this woman chief has done [57] all she could to save us, all our women owe her their lives, they would have been killed without her.

We would still not know about the retreat of the Natchez without the one named Forbant who while going for a walk saw a large number of vultures, animals that eat human flesh, flying above the fort, which made him think that the enemies had withdrawn, he approached, he saw no one, he entered as there were many boxes, and plunder, he hid it, and then went to bring the news to the commandant of what he had found. The officer, and the soldier had never displayed such eagerness as on this occasion, they fills their boats with goods that they said they had purchased from the soldier, Mr. Broutin went to the d'Asfeld concession of which he had previously been manager, he forbade the soldiers from touching anything at pain of death, in order to get a better price, he hid a number of things that the soldier had tried to take for himself. This war brought little honor to these gentlemen for whom the principal occupation was to trade, and to pillage, from start to finish, I except Mr. Dartaguiette, Mr. Chambellan, and Mr. de Louboys, these three officers seemed to me to be very disinterested, especially the first who has the true character of an officer; Mr. Villainville, Mr. Saint Thérèse, Mr. Latour, Mr. Yens, and Mr. Beslant seemed very disinterested during my sojourn at the Natchez; this in brief is all that happened there from the beginning of the war to the end.

Let us present the cause of so many misfortunes, which came only from a shot of desperation on the part the Natchez, there has never been a single good commandant in this post, we are seen as nothing but drunkards, tyrants, and misers. The last two were subject to all of these vices, Mr. Merveilleux distinguished himself by his avarice, and the tyranny that he exercised [58] upon the savages as well as toward the French. He was seen perpetrating a thousand actions unworthy of an honest man, such as ordering the arrest by his soldiers of savages carrying game, taking the best pieces, and sending them away without giving them anything, the last imitated his example and held them for ransom just like the French; all the settlers who survived the massacre reported that he forced them all to bring him as a present a half-dozen tobacco andouilles [locally grown tobacco leaves rolled and pressed tightly together, with the appearance of andouilles sausages], which no doubt brought him a fortune given the number of settlers who were established in that place, he promised them his protection, and to let them have negroes from the Company, these poor wretches were left deep in debt to him for they did not hesitate to give him all he asked in hope of getting some negroes, he made the same promise to the Natchez; but they found they were working for the Company, he gave them only half of what was coming to them, and when they complained he would extract the payment by the blows of clubs; the savage born free found himself abused, and reduced to slavery attached to us by naught but fear, not by inclination, everyone since the other war was full of praise for these savages, if a resident needed two men, he could find them, and have them for very little, if he needed forty, he could also have them easily, and get them to do whatever he wanted, never had a nation seemed more affectionate toward the French, it was so strong compared to the other savages they called them slaves, the sole cause of this massacre wast that Mr. Chepare desiring to build a settlement on the land of the chief of Apple told the savages of this village to go elsewhere, and that he needed that place, that speech did not please them, especially not that chief who is [59] a great rebel, and who had never liked the French, he asked why they wanted to chase him from his home, the commandant gave him no reason, he ordered him to leave immediately under pain of being put in irons, he threatened to burn his village, and made other threats which irritated him so much that he looked for means of getting revenge. Mr. Chepare sent the negroes to seize the cabins of this chief which they tore down, and put out, this forced him to engage the chiefs of all the villages in his quarrel, they had little difficulty deciding because of the discontent that each of them had, at last they counseled together the loss of our post, and in case the commandant had any suspicions, they made him a present of a beautiful bunch of poultry, and wheat, they resolved among themselves to be more friendly than ever toward the French, so as to have their trust.

This officer boasted of the power he had over this nation which he imagined to be fear, saying that he had made these harsh moves so as to make them pliable, and obedient, and to obtain what he wanted from them; these savages had more finesse than he, they had other designs, knowing his character, and his avarice, they hoped to dazzle him with gratification, and thereby achieve the end of their design, they resolved among themselves to trade for all the merchandise of the settlers, and especially their arms, they promised all that was asked of them; in a word they were double dealing, they discovered by this means the secret of disarming two thirds of the settlers, after which they chose the day to assassinate everyone, as they did the 28th of November 1729 as we have seen at the beginning of this account, we could have prevented this massacre if this officer had followed the warnings he was given, we see that [60] this nation has given to us naught but a stroke of desperation, and that it was not a general conspiracy as many claim. Several want it to be that the English excited them to strike this blow, I would like to believe this, however, if they had not had so much dissatisfaction from us they would have done nothing.

I am surprised that all the settlers having been warned were not put in a defensive state, they were all killed like women, there was none but the ones named Jappio, and Brisebois, who defended themselves, and who have held against fifty whom they repulsed with the loss of three men, they had saved their beards and stole a canoe in the presence of over one hundred and fifty of these barbarians on whom they fired as they departed, these are the only people who defended themselves, all those that were saved said that all the settlers would have been poorly guarded without these gentlemen who were in a different village the previous day, they declared that they had found the savages very peaceful, and that they had nothing to worry about, that if they had had any bad intentions, they would have killed them, it was necessary that all of these people were devoid of good sense; this destruction serves as an example to the settlers, and for them to learn to stand more on guard. These same people also said that if the commandant had wanted he could have prevented this misfortune, there is no doubt.

Everyone was surprised by the latter conduct of the officer who always distinguished himself while he was in the colony, and that it was because of the good relations he made with it that he was sent as commandant to the Natchez, he went down three months before the massacre, the settlers learned that he sent back [61] a request to Mr. Perrier pleading with him strongly to not deprive them of their commandant, whom they were content; it must be absolutely that this officer had been corrupted by certain flatterers, who made him understand that all these vexations were little duties that required his power as commandant, and, not being aware of the true situation, he followed the advice that was given him, a sad effect of flattery. I knew him for a very long time; he always appeared very wise, it was said that he was filled with a prejudice without equal, and that he had become very drunk, this could well be true, the officer always had a habit of relaxing, when he was not under the eyes of his commanding officer.

Let's see at how the Tioux struck us; we usually see that when evil comes, it always brings some other, of the kind that there are at times, it appears that we are besieged by trouble, or at least so heavily blockaded by an army of calamities, that every passage by which we might receive help is entirely closed. This is the state where a few miserable refugees who escaped found themselves, some on pieces of wood, letting themselves go with the flow, and others by land in spite of the difficulties of the way to make it to the Tioux, the former were happy to be well enough received by this little nation who did not know of the massacre except by the report of our people, they appeared at the outset to share in the pain of those unfortunates and gave them food, however, after having reflected on this situation, they resolved to go to the Natchez to see what was happening, the Natchez persuaded them to enter into their cause, by giving them presents. They came back into their village, where they stayed for a few days waiting for those who came down there whom they killed as [62] they disembarked, thinking that there were no more coming down from the Natchez, they went to the Tunicas to engage them to kill the settlers who were in their village, and those at Pointe Coupée, they offered presents on behalf of the Natchez to enter into their cause, they swung back and forth for a time on the threats made on them by the others that the Natchez would destroy them if they did not attack us, not knowing which side to take because the greater part of their men were away hunting, the elders, and the most experienced resolved to keep the minds of the Tioux in suspense, to have time to save our people, and when they were saved to declare themselves neutral until the arrival of their warriors, and the French, this they did with much zeal, when our people had gone, they said that they did not want to dip their hands in the blood of the French, however, there were five of this nation who joined with the Tioux who seeing that they could do nothing more there went on the Black River, where they destroyed a concession belonging to Madame La Marquise de Mezières and assassinated eighteen people who had settled in that area, from there they went to the Natchez to see their comrades and to enjoy the fruits of their cruelty, and their treachery, for all these barbarians who had killed our people joined hands with them.

It can be seen that the Tioux were not complicit in the initial massacre which they had no knowledge of in the beginning, for if they had been part of the plot, and if they had been riled up by the English, they would have killed some thirty more people whom they instead saved.

[63] Fourteen Yazoos found themselves at the Natchez the day of the massacre, they were returning from the Houmas to whom they had brought a peace pipe, they seemed to be very touched by our suffering in the beginning of this affair, the chief of the nation even helped to save one named Fonder by giving him a dugout, and something to eat, he recommended that he tell Mr. Perrier what he had done for him, that he was going to go to up into his village, where he would warn all the French to be on their guard, and that he was figure on avenging their death, after all these signs of friendship, it would never have been believed that these savages had plotted anything against us; the next day was another thing completely, this good will was transformed into cruelty, and of the worst, for they burned the people who unfortunately fell into their hands, these poor unfortunates who counted on prolonging their lives by trusting them to these savages whom they regarded as our friends instead shortened them, for in them they found the most cruel executioners. It was reported that the Yazoos had great difficulty in declaring themselves our enemies and that the Natchez pushed them into it for gifts, and also by threats, claiming that all the nations had struck together, and that all the French were dead, they showed them the large quantity of merchandise that they had won, and the number of slaves that they taken, they gave them various presents, and especially brandy, and munitions which had a greater effect than all their words; finally their own interests prevailed over this affection, and this attachment that had previously testified toward us; we should not be astonished that these barbarians are won over by this appeal, because we see every day how it also corrupts the most civilized people.

[64] Several days later they fled to their village, they used the same method as the Natchez to assassinate all our people in presenting the peace pipe to Mr. Desroches, who commanded that area, they killed him and all the French of the post at the same time.

It can be seen by the conduct of this nation that it was not at all complicit in the massacre that the Natchez have committed, and that it was only the gifts, and the fear of being destroyed which got them to attack us, because the others made them think that all the nations had done the same; some absolutely want them to be blamed in this case, and that they had gone to carry the word to the Houmas, those who talk in this fashion are not paying attention or do not know what these savages have done since the beginning of the war; these Yazoos had gone to the Houmas carrying a peace pipe following their annual custom to make trade, and to renew their ancient friendship; if they had been part of the plot, they would not have been so foolish as to communicate to the Houmas, where there was a large number of Frenchmen who would have received word from one moment to another, they may well have told them that the Frenchmen would sell them their goods at very high prices, and that the English would give them a better value, this is the talk that I heard for the five years I was at the Witchitas where they came very often, a reason with proves even better that the savages knew nothing of it, and that they had no desire to attack us, is that they lent a settler from my district two people to help them hunt in the winter, in a word they would not have saved Fonder, and the Tioux [65] among whom there was a Yazoo, and a Courois would not save a party of fugitives, if the latter had been part of the plot, because they would have worked with the others to kill them; I am fully persuaded that if these savages had not found themselves at the Natchez that day the post of the Yazoos would not have been destroyed.

After having massacred all these poor unfortunates, they sent three of their men to carry some scalps to the Chickasaws, these they refused, why I don't know, for they did not like us at all, I believe they did this, because they saw that the Choctaws were for us, they sent back the three Yazoos who were killed by the Chacchoumas who after having struck this blow joined with the Tapoux and the Choctaws who came in a party of two hundred by order of Mr. Perrier for the destruction of the Yazoos, on whom they all made their attack together, they killed twenty or twenty-five, both men and women, and children, and removed our women whom they made slaves, and all their ammunition.

La Pezée, wife of a settler at Yazoo, reports that some time after the barbarians had made their attack, two of their people arrived with a letter; they said that the French were at the Tunicas, and that they were soon going to come up to destroy Natchez, this news made them very depressed, they believed all the Frenchmen were dead, the Natchez had assured them it was so, they cast blame on one another, their women, and their children were crying, finally they left their village, and went to hide in a bayou, where our allies attacked them, from there they crossed the river and went on the Black River into a place where they [66] once had made a village, the two Yazoos who carried this letter were the two savages that I've already cited, whom Mr. Merveilleux took at Point Coupée to send to their home to warn the commandant of the post to whom he wrote.

If this had been a general affair the Chacchoumas would have been invited to join it as friends of the Chickasaws, they attacked the Yazoos without orders by pure affection for the Frenchmen to avenge their dead, they brought their scalps to Mr. Perrier, they say that the Yazoos have no more than forty men.

The Offos, neighbors of the Yazoos, did not attack us, they were out hunting when the others struck the blow, if they had been in their village, they would have tried to prevent this massacre, these are savages who are strongly attached to us, they took a French women from the hands of the enemies, they retreated downriver to a place near Grand Gouffre, where they stayed until they saw some of our people, they came down by chance in a boat from the Illinois to come to the Tunicas, old friends of theirs among whom they have made a village.

Several want this to be a general conspiracy, and incited by the English, and that the Choctaw were expected to attack New Orleans at the same time as the Natchez, and that the latter attacked too early, those who are of this sentiment know nothing of the colony, nor of the savages, nor do they know anything of what has happened since the beginning of this affair, the Choctaws are the enemies of the Natchez and have been for a long time, if they had told them, it would have been to [67] get them to make this move, to bring about their defeat, they did not do this, and they knew nothing, for they only learned of the massacre through the French, the Natchez kept this plan very secret, they did not want to tell any other nation for fear of being betrayed, and when the blow was made, they told them, to engage the others in declaring themselves our enemies, that all nations would strike at the same hour, and that if they did not attack us as they themselves had done, they would all be destroyed waiting for support from the French. This is the reason which has caused the Tioux, and the Yazoos to declare themselves our enemies, and which would have caused all the other savages to do the same, and it was the foresight of Mr. Perrier who disrupted all their plans by reassuring the Choctaws.

Fifteen days after the massacre the Natchez sent fifteen of their number to go to the Choctaws carrying a peace pipe to win them over to their side, after having made it halfway there, they reflected on their mission, and thought that the Choctaws might have been alerted, and might capture them to take them to Mr. Perrier, this caution caused them to return home; there is strong proof that the Choctaws were not part of the plot; these former with order from Mr. Perrier to go make a raid on the Natchez went with a party of fifteen Choctaws with a peace pipe to examine their forts, and see by what means they could attack them, there were a few of them who spoke with some of our women to whom they said that shortly they would rescue them from the hands of those dogs, some time after they did attack, as we have [68] already said, they would have succeeded, and the defeat would have been certain, if they had had another man with them, and one with better judgment, if these savages have offended us, it is we who have are the authors it by our bad conduct.

There are people who say that if we had employed only the small nations with us, we would have defeated the Natchez without any difficulty, those who talk this way do not understand the savages, nor the colony, and know nothing about what happened since the beginning of our settlement, it is true that we might have been able to do everything that we wanted, and that they would not have shown such insolence, and they would have stayed with us as we had wanted; all of that is very good, but they could not give courage, and good will to our people, this is the one thing missing to vanquish the enemy with which we would have succeeded despite the disasters that came our way, if we our conduct had been the complete opposite, and if we had attacked the other side.

These same people who so exalt the valor of these small nations should think about the prowess those nations made in the time of Mr. de Bienville, when he took them with him to make war at the Natchez who had killed several Frenchmen at that time, and who had consulted among themselves the demise of the post, if those barbarians had been properly punished they would never have undertaken anything against the French; the current misfortune of this colony comes only from the softness of the former governor, [69] for these savages have said to one another, kill the French and steal from them, after this we will make peace with them as we have done before.

Mr. Perrier took the right course in employing the Choctaws in this affair, if he had not done so they would have been envious, and jealous, they would have taken our distrust as evidence of our enmity, they would have waited for the time when we were at the Natchez to attack us at New Orleans, and all the neighboring settlements they would have easily defeated;
Mr. Perrier foreseeing in advance what could happen invited them to attack our enemies, promising them rewards, and kept the small militia he had formed, to protect the lower part of the river, he acted very wisely because if he had done otherwise, he would have exposed the colony to the outbreaks of the savages who would have not missed the opportunity to attack in the hope of pillaging us, all that we have done wrong was permitting these savages down the river, they saw the situation of the colony that could harm us in the future, the colony has come within two fingers of its loss not only by the invasion of the savages, but also by this panic

that seized all the settlers of the river who ran away from their homes. Mr. Perrier, seeing the sad situation in this country has acted as if he had to fight every nation and has immediately formed a militia, and has made forts to be built from post to post, where he has established district captains to protect life, and the property of all the settlers, whom he has quickly armed as best as he could, and these forts are held held in respect by all the nations, especially those of the Mississippi which were very well built, finally, he made them return to their duty to each other, we now have no one for enemies but the Yazoos, and the Natchez. Mr. Perrier [70] has harassed them without ceasing; they cannot be completely destroyed except by the means of a strong reinforcement of troops, those of this colony cannot be counted on to fight, of whom the greater part are lacking in will and in honor; these barbarians used all sorts of trickery to massacre us at the Natchez; they know that their crime is so great that it will never be pardoned, they don't count on peace, and they are not even interested in it, because they believe themselves invincible, they will push their rage to the last extremity, it is absolutely necessary to destroy them to serve as an example to the other savages, no doubt we will always be exposed to such troubles.

It can be seen that this account shows that this colony survives, it requires only valor, attention, and the wisdom of our commandant who alone has borne the burden of everything.

At the bluffs the first of June 1730

Delaye

Appendix Two
Fr. Philiberts List of Victims of the Natchez Massacre

Victims of the 1729 Massacre at Natchez

From Ministry of the Colonies, National Archives of France, C. 13, V. 12, General Correspondence of Louisiana, pages 57 to 58 v.; copy Vol. XIX, pages 241 to 245.)

Post of the Natchez . Register of the persons of the post of the Natchez massacred on the 28th of November, 1729, by the neighboring Indians whose name the said post bears.

Gentlemen and Ladies to wit:

De Chepart,
Commandant Masse, his lieutenant, his wife and niece
Desnoyers, second-lieutenant, commandant of the town and director of the White Earth concession.

The garrison composed of twenty-four men of whom the soldier named Belair alone escaped

Bailly, director
La Sonde, surgeon-major
Laurent Hurlot, assistant surgeon
Kneper, notary
Francois Dubrey, sacristan
De Longrais, director of the Concession of Saint Catherine
La Renaudais, keeper of the warehouse of the White Earth
Pascal, captain of the Company's galley, who arrived two days before
Caron, captain of the Company's boat, who arrived two days before
La Loire Desursins, formerly councillor
Sabanier, his wife and one of his children
Villeneuve, his wife and one of his children
Louis Mirault, tailor and his child (called "St. Louis")
Louis Le Tortillier called "La Marche", his wife, his child
Livernais and one of his children, his wife
Antoine Gavignon called "rape du Bor" and two of his children
Julien Chartier
Jean Despace called "Beausejour" and his child
Jean Charles Le Maire called "Cambrelot"
Louis Henry called "little St. Louis" and two of his children
Picard, his wife and son-in-law, copper-smith
Leonard Charante and four of his children
Antoine Jouard called "Mouton"
Jean George Schutz called "Jean L'Allemand"
Jean Roussin and his child
Pierre Billy called "La Jeunesse"
Joseph Ducrot, cooper for the Company
Pierre Dauvido called "Le Bleu"
La Forc and his wife
Grimault La Plaine, his wife, his child, his niece
Le Houx, his child, his niece; formerly keeper of the warehouse at the Arkansas
Anselme Foucault called "La Fleur"

Francois Censier
Jean Delon and his child Francois
Fertin and two of his children and his brother-in-law Gabriel
Poulin L'Evesque and his child
Pierre Lambremont and his child
Jean Louis Dupin
Jean Flandrin, his wife and two of his children.
The wife of Michel Beau Papin, interpreter, his wife and his two children
Louis Longueville
La Ferte
Jean Evrard, Bohemian
Stroup, Bohemian, his wife and his child
Estienne Rene Lartault, tailor
Bideau, his wife and his child
Ponconet, his wife and his two children
Modeste Le Brasseur by trade and his wife Barbier Massiot
The wife of Canterelle, mid-wife
Guerin, his wife and two of his children
The wife of Sondu, goldsmith, and her child
Pimon Robinet Duchesne of the invalides
Quidor and Pierre his servant
Foulian, his wife and child
Le Clerc and his wife
The nephew of Mr. De Longrais
Madame, commander of the negroes of the White Earth
Pouvalin, his wife and his child
Robichon, his wife and his child
Auberlet, his wife and his child
Pierre Schmitt, his wife, his child and his brother-in-law
Gaspard Tilly, his wife, two children and his brothers
Rosser, his wife and his child
La Douceur
A child of Nicolas La Cour
Le Grand, mason, his wife and two of his children
Sans Soucy, servant of Mr. Guyot
Estiene, blacksmith with Mr. De Longrais
The wife of Mirly, and her child

Pierre Le Blanc
Ducorroir, cooper
La Lande Goupil
Bonaventure
La Vielle, Bohemian Knight
La Miette and her three children
Joly, cabinet-maker and his wife
Leger, cabinet-maker and his wife
Isbra, carpenter,
Jean Jouan, carpenter,
Ribert, carpenter,
Picard, carpenter,
Monthuy, his wife and his child
Pierre Toudou, his wife and his child
Beausoleil, servant of Sabanier
Cornseret, cooper.
The widow Ricard and her child
Pierre Letant
Benichon Badeau Le Maire, cooper
The Dauphine woman
The Montauban woman and her two children
Alain Duquay called "the little mason"
Francois Hyacinthe
Giles Jossian
A Pierre called "Chatelain."

Voyageurs who had arrived there a few days before:
Ducodere, commandant at the Yazoos
The Reverend Father Poisson, Jesuit missionary
Kolly and his son from New Orleans
Langlois, clerk
Monsieur Kolly, ditto
Charlot Verlug,
Son of the Chapitoula Bourbeau, colonist of New Orleans
St. Pierre, workman of the said
Bourbeau, colonist of New Orleans
Soupar of the Yazoos
Bompugnon of the Yazoos.

Detachment from the Tunicas for scouting consisting of seven men, only one of whom escaped with his life:
Mesplet, who was burnt and tortured with Dominique
St. Amant, killed in the combat
Busebois and Navarre and another volunteer

TOTALS: 144 Men, 35 Women, 56 Children

Among the number of women massacred there were four women whose abdomens the savages ripped open and whose children,included in the above register, they killed.

I, the undersigned Father Philibert, priest and missionary to the said Natchez, certify that the present register, is correct.

On board the Duc de Bourbon.
The 9th of June, 1730
F. Philibert,
(Autograph signature)
Capuchin priest and missionary.

Appendix Three
Letter from Father le Petit, Missionary, to Father d'Avaugour, Procurator of the Missions in North America

Note: The Jesuit priest Mathurin le Petit was the first missionary to the Choctaw who served in that mission for three years, from 1727 to 1730, when he was appointed Superior for all the Jesuit missions in Louisiana and relocated to New Orleans.

At NEW ORLEANS,
the 12th of July, 1730.

MY REVEREND FATHER,

The peace of Our Lord.

You cannot be ignorant of the sad event which has desolated that part of the French Colony established at *Natchez,* on the right bank of the Mississipi river, at the distance of a hundred and twenty leagues from its mouth. Two of our Missionaries who were engaged in the conversion of the Savages, have been included in the almost general massacre which this barbarous Nation made of the French, at a time too when they had not the least reason to suspect their perfidy. A loss so great as this infant Mission has sustained, will continue for a long time to excite our deepest regrets.

As you could only have learned in a confused manner the events of this dark treachery, I will endeavor to relate to you all the circumstances; but first I think that it would be best to make you acquainted with the character of these perfidious Savages, called the *Natchez.* When I have described to you the Religion, the manners, and the customs of these barbarians, I will proceed to the history of the tragical event which I design to narrate, and will in detail recount all those circumstances, of which I am certain you have hitherto had no knowledge.

This Nation of Savages inhabits one of the most beautiful and fertile countries in the World, and is the only one on this continent which appears to have any regular worship. Their Religion in certain points is very similar to that of the ancient Romans. They have a Temple filled with Idols, which are different figures of men and of animals, and for which they have the most profound veneration. Their Temple in shape resembles an earthen oven, a hundred feet in circumference. They enter it by a little door about four feet high, and not more than three in breadth. No window is to be seen there. The arched roof of the edifice is covered with three rows of mats, placed one upon the other, to prevent the rain from injuring the masonry, Above on the outside are three figures of eagles made of wood, and painted red, yellow, and white. Before the door is a kind of shed with folding-doors, where the Guardian of the Temple is lodged; all around it runs a circle of palisades, on which are seen exposed the skulls of all the heads which their Warriors had brought back from the battles in which they had been engaged with the enemies of their Nation.

In the interior of the Temple are some shelves arranged at a certain distance from each other, on which are placed cane baskets of an oval shape, and in these are enclosed the bones of their ancient Chiefs, while by their side are those of their victims who had caused themselves to be strangled, to follow their masters into the other world. Another separate shelf supports many flat baskets very gorgeously painted, in which they preserve their Idols. These are figures of men and women made of stone or baked clay, the heads and the tails of extraordinary serpents, some stuffed owls, some pieces of crystal, and some jaw-bones of large fish. In the year 1699, they had there a bottle and the foot of a glass, which they guarded as very precious.

In this Temple they take care to keep up a perpetual fire, and they are very particular to prevent its ever blazing; they do not use anything for it but dry wood of the walnut or oak. The old men are obliged to carry, each one in his turn, a large log of wood into the enclosure of the palisade. The number of the Guardians of the Temple is fixed, and they serve by the quarter. He who is on duty is placed like a sentinel under the shed, from whence he examines whether the fire is not in danger of going out. He feeds it with two or three large logs, which do not burn except at the extremity, and which they never place one on the other, for fear of their getting into a blaze.

Of the women, the sisters of the great Chief alone have liberty to enter within the Temple. The entrance is forbidden to all the others, as well as to the common people, even when they carry something there to feast to the memory of their relatives, whose bones repose in the Temple. They give the dishes to the Guardian, who carries them to the side of the basket in which are the bones of the dead; this ceremony lasts only during one moon. The dishes are afterward placed on the palisades which surround the Temple, and are abandoned to the fallow-deer.

The Sun is the principal object of veneration to these people; as they cannot conceive of anything which can be above this heavenly body, nothing else appears to them more worthy of their homage. It is for the same reason that the great Chief of this Nation, who knows nothing on the earth more dignified than himself, takes the title of brother of the Sun, and the credulity of the people maintains him in the despotic authority which he claims. To enable them better to converse together, they raise a mound of artificial soil, on which they build his cabin, which is of the same construction as the Temple. The door fronts the East, and every morning the great Chief honors by his presence the rising of his elder brother, and salutes him with many howlings as soon as he appears above the horizon. Then he gives orders that they shall light his calumet; he makes him an offering of the first three puffs which he draws; afterward raising his hand above his head, and turning from the East to the West, he shows him the direction which he must take in his course.

There are in this cabin a number of beds on the left hand at entering: but on the right is only the bed of the great Chief, ornamented with different painted figures. This bed consists of nothing but a mattress of canes and reeds, very hard, with a square log of wood, which serves for a pillow. In the middle of the cabin is seen a small stone, and no one should approach the bed until he has made a circuit of this stone. Those who enter salute by a howl, and advance even to the bottom of the cabin, without looking at the right side, where the Chief is. Then they give a new salute by raising their arms above the head, and howling three times. If it be any one whom the Chief holds in consideration, he answers by a slight sigh and makes a sign to him to be seated. He thanks him for his politeness by a new howl. At every question which the Chief puts to him, he howls once before he answers, and when he takes his leave, he prolongs a single howl until he is out of his presence.

When the great Chief dies, they demolish his cabin, and then raise a new mound, on which they build the cabin of him who is to replace him in this dignity, for he never lodges in that of his predecessor. The old men prescribe the Laws for the rest of the people, and one of their principles is to have a sovereign respect for the great Chief, as being the brother of the Sun and the master of the Temple. They believe in the immortality of the soul, and when they leave this world they go, they say, to live in another, there to be recompensed or punished. The rewards to which they look forward, consist principally in feasting, and their chastisement in the privation of every pleasure. Thus they think that those who have been the faithful observers of their laws will be conducted into a region of pleasures, where all kinds of exquisite viands will be furnished them in abundance that their delightful and tranquil days will flow on in the midst of festivals, dances, and women; in short, they will revel in all imaginable pleasures. On the contrary, the violators of their laws will be cast upon lands unfruitful and entirely covered with water, where they will not have any kind of corn, but will be exposed entirely naked to the sharp bites of the mosquitoes, that all Nations will make war upon them, that they will never eat meat, and have no nourishment but the flesh of crocodiles, spoiled fish, and shell-fish.

These people blindly obey the least wish of their great Chief. They look upon him as absolute master, not only of their property but also of their lives, and not one of them would dare to refuse him his head, if he should demand it; for whatever labors he commands them to execute, they are forbidden to exact any wages. The French, who are often in need of hunters or of rowers for their long voyages, ' never apply to any one but the great Chief. He furnishes all the men they wish, and receives payment, without giving any part to those unfortunate individuals, who are not permitted even to complain. One of the principal articles of their Religion, and particularly for the servants of the great Chief, is that of honoring his funeral rites by dying with him, that they may go to serve him in the other world. In their blindness they willingly submit to this law, in the foolish belief that in the train of their Chief they will go to enjoy the greatest happiness.

To give an idea of this bloody ceremony, it is necessary to know that as soon as an heir presumptive has been born to the great Chief, each family that has an infant at the breast is obliged to pay him homage. From all these infants they choose a certain number whom they destine for the service of the young Prince, and as soon as they are of a competent age, they furnish them with employments suited to their talents. Some pass their lives in hunting, or in fishing, to furnish supplies for the table; others are employed in agriculture, while others serve to fill up his retinue. If he happen to die, all these servants sacrifice themselves with joy to follow their dear master. They first put on all their finery, and repair to the place opposite to the Temple, where all the people are assembled. After having danced and sung a sufficiently long time, they pass around their neck a cord of buffalo hair with a running knot, and immediately the Ministers appointed for executions of this kind, come forward to strangle them, recommending them to go to rejoin their master, and render to him in the other world services even more honorable than those which had occupied them in this.

The principal servants of the great Chief having been strangled in this way, they strip the flesh off their bones, particularly those of their arms and thighs, and leave them to dry for two months, in a kind of tomb, after which they take them out to be shut up in the baskets which are placed in the Temple by the side of the bones of their master. As for the other servants, their relatives carry them home with them, and bury them with their arms and clothes.

The same ceremony is observed in like manner on the death of the brothers and sisters of the great Chief. The women are always strangled to follow the latter, except when they have infants at the breast, in which case they continue to live, for the purpose of nourishing them. And we often see many who endeavor to find nurses, or who themselves strangle their infants, so that they shall not lose the right of sacrificing themselves in the public place, according to the ordinary ceremonies, and as the law prescribes.

This Government is hereditary; it is not, however, the son of the reigning Chief who succeeds his father, but the son of his sister, or the first Princess of the blood. This policy is founded on the knowledge they have of the licentiousness of their women. They are not sure, they say, that the children of the chief's wife may be of the blood Royal, whereas the son of the sister of the great Chief must be, at least on the side of the mother.

The Princesses of the blood never espouse any but men of obscure family, and they have but one husband, but they have the right of dismissing him whenever it pleases them, and of choosing another among those of the Nation, provided he has not made any other alliance among them. If the husband has been guilty of infidelity, the Princess may have his head cut off in an instant; but she is not herself subject to the same law, for she may have as many Lovers as she pleases, without the husband having any power to complain. In the presence of his wife he acts with the most profound respect, never eats with her, and salutes her with howls, as is done by her servants. The only satisfaction he has is, that he is freed from the necessity of laboring, and has entire authority over those who serve the Princess.

In former times the Nation of the *Natchez* was very large. It counted sixty Villages and eight hundred Suns or Princes; now it is reduced to six little Villages and eleven Suns. In each of these Villages there is a Temple where the fire is always kept burning as in that of the great Chief, whom all the other Chiefs obey.

The great Chief nominates to the most important offices of the State; such are the two war-Chiefs, the two Masters of ceremony for the worship of the Temple, the two Officers who preside over the other ceremonies which are observed when foreigners come to treat of peace, another who has the inspection of the public works, four others charged with the arrangement of the festivals with which they publicly entertain the Nation, and such Strangers as come to visit them. All these Ministers, who execute the will of the great Chief are treated with the same respect and obedience as if he personally gave the orders.

Each year the people assemble to plant one vast field with Indian corn, beans, pumpkins, and melons, and then again they collect in the same way to gather the harvest. A large cabin situated on a beautiful prairie is set apart to hold the fruits of this harvest. Once in the summer, toward the end of July, the people gather by order of the great Chief, to be present at a grand feast which he gives them. This Festival lasts for three days and three nights, and each one contributes what he can to furnish it; some bring game, others fish, etc. They have almost constant dances, while the great Chief and his sister are in an elevated lodge covered with boughs, from whence they can see the joy of their subjects. The Princes, the Princesses, and those who by their office are of distinguished rank, are arranged very near the Chief, to whom they show their respect and submission by an infinite variety of ceremonies.

The great Chief and his sister make their entrance in the place of the assembly on a litter borne by eight, of their greatest men: the Chief holds in his hand a great scepter ornamented with painted plumes, and all the people dance and sing about him in testimony of the public joy. The last day of this Feast he causes all his subjects to approach, and makes them a long harangue, in which he exhorts them to fulfill all their duties to Religion; he recommends them above all things to have a great veneration for the spirits who reside in the Temple, and carefully to instruct their children. If any one has distinguished himself by some act of zeal, he is then publicly praised. Such a case happened in the year 1702. The Temple having been struck by lightning and reduced to ashes, seven or eight women cast their infants into the midst of the flames to appease the wrath of Heaven. The great Chief called these heroines, and gave them great praises for the courage with which they had made the sacrifice of that which they held most dear; he finished his panegyric by exhorting the other women to imitate so beautiful an example in similar circumstances.

The fathers of families do not fail to carry to the Temple the first of their fruits, their corn and vegetables. It is the same even with presents which are made to this Nation; they are immediately offered at the gate of the Temple, when the guardian, after having displayed and presented them to the spirits, carries them to the house of the great Chief, who makes a distribution of them as he judges best, without any person testifying the least discontent.

They never plant their fields without having first presented the seed in the Temple with the accustomed ceremonies. As soon as these people approach the Temple, they raise their arms by way of respect, and utter three howls, after which they place their hands on the earth, and raise themselves again three times with as many reiterated howls — When any one has merely to pass before the Temple, he only pauses to salute it by his downcast eyes and raised arms. If a father or mother see their son fail in the performance of this ceremony, they will punish him immediately with repeated blows of a stick.

Such are the ceremonies of the *Natchez* Savages with regard to their Religion. Those of marriage are very simple. When a young man thinks of marrying he has only to address himself to the father of the girl, or if she have none, to her eldest brother, and they agree on the price, which he pays in skins or merchandise. When a girl has even lived a licentious life, they make no difficulty in receiving her, if there is the least idea that she will change her conduct when she is married. Neither do they trouble themselves as to what family she belongs, provided that she pleases them. As to the relatives of the girl, their only care is to inform themselves whether he who asks her is an able hunter, a good warrior, and an excellent workman. These qualities diminish the price which they have a right to ask on the marriage.

When the parties have agreed, the future husband goes to the chase with his friends; and when he has sufficient either of game or of fish, to feast the two families who have contracted the alliance, they assemble at the house of the parents of the girl. They particularly serve the newly married pair, who eat from the same dish. The repast being ended, the bridegroom smokes the calumet toward the parents of his wife, and then toward his own parents, after which all the guests retire. The newly married people remain together until the next day, and then the husband conducts his wife to the residence of her father-in-law, where they live until the family has built for him a cabin of his own, While they are constructing it, he passes the whole day in the chase to furnish food, which he gives to those who are employed in this work.

The laws permit the *Natchez* to have as many wives as they choose, nevertheless the common people generally have but one or two. This however is not the case with the Chiefs, their number is greater, because having the right to oblige the people to cultivate their fields, without giving them any wages, the number of their wives is no expense to them.

The marriage of the Chiefs is made with less ceremony. They content themselves with sending to fetch the father of the girl whom they wish to espouse, and they declare to him that they will give her the rank of their wives. They do not fail however, as soon as the marriage is consummated, to make a present to the father and mother. Although they have many wives, they keep but one or two in their own cabins; the rest remain at the houses of their parents, where they go to see them when they wish.

At certain periods of the moon these Savages never live with their wives. Jealousy has so little place in their hearts, that many find no difficulty in lending their wives to their friends. This indifference to the conjugal union results from the liberty they have of changing when it seems good to them, provided however that their wives have never borne children to them, for if any have been born of the marriage, nothing but death can separate them.

When this Nation sends out a detachment for war, the Chief of the party erects two kinds of poles painted red from the top to the bottom, ornamented with red plumes, and arrows and tomahawks, also painted red. These poles are pointed to the side to which they are to carry the war. Those who wish to join the party, after having ornamented and daubed themselves with different colors, come to harangue the war-Chief. This harangue, which one makes after the other, and which lasts nearly half an hour, consists of a thousand protestations of service, by which they assure him that they ask nothing more than to die with him, that they are charmed to learn from so able a warrior the art of taking scalps, and that they fear neither the hunger nor fatigues to which they are going to be exposed.

When a sufficient number of braves have presented themselves to the war-Chief, he causes to be made at his house a beverage which they call the "war medicine."[15] This is an emetic, which they make from a root they boil in large kettles full of water. The warriors, sometimes to the number of 300, having seated themselves about the kettle, they serve each one with two pots of it. The ceremony is to swallow them with a single effort, and then to throw them up immediately by the mouth, with efforts so violent that they can be heard at a great distance.

After this ceremony, the war-Chief appoints the day of departure, that each one may prepare provisions necessary for the campaign. During this time, the warriors repair evening and morning to the place before the Temple, where, after having danced and related in detail the brilliant actions in which their bravery was conspicuous, they chant their death-songs.

To see the extreme joy which they show at their departure, we should say that they had already signalized their valor by some great victory, but a very small thing alone is necessary to disconcert their plans. They are so superstitious with respect to dreams, that a single one of evil augury can arrest the execution of their enterprise, and oblige them to return when they are on the march. We see parties, who after having gone through with all the ceremonies I have mentioned, immediately break off from their expedition, because they have heard a dog bark in an extraordinary manner: in an instant their ardor for glory is changed into a perfect panic,

When on the war-path, they march in single file: four or five men who are the best walkers lead the way, and keep in advance of the army a quarter of a league, to observe everything, and give immediate notice. They encamp every evening an hour before sunset, and lie down about a large fire, each one with his arms near him. Before they encamp, they take the precaution to send out twenty warriors to the distance of half a league around the camp, for the purpose of avoiding all surprise. They never post sentinels during the night, but as soon as they have supped, they extinguish all the fires. At night the war-Chief exhorts them not to give themselves up to a profound sleep, and to keep their arms always in a state of readiness. He appoints a place where they shall rally in case they are attacked during the night and put to flight.

As the war-Chiefs always carry with them their idols, or what they call their spirits, well secured in some skins, at night they suspend them from a small pole painted red, which they erect in a Slanting position, so that it may be bent on the side of the enemy. The warriors, before they go to sleep, with war-club in hand, pass one after the other in a dance before these pretended spirits, at the same time uttering the fiercest threats toward the side on which are their enemies.

When the war-party is considerable, as it enters the enemy's country, they march in five or six columns. They have many spies, who go out on scouting expeditions. If they perceive that their march is known, they ordinarily adopt the resolution of retracing their steps, leaving a small troop of from ten to twenty men who detach themselves, and endeavor to surprise some Hunters at a distance from the Villages: on their return they chant their songs with reference to the scalps they have taken. If they have taken any prisoners, they force them to sing and dance for some days before the Temple, after which they present them to the relatives of those who have been killed. These relatives are dissolved in tears during this ceremony, and drying their eyes with the scalps which have been taken, they contribute among themselves to recompense the warriors who have taken these captives, whose lot is to be burned.

The *Natchez,* like all the other Nations of Louisiana, distinguish by particular names those who have killed a greater or less number of the enemy. The old war-Chiefs distribute these names according to the merit of the warriors. To deserve the title of a great man-slayer, it is necessary to have taken 10 slaves or to have carried off 20 scalps. When a person understands their language, the name itself of a warrior enables him to learn all his exploits. Those who, for the first time, have taken a scalp or made a captive, do not sleep at their return with their wives, and do not eat any meat; they ought not to partake of anything but fish and thickened milk. This abstinence lasts for six months. If they fail to observe it, they imagine that the soul of him whom they have killed will cause them to die through sorcery, that they will never again obtain any advantage over their enemies, and that the slightest wounds they may receive will prove fatal.

They take extreme care that the great Chief shall not in any way expose his life when he goes to war. If, carried away by his valor, he should happen to be killed, the Chiefs of the party and the other principal warriors would be put to death on their return; but executions of this kind are almost without example, on account of the precautions they take to preserve him from this evil.

This Nation, like the others, has its Medicine- men; these are generally old men, who without study or any science, undertake to cure all complaints. They do not attempt this by simples, or by drugs; all their art consists in different juggleries; that is to say, that they dance and sing night and day about the sick man, and smoke without ceasing, swallowing the smoke of the tobacco. These Jugglers eat scarcely anything during all the time that they are engaged in the cure of the sick, but their chants and their dances are accompanied by contortions so violent that, although they are entirely naked and should naturally suffer from cold, yet they are always foaming at the mouth. They have a little basket in which they keep what they call their Spirits, that is to say, small roots of different kinds, heads of owls, small parcels of the hair of fallow-deer, some teeth of animals, some small stones or pebbles, and other similar trifles.

It appears that to restore health to the sick, they invoke without ceasing that which they have in their basket. Some of them have there a certain root, which by its smell can put serpents to sleep and render them senseless. After having rubbed their hands and body with this root, they take hold of these reptiles without fearing their bite, which is mortal. Sometimes they cut, with a flint, the part affected with the malady, and then suck out all the blood they can draw from it, and in returning it immediately into a dish, they at the same time spit out a little piece of wood, or straw, or leather, which they have concealed under the tongue. Drawing to it the attention of the relatives of the sick man, "There," say they, "is the cause of the sickness." These Medicine-men are always paid in advance. If the sick man recovers, their gain is very considerable, but if he should die, they are sure to have their heads cut off by the relatives or friends of the deceased. This never fails to be done, and even the relatives of the Medicine-man find nothing at all of which to complain, and do not testify any concern.

There is the same rule with some other Jugglers, who undertake to procure rain or fair weather. These are commonly indolent, old men, who, wishing to avoid the labor which is required in hunting, fishing, and the cultivation of the fields, exercise this dangerous trade to gain a support for their families. Toward spring, the Nation taxes itself to purchase from these Jugglers favorable weather for the fruits of the earth. If the harvest prove abundant, they gain a handsome reward, but if it is unfortunate, they take it from them, and cut off their heads. Thus those who engage in this profession risk everything to gain everything. In other respects their life is very idle; they have no other convenience than that of fasting and dancing with a pipe in their mouth, full of water and pierced like a watering-pot, which they blow into the air on the side where the clouds are thickest. In one hand they hold the *sicicouet*, which is a kind of rattle, and in the other their spirits, which they stretch out toward the clouds, uttering frightful cries to invite them to burst upon their fields.[16]

If it is pleasant weather for which they ask, they do not use these pipes, but they mount on the roof of their cabins, and with their arms make signs to the clouds, blowing with all their strength, that they shall not stop over their lands, but pass beyond. When the clouds are dissipated according to their wish, they dance and sing about their spirits, which they place reverently on a kind of pillow; they redouble their fasts, and when the cloud has passed, they swallow the smoke of tobacco, and hold up their pipes to the Sky.

Although they never show any favor to these Charlatans, when they do not obtain what they ask, yet the profit they receive is so great, when by chance they succeed, that we see a great number of these Savages who do not at all fear to run the risks. It is to be observed that he who undertakes to furnish rain never engages to procure pleasant weather. There is another kind of Charlatans to whom this privilege belongs, and when you ask them the reason, they answer boldly that their spirits can give but the one or the other.

When one of these Savages dies, his relatives come to mourn his death during an entire day, then they array him in his most beautiful dresses, they paint his face and his hair, and ornament him with plumes, after which they carry him to the grave prepared for him, placing by his side his arms, a kettle, and Some provisions. For the space of a month, his relatives come at the dawn of day and at the beginning of the night, to weep for half an hour at his grave Each one names his degree of relationship, If he were the father of a family, the wife cries, "My dear husband, Ah ! how I regret you!" The children cry, "My dear father!" The others, "My uncle ! my cousin!" etc. The nearest relatives continue this ceremony for three months; they cut off their hair in sign of grief, they abstain from painting the body, and are never found at any assembly for festivity.

When any foreign Nation comes to treat of peace, with the *Natchez* Savages, they send their couriers to give notice of the day and hour when they shall make their entrance. The great Chief orders the Masters of ceremony to prepare all things for this grand occasion. They begin by naming those who during each day should support the strangers, for the expense never falls upon the Chief, but always on his subjects. Then they clear the roads, they sweep the cabins, they arrange the seats in a large hall. which is on the mound of the great Chief by the side of his cabin. His throne, which is on an elevation, is painted and ornamented, and the bottom is furnished with beautiful mats.

On the day that the Ambassadors are to make their entrance, all the Nation assembles. The Masters of ceremony Place the

Princes, the Chiefs of the Villages, and the old Chiefs of quality near the great Chief On particular seats. When the Ambassadors arrive, and are within five hundred steps of the great Chief, they stop and chant the song of peace. The ambassage ordinarily consists of thirty men and six women. six of the best made, and who have the finest voices, march in front; they are followed by the others who chant in like manner, regulating the cadence with the *sicicouet*. The six women are the last.

When the Chief has directed them to approach, they advance; those who have the calumets, chant and dance with much agility, now turning around each other, and now presenting themselves in front, but always with violent movements and extraordinary contortions. When they have entered the circle, they dance about the chair on which the Chief is seated, they rub him with their calumets from his feet even to his head, and after that go back to find those who belong to their suite. Then they fill one of their calumets with tobacco, and holding the fire in one hand, they advance all together before the Chief and smoke it: they direct the first puff of smoke toward the Heavens, the second toward the Earth, and the others around the horizon, after which they without ceremony present the pipe to the Princes and to the other Chiefs.

The ceremony having been finished, the Ambassadors, as a token of alliance, rub their hands on the stomach of the Chief, and rub themselves over the whole body; they then place their calumets before the Chief on small forks, while the person among the Ambassadors who is particularly charged with the orders of his Nation, delivers a harangue which lasts for an entire hour.: When he has finished, they make a sign to the strangers to be seated on the benches ranged near the great Chief, who responds to them by a discourse of equal length. Then the Master of ceremonies lights the great calumet of peace, and makes the strangers smoke, who swallow the tobacco smoke. The great Chief inquires of them whether they arrived safe, — that is, whether they are well, and those who are around them go one after the other to discharge the same office of politeness. After which they conduct them to the cabin which has been prepared for them, and where they are feasted.

That same evening at Sunset, the Ambassadors, with the calumet in their hands, go with singing to find the great Chief, and having raised him on their shoulders, they transport him to the quarter in which their cabin is situated. They spread on the ground a large skin, on which they cause him to sit down. One of them places himself behind him, and putting his hands on the Chief's shoulders he agitates all his body, while the others, seated in a circle on the ground, chant the history of their distinguished deeds. After this ceremony, which is repeated night and morning for four days, the great Chief returns to his cabin. When he pays his last visit to the Ambassadors, these place a stake at his feet, about which they seat themselves: The Warriors of the Nation having arranged themselves in all their finery dance around, striking the stake, and in turn recounting their great exploits, then follows the giving of Presents to the Ambassadors, which consist of kettles, hatchets, guns, powder, balls, etc.

The day following this last ceremony, it is permitted to the Ambassadors to walk through the whole Village, which before they were not able to do. Then every evening they give them spectacles, — that is to say, the men and women in their most beautiful dresses assemble at the public place, and dance until the night is far advanced. When they are ready to return home, the Masters of the ceremonies furnish them with the provisions necessary for the journey.

After having thus given you a slight idea of the character and customs of the Natchez Savages, I proceed, my Reverend Father, as I have promised you, to enter on a detail of their perfidy and treason. It was on the second of December of the year 1729, that we learned they had surprised the French, and had massacred almost all of them. This sad news was first brought to us by one of the planters, who had escaped their fury. It was confirmed to us on the following day by other French fugitives, and finally, some French women whom they had made slaves, and were forced afterward to restore, brought us all the particulars.

At the first rumor of an event so sad, the alarm and consternation was general in New Orleans. Although the massacre had taken place more than a hundred leagues from here, you would have supposed that it had happened under our own eyes. Each one was mourning the loss of a relative, a friend, or some property; all were alarmed for their own lives, for there was reason to fear that the conspiracy of the Savages had been general.

This unlooked-for massacre began on Monday, the 28th of November, about nine o'clock in the morning. Some cause of dissatisfaction which the Natchez thought they had with Monsieur the Commandant,[127] and the arrival of a number of richly-loaded boats for the garrison and the colonists, determined them to hasten their enterprise, and to strike their blow sooner than they had agreed with the other confederate Tribes. And it was thus that they carried their plan into execution. First they divided themselves, and sent into the Fort, into the Village, and into the two grants, as many Savages as there were French in each of these places; then they feigned that they were going out for a grand hunt, and undertook to trade with the French for guns, powder, and ball, offering to pay them as much, and even more than was customary; and in truth, as there was no reason to suspect their fidelity, they made at that time an exchange of their poultry and corn, for some arms and ammunition which they used advantageously against us. It is true that some expressed their distrust, but this was thought to have so little foundation, that they were treated as cowards who were frightened at their own shadows. They had been on their guard against the *Tchactas,* but as for the *Natchez,* they had never distrusted them, and they were so persuaded of their good faith that it increased their hardihood. Having thus posted themselves in different houses, provided with the arms obtained from us, they attacked at the same time each his man, and in less than two hours they massacred more than two hundred of the French. The best known are Monsieur de Chepar, Commandant of the post, Monsieur du Codère, Commandant among the *Yazous,* Monsieur des Ursins, Messieurs de Kolly, father and son, Messieurs de Longrays, des Noyers, Bailly, etc.

Father du Poisson had just performed the funeral rites of his associate, Brother Crucy, who had died very suddenly of a Sunstroke; he was on his way to consult Monsieur Perrier, and to adopt with him proper measures to enable the *Akensas* to descend to the banks of the Mississipi, for the accommodation of the voyageurs. He arrived among the *Natchez* on the 26th of November, that is, two days before the massacre. The next day, which was the first Sunday of Advent, he said Mass in the parish and preached in the absence of the Curé He was to have returned in the afternoon to his Mission among the *Akensas*, but he was detained by some sick persons, to whom it was necessary to administer the Sacraments. On Monday, he was about to say Mass, and to carry the holy Viaticum to one of those sick persons whom he had confessed the evening before, when the massacre began; a gigantic Chief six feet in height, seized him, and having thrown him to the ground, cut off his head with blows of a hatchet. The Father in falling only uttered these words, "Ah, my God! ah, my God!" Monsieur du Codère drew his sword to defend him, when he was himself killed by a musket-ball from another Savage, whom he did not perceive.

These barbarians spared but two of the French, a Tailor and a Carpenter, who were able to serve their wants. They did not treat badly either the Negro Slaves, or the Savages who were willing to give themselves up; but they ripped up the belly of every pregnant woman, and killed almost all those who were nursing their children, because they were disturbed by their cries and tears, They did not kill the other Women, but made them Slaves, and treated them with every indignity during the two or three months that they were their masters, The least miserable were those who knew how to sew, because they kept them busy making shirts, dresses, etc. The others were employed in cutting and carrying wood for cooking, and in pounding the corn of which they make their sagamité. But two things, above all, aggravated the grief and hardness of their slavery; it was, in the first place, to have for masters those same persons whom they had seen dipping their cruel hands in the blood of their husbands; and, in the second place, to hear them continually saying that the French had been treated in the same manner at all the other posts, and that the country was now entirely freed from them.

During the massacre, the great Chief of the *Natchez* was seated quietly under the tobacco shed of the Company. His Warriors brought to his feet the head of the Commandant, about which they ranged those of the principal French of the post, leaving their bodies a prey to the dogs, the buzzards, and other carnivorous birds,

When they were assured that not another Frenchman remained at the post, they applied themselves to plunder the houses, the magazine of the Company of the Indies, and all the boats which were still loaded by the bank of the river. They employed the Negroes to transport the merchandise, which they divided among themselves, with the exception of the munitions of war, which they placed for security in a separate cabin. While the brandy lasted, of which they found a good supply, they passed their days and nights in drinking, singing, dancing, and insulting in the most barbarous manner, the dead bodies and the memory of the French. The *Tchactas*, and the other Savages being engaged in the plot with them, they felt at their ease, and did not at all fear that they would draw on themselves the vengeance which was merited by their cruelty and perfidy. One night when they were plunged in drunkenness and sleep, Madame des Noyers wished to make use of the Negroes to revenge the death of her husband and the French, but she was betrayed by the person to whom she confided her design, and came very near being burned alive.

Some of the French escaped the fury of the Savages by taking refuge in the woods, where they suffered extremely from hunger and the effects of the weather. One of them, on arriving here, relieved us of a little disquietude we felt with regard to the post we occupy among the *Yazous*, which is not more than forty or fifty leagues above the *Natchez* by water, and only from 15 to 20 by land. Not being able longer to endure the extreme cold from which he suffered, he left the woods under cover of night, to go to warm himself in the house of a Frenchman. When he was near it he heard the voices of Savages and deliberated whether he should enter. He determined, however, to do so, preferring rather to perish by the hand of these barbarians, than to die of famine and cold. He was agreeably surprised when he found these Savages eager to render him a service, to heap kindnesses upon him, to commiserate him, to console him, to furnish him with provisions, clothes, and a boat to make his escape to New Orleans. These were the *Yazous* who were returning from chanting the calumet at *Oumas*. The Chief charged him to say to Monsieur Perrier, that he had nothing to fear on the part of the *Yazous*, that "they would not lose their sense," that is, that they would always remain attached to the French, and that he would be constantly on the watch with his tribe to warn the French pirogues that were descending the river to be on their guard against the *Natchez*.

We believed for a long time that the promises of this Chief were very sincere, and feared no more Indian perfidy for our post among the *Yazous*. But learn, my Reverend Father, the disposition of these Savages, and how little one is able to trust their words, even when accompanied by the greatest demonstrations of friendship. Scarcely had they returned to their own village, when, loaded with the presents they received from the *Natchez*, they followed their example and imitated their treachery. Uniting with the Corroys,[19] they agreed together to exterminate the French. They began with Father Souel, the Missionary of both tribes, who was than living in the midst of them, in their own village. The fidelity of the *Ofogoulas*, who were then absent at the chase, has never been shaken, and they now compose one Village with the *Tonikas*.

On the 11th of December, Father Souel was returning in the evening from visiting the Chief, and while in a ravine, received many musket-balls, and fell dead on the spot. The Savages immediately rushed to his cabin to plunder it. His Negro, who composed all his family and all his defense, armed himself with a wood-cutter's knife, to prevent the pillage, and even wounded one of the Savages. This zealous action cost him his life, but, happily, he had received Baptism less than a month before, and was living in a most Christian manner.

These Savages, who even to that time had seemed sensible of the affection which their Missionary bore them, reproached themselves for his death as soon as they were capable of reflection;

but returning again to their natural ferocity, they adopted the resolution of putting a finishing stroke to their crime by the destruction of the whole French post. "Since the black Chief is dead," said they, "it is the same as if all the French were dead — let us not spare any."

The next day, they executed their barbarous plan. They repaired early in the morning to the Fort, which was not more than a league distant, and whose occupants supposed, on their arrival, that the Savages wished to chant the calumet to the Chevalier des Roches, who commanded that post in the absence of Monsieur de Codère. He had but seventeen men with him, who had no suspicion of any evil design on the part of the Savages, and were therefore all massacred, not one escaping their fury. They, however, granted their lives to four women and five children, whom they found there, and whom they made slaves.

One of the *Yazous*, having stripped the Missionary, clothed himself in his garments, and shortly afterward announced to the *Natchez*, that his Nation had redeemed their pledge, and that the French settled among them were all massacred. In this city there was no longer any doubt on that point, as soon as they learned what came near being the fate of Father Doutreleau. This Missionary had availed himself of the time when the Savages were engaged in their winter occupations, to come to see us, for the purpose of regulating some matters relating to his Mission. He set out on the first day of this year, 1730 and not expecting to arrive at the residence of Father Souel, of whose fate he was ignorant, in time to say Mass, he determined to say it at the mouth of the little river of the *Yazous*, where his party had cabined.

As he was preparing for this sacred office, he saw a boat full of Savages landing. They demanded from them of what Nation they were. "*Yazous*, comrades of the French," they replied, making a thousand friendly demonstrations to the voyageurs who accompanied the Missionary, and presenting them with provisions. While the Father was preparing his altar, a flock of bustards passed, and the voyageurs fired at them the only two guns they had, without thinking of reloading, as Mass had already commenced. The Savages noted this and placed themselves behind the voyageurs, as if it was their intention to hear Mass, although they were not Christians.

At the time when the Father was saying the *Kyrie elision*, the Savages made their discharge. The Missionary perceiving himself wounded in his right arm, and seeing one of the voyageurs killed at his feet, and the four others fled, threw himself on his knees to receive the last fatal blow, which he regarded as inevitable. In this posture he received two or three discharges. But although the Savages fired while almost touching him, yet they did not inflict on him any new wounds. Finding himself, then, as it were, miraculously escaped from so many mortal blows, he took to flight, having on still his Priestly garments, and without any other defense than an entire confidence in God, whose particular Protection was given him, as the event proved, He threw himself into the water, and after advancing some steps, gained the pirogue in which two of the voyageurs were making their escape. They had supposed him to be killed by some of the many balls which they had heard fired on him. In climbing up into the pirogue, and turning his head to see whether any one of his pursuers was following him too closely, he received in the mouth a discharge of small shot, the greater part of which were flattened against his teeth, although some of them entered his gums, and remained there for a long time. I have myself seen two of them there. Father Doutreleau, all wounded as he was, undertook the duty of steering the pirogue, while his two companions placed themselves at the paddles. Unfortunately, one of them, at setting out, had his thigh broken by a musket-ball, from the effects of which he has since remained a cripple.

You may well imagine, my Reverend Father, that the Missionary and his companions had no thoughts of ascending the river. They descended the Mississipi with all the speed possible, and at last lost sight of the pirogue of their enemies, who had pursued them for more than an hour, keeping up a continual fire upon them, and who boasted at the Village that they had killed them. The two paddlers were often tempted to give themselves up, but encouraged by the Missionary, they in their turn made the

Savages, fear. An old gun which was not loaded, nor in a condition to be, which they pointed at them from time to time, made them often dodge in their boat, and at last obliged them to retire.

As soon as they found themselves freed from their enemies, they dressed their wounds as well as they could, and for the purpose of aiding their flight from that fatal shore, they threw into the river everything they had in their boat, preserving only some pieces of raw bacon for their nourishment.

It had been their intention to stop in passing at the *Natchez*, but having seen that the houses of the French were either demolished or burned, they did not think it advisable to listen to the compliments of the Savages, who from the bank of the river invited them to land. They placed a wide distance between them as soon as possible; and thus shunned the balls which were ineffectually fired at them. It was then that they began to distrust all these savage Nations, and therefore resolved not to go near the land until they reached New Orleans, and supposing that the barbarians might have rendered themselves masters of it, to descend even to the Balize, where they hoped to find some French vessel provided to receive the wreck of the Colony.

In passing the *Tonikas*, they separated themselves as far as possible from the shore, but they were discovered, and a pirogue which had been despatched to reconnoiter them, was not a long time in approaching. Their fear and distrust were renewed, and they did not decide to stop, until they perceived that the persons in that boat spoke very good French, when they overcame their fears, and in the weak state they were, gladly availed themselves of the opportunity to land. There they found the little French army which had been formed, the Officers compassionate and every way kind, a Surgeon, and refreshments. After recovering a little from the great dangers and miseries they had endured, they on the next day availed themselves of a pirogue which had been fitted out for *New Orléans*.

I cannot express to you, my Reverend Father, the great satisfaction I felt at seeing Father Doutreleau, his arm in a scarf, arrive after a voyage of more than four hundred leagues, all the clothes he had on having been borrowed, except his cassock. My surprise was increased at the recital of his adventures. I placed him immediately in the hands of brother Parisel, who examined his wounds, and who dressed them with great care and speedy success.

The Missionary was not yet entirely cured of his wounds, when he departed to act as Chaplain to the French army, as he had promised Messieurs the Officers, in accordance with their request. He endured with them the fatigues of the campaign against the *Natchez*, and there gave new proofs of his zeal, his wisdom, and his courage.

On his return from the *Natchez*, he came to recruit himself here for six weeks, which he found very long, but which appeared to me very short. He was impatient to return to his dear Mission, but it was necessary for me to fit him out generally with everything proper for a Missionary, and he was obliged to wait for the escort which was going to the Illinois. The risks which they ran on the river during this insurrection of the Savages, induced Monsieur the Commandant to forbid voyageurs going in separate companies. He set out, therefore, on the 16th of April, with many others, in a body sufficiently large to relieve them from all fear of their enemies. I learned, in fact, that they had proceeded above the *Akensas*, without any accident.

The pleasure of seeing Father Doutreleau for the first time, and seeing him, too, after his escape from such imminent perils, was much impaired by the vivid grief I felt for the loss of two Missionaries, with whose merit you were as well acquainted as myself. you know that to a most amiable disposition, they united the appropriate qualifications for apostolic men, that they were very much attached to their Mission, that they had already become well acquainted with the language of the Savages, that their earliest labors had produced great fruits, and they gave the promise of still greater results, since neither of them was more than thirty-five or thirty- six years of age. This deprivation, which entirely occupied my thoughts, gave me no time for thinking of the loss we had sustained of their Negroes and their effects, although it very much deranged a Mission which had just been commenced, and whose necessities you know better than any one else.

But nothing has happened to these two excellent Missionaries for which we should mourn, or for which they were not prepared when they devoted themselves to the Savage Missions in this Colony. This disposition alone, independent of everything else, has without doubt placed a great difference in the eyes of God between their death and that of the others, who have fallen martyrs to the French name. But I am well persuaded that the fear of a similar fate will not in the least diminish the zeal of those of our fathers who had thought of following them, neither will it deter OUT Superiors from responding to the holy desires they may have of sharing our labors.

Knowing, as you do, my Reverend Father, the vigilance and the foresight of Monsieur our Commandant, you can well imagine that he did not sleep in this sad crisis in which we now found ourselves. We may say without flattery that he surpassed himself by the rapid movements he made, and by the wise measures he adopted to revenge the French blood which had been shed, and to prevent the evils with which almost all the posts of the Colony were threatened.

As soon as he was apprised of this unexpected attack by the *Natchez* Savages, he caused the news to be carried to all the posts, and even as far as the Illinois, not by the direct and ordinary route of the river, which was closed, but on one side by the *Natchitoches* and the *Akensas*, and on the other by Mobile and the *Tchicachas*. He invited the neighbors who were our allies, and particularly the*Tchactas*, to avenge this perfidy,[20] He furnished arms and ammunition, to all the houses of this City and to the plantations. He caused two ships, that is, the *Duc de Bourbon* and the *Alexandre*, to ascend the river as far as the *Tonikas*. These ships were like two good fortresses against the insults of the Savages, and in case of attack, two certain asylums for the women and children. He caused a ditch to be dug entirely around the City, and placed guard-houses at the four extremities. He organized for its defense many companies of city militia who mounted guard during the whole night. As there was more to fear in the grants and in the plantations than in the City, he fortified them with the most care. He had good forts erected at *Chapitoulas*, at *Cannes brûlées*, at *les Allemands*, at *Bayagoulas*, and at *Pointe coupée*.

At first, Monsieur our Commandant, listening only to the dictates of his own courage, adopted the design of Placing himself at the head of the troops, but it was represented to him that he ought not to quit *New Orleans*, where his presence was absolutely necessary, that there was danger of the *Tchactas* determining to fall upon the City, if it should be deprived of its troops; and the Negroes, to free themselves from slavery, might join them, as some had done with the *Natchez*. Moreover he could feel perfectly easy with regard to the conduct of the troops, as Monsieur the Chevalier de Loubois, with whose experience and bravery he was well acquainted, had been appointed to command them,

While our little army was repairing to the *Tonikas*, seven hundred *Tchactas* mustered, and conducted by Monsieur le Sueur, marched toward the *Natchez*. We were informed by a party of these people that the Savages were not at all on their guard, but passed all their nights in dancing. The *Tchactas* took them therefore by surprise, and made a descent on them on the 27th of January, at the break of day. In less than three hours they had delivered 59 persons, both women and children, with the Tailor and Carpenter, and 106 Negroes or Negro women with their children; they made 18 of the *Natchez* prisoners and took 60 scalps. They would have taken more, if they had not been intent on freeing the slaves, as they had been directed. They had but two men killed and seven or eight wounded. They encamped with their prizes at the grant of Sainte Catherine, in a bare cattle-yard enclosed with stakes. The victory would have been complete if they had waited for the arrival of the French army, as had been agreed upon with their Deputies.

The *Natchez* seeing themselves attacked by the formidable *Tchactas*, regarded their defeat as certain, and shutting themselves up in two forts, passed the following nights in dancing their death-dance, In their speeches we heard them reproaching the *Tchactas* for their perfidy, in declaring in favor of the French, contrary to the pledge they had given, to unite with them for our destruction.

Three days before this action, the sieur Mesplex landed among the *Natchez* with five other Frenchmen. They had volunteered to Monsieur de Loubois to carry to the Savages negotiations for peace, that they might be able under this pretext to gain information with regard to their force, and their present situation. But in descending from their boat, they encountered a party, who without giving them time to speak, killed three of their men, and made the other three prisoners. The next day they sent one of these prisoners with a letter, in which they demanded as hostages the sieur Broutin, who had formerly been commandant among them, and the chief of the *Tonikas*. Besides, they demanded as the ransom for the women, children, and slaves, two hundred guns, two hundred barrels of powder, two hundred barrels of balls, two thousand gun-flints, two hundred knives, two hundred hatchets, two hundred pickaxes, twenty quarts of brandy, twenty casks of wine, twenty barrels of vermilion, two hundred shirts, twenty pieces of limbourg, twenty pieces of cloth, twenty coats with lace on the seams, twenty hats bordered with plumes, and a hundred coats of a plainer kind. Their design was to massacre the French who should bring these goods. On the very same day, with every refinement in cruelty they burned sieur Mesplex and his companion.

On the 8th of February, the French, with the *Tonikas*, and some other small Tribes from the lower end of the Mississipi, arrived at the *Natchez*, and seized their Temple dedicated to the Sun. The impatience and intractability of the *Tchactas*, who like almost all Savages are capable of striking only one blow, and then disperse; the small number of French soldiers who found themselves worn down by fatigues; the want of provisions which the Savages stole from the French; the failure of ammunition with which they were not able to satisfy the *Tchactas*, who wasted one part of it, and placed the other in reserve to be used in hunting; the resistance of the *Natchez*, who were well fortified, and who fought in desperation, — all these things decided us to listen to the propositions which the besieged made, after the trenches had been opened for seven days. They threatened, if we persisted in the siege, to burn those of the French who remained, while on the other hand, they offered to restore them, if we would withdraw our seven pieces of cannon. These, in reality, for want of a good gunner, and under present circumstances, were scarcely in a fit state to give them any fear.

These propositions were accepted, and fulfilled on both sides. On the 25th of February, the besieged faithfully restored all that they had promised, while the besiegers retired with their cannon to a small fort which they had hastily built on the Escôre [bluff] near the river, for the purpose of always keeping the *Natchez* in check, and insuring a passage to the voyageurs. Monsieur Perrier gave the command of it to Monsieur Dartaguette, as an acknowledgment of the intrepidity with which, during the siege, he had exposed himself to the greatest dangers, and everywhere braved death.

Before the *Tchactas* had determined to fall upon the *Natchez,* they had gone to them to carry the calumet, and were received in a very novel manner, They found them and their horses adorned with chasubles and drapery of the altars, many wore patens about their necks, and drank and gave to drink of brandy in the chalices and the ciboria. And the *Tchactas* themselves, when they had gained these articles by pillaging our enemies, renewed this profane sacrilege, by making the same use of our ornaments and sacred vessels in their dances and sports. We were never able to recover more than a small portion of them. The greater part of their chiefs have come here to receive payment for the scalps they have taken, and for the French and Negroes whom they have freed. It is necessary for us to buy very dearly their smallest services, and we have scarcely any desire to employ them again, particularly as they have appeared much less brave than the small Tribes, who have not made themselves feared by their great number. Every year disease diminishes this Nation, which is now reduced to three or four thousand warriors. Since these Savages have betrayed their disposition here, we have not been able to endure them longer. They are insolent, ferocious, disgusting, importunate, and insatiable. We compassionate, and at the same time, we admire our Missionaries, that they should renounce all society, to have only that of these Barbarians.

I have renewed my acquaintance with *Paatlako,* one of the chiefs, and with a great number of other *Tchactas*. They have made me many interesting visits and have often repeated to me very nearly the same compliment which they paid me more than a year ago when I left them. "Our hearts and those of our children weep," they said to me, "since we shall not see you more; you were beginning to have the same spirit with us, you listened to us, and we listened to you, you loved us and we loved you: why have you left us? will you not return? come, go with us!" You know, my Reverend Father, that I was not able to yield to their wishes. I therefore merely said that I would come to rejoin them as soon as it was in my power, but that after all, I should be here only in the body, while my heart was with them, "That is good," replied one of these Savages, "but, nevertheless, your heart will say nothing to us, it will give us nothing." Thus it is that everything comes to that point; they do not love us, and do not find us of the same spirit as themselves, except when we are giving them something.

It is true that *Paatlako* has fought with much courage against the *Natchez,* and has even received a musket-ball in the loins, while to console him for this wound he has had more esteem and friendship shown him than the rest. Scarcely was he seen in his Village, when, inflated with these trifling marks of distinction, he said to Father Baudouin that all *New Orléans* has been in a wonderful state of alarm on account of his illness, and that Monsieur Perrier had informed the King of his bravery and the great services he had rendered in the last expedition. In these traits I recognize the genius of this Nation: it is presumption and vanity itself.

They had abandoned to the Tchactas three Negroes who had been most unruly, and who had taken the most active part in behalf of the *Natchez.* They have been burned alive with a degree of cruelty which has inspired all the Negroes with a new horror of the Savages, but which will have a beneficial effect in securing the safety of the Colony.[23] The *Tonikas* and other smaller Tribes have gained some new advantages over the *Natchez*, and have taken many prisoners, of whom they have burned three women and four men, after having taken their scalps. Our own people, it is said, begin to be accustomed to this barbarous spectacle.

We could not forbear being affected, when we saw arrive in this City the French women whom the *Natchez* had made slaves. The miseries which they had suffered were painted on their countenances. But it seems as if they shortly forgot them; at least, many of them were in great haste to marry again, and we are told there were great demonstrations of joy at their weddings.

The little girls, whom none of the inhabitants wish to adopt, have greatly enlarged the interesting company of orphans whom the Nuns are bringing up. The great number of these children only serves to increase their charity and attentions. They have formed them into a separate class, and have appointed two special matrons for their care.

There is not one of this holy Community but is delighted at having crossed the ocean, nor do they seek here any other happiness than that of preserving these children in their innocency, and giving a polished and Christian education to these young Frenchmen, who are in danger of being almost as degraded as the slaves. We may hope, with regard to these holy women, that before the end of the year they will occupy the new mansion which, is destined for them, and which they have for so long a time desired.

When they shall once be settled there, to the instruction of the boarders, the orphans, the girls who live without, and the Negro women, they will add also the care of the sick in the hospital, and a house of refuge for women of questionable character, Perhaps they will even at length be able to aid in affording regularly each year the retreat to a large number of women, in accordance with the taste with which we have inspired them.

So many works of charity would, in France, be sufficient to occupy many associations and different institutions. But what cannot great zeal effect? These different labors do not at all startle seven Ursulines, and by the grace of God they are able to sustain them, without infringing at all on the observance of their religious rules. But for myself, I very much fear that, if some assistance do not arrive, they may sink under the weight of such great fatigues. Those who, before they were acquainted with them, said they had come out too soon and in too great a number, have entirely changed their views and their language; witnesses of their edifying conduct and the great services which they render to the Colony, they find that they have not arrived soon enough, and that there could not come too much of the same virtue and the same merit.

The *Tchikachas*, a brave Nation but treacherous, and little known to the French, have endeavored to seduce the Illinois Tribes from their allegiance: they have even sounded some particular persons to see whether they could not draw them over to the party of those Savages who were enemies of our Nation. The Illinois have replied to them that they were almost all "of the prayer" (that is, according to their manner of expression, that they are Christians); and that in other ways they are inviolably attached to the French, by the alliances which many of that, Nation had contracted with them, in espousing their daughters.

"We always place ourselves," added they, "before the enemies of the French; it is necessary to pass over our bodies to go to them, and to strike us to the heart before a single blow can reach them." Their conduct is in accordance with this declaration, and has not in the least contradicted their words. At the first news of the war with the *Natchez* and the *Yazous*, they came hither to weep for the black Robes and the French, and to offer the services of their Nation to Monsieur Perrier, to avenge their death. I happened to be at the governor's house when they arrived, and was charmed with the harangues they made. Chikagou, whom you saw in Paris, was at the head of the *Mitchigamias*, and *Mamantouensa* at the head of the *Kaskaskias*.

Chikagou spoke first. He spread out in the hall a carpet of deerskin, bordered with porcupine quills, on which he placed two calumets, with different savage ornaments, accompanying them with a present according to the usual custom. "There," said he, in showing these two calumets, "are two messages which we bring you, the one of Religion, and the other of peace or war, as you shall determine. We have listened with respect to the Governors, because they bring us the word of the King our Father, and much more to the black Robes, because they bring us the word of God himself, who is the King of Kings. We have come from a great distance to weep with you for the death of the French, and to offer our Warriors to strike those hostile Nations whom you may wish to designate. You have but to speak. When I went over to France, the King promised me his protection for the Prayer, and recommended me never to abandon it. I will always remember it. Grant then your protection to us and to our black Robes." He then gave utterance to the edifying sentiments with which he was impressed with regard to the Faith, as the Interpreter Baillarjon enabled us to half understand them in his miserable French.

Mamantouensa spoke next. His harangue was short, and in a style widely different from that which is usual among the Savages, who a hundred times repeat the same thing in the same speech.

"There," said he, addressing Monsieur Perrier, "are two young *Padouka* slaves, some skins, and some other trifles. It is but a small present which I make you; nor is it at all my design to induce you to make me one more costly, All that I ask of you is your heart and your protection. I am much more desirous of that than of all the merchandise of the world, and when I ask this of you, it is solely for the Prayer. My views of the war are the same as those of *Chikagou*, who has already spoken. It is useless therefore for me to repeat what you have just heard."

Another old Chief, who had the air of an ancient Patriarch, then rose. He contented himself with saying that he wished to die as he had lived, in the Prayer. "The last words," added he, "which our Fathers have spoken to us, when they were on the point of yielding up their last breath, were to be always attached to the Prayer, and that there is no other way of being happy in this life, and much more in the next which is after death."

Monsieur Perrier, who has the deepest Religious feelings, listened with evident pleasure to these savage harangues. He abandoned himself to the dictates of his own heart, without taking the precaution to have recourse to the evasion and disguises which are often necessary when one is treating with the generality of Savages. To each harangue he made such an answer as good Christians should desire. He declined with thanks their offers of service for the war, since we were sufficiently strong against the enemies who lived at the lower end of the river, but advised them to be on their guard, and to undertake our defense against those who dwelt on the upper part of the same river.

We always felt a distrust of the *Renard* Savages, although they did not longer dare to undertake any thing, since Father Guignas has detached from their alliance the Tribes of the *Kikapous* and the*Maskoutins*. You know, my Reverend Father, that, being in Canada, he had the courage to penetrate even to the *Sioux*, wandering Savages near the source of the Mississipi, at the distance of about eight hundred leagues from *New Orleans*, and six hundred leagues from Quebec. Obliged to abandon this infant Mission, by the unfortunate result of the enterprise against the *Renards*, he descended the river to repair to the Illinois. On the 15th of October in the year 1728, he was arrested when half-way, by the *Kikapous* and the *Maskoutins*. For five months he was a captive among these Savages, where he had much to suffer and everything to fear. The time at last Came when he was to be burned alive, and he prepared himself to finish his life in this horrible torment, when he was adopted by an old man, Whose family saved his life, and procured him his liberty. our Missionaries, who were among the Illinois, were no sooner acquainted with his sad situation, than they procured him all the alleviations they were able. Everything which he received he employed to conciliate the Savages, and succeeded even to the extent of engaging them to conduct him to the Illinois, and while there to make peace with the French and the Savages of that region. Seven or eight months after this peace was concluded, the *Maskoutins* and the *Kikapous* returned again to the Illinois country, and took away Father Guignas to spend the winter with them, from whence, in all probability, he will return to Canada. He has been exceedingly broken down by these fatiguing journeys, but his zeal, full of fire and activity, seems to give him new strength.[27]

The Illinois had no other residence but with us, during the three weeks they remained in this city. They charmed us by their piety, and by their edifying life. Every evening they recited the rosary in alternate choirs, and every morning they heard me say Mass; during which, particularly on Sundays and Feast-days, they chanted the different prayers of the Church suitable to the Offices of the day. At the end of the Mass, they never fail to chant with their whole heart the prayer for the King — The Nuns chanted the first Latin couplet in the ordinary tone of the Gregorian chant, and the Illinois continued the other couplets in their language in the same tone. This spectacle, which was novel, drew great crowds to the Church, and inspired a deep devotion. In the course of the day, and after supper, they often chant, either alone or together, different prayers of the Church, such as the *Dies iræ*, etc., *Viexilla Regis*, etc., *Stabat Mater*, etc. To listen to them, you would easily perceive that they took more delight and pleasure in chanting these holy Canticles, than the generality of the Savages, and even more than the French receive from chanting their frivolous and often dissolute songs.

You would be astonished, as I myself have been, on arriving at this Mission, to find that a great number of our French are not, by any means, so well instructed in Religion as are these Neophytes; they are scarcely unacquainted with any of the histories of the old and new Testament; the manner in which they hear the holy Mass and receive the Sacraments, is most excellent; their Catechism, which has fallen into my hands, with the literal translation made by Father Boullanger, is a perfect model for those who have need of such works in their new Missions. They do not leave these good Savages to be ignorant of any of our Mysteries, or of our duties, but attach them to the foundation and the essentials of Religion, which they have displayed before them in a manner equally instructive and sound.

The first thought which is suggested to those who become acquainted with these Savages is, that it must have been at great cost of labor to the Missionaries, and that it will be still more so, to form them into any kind of Christianity. But their assiduity and patience is abundantly recompensed by the blessings which it has pleased God to pour out upon their labors. Rather le Boullanger has written me word that he is obliged, for the second time, considerably to enlarge his Church, on account of the great number of Savages who each year have received Baptism.

The first time that the Illinois saw the Nuns, *Mamantouensa*, perceiving before them a troop of little girls, remarked, "I see, indeed, that you are not Nuns without an object." He wished to say, that they were not mere solitaries, laboring only for their own perfection. "You are," he added, "like the black Robes, our Fathers; you labor for others. Ah! if we had above there two or three of your number, our wives and daughters would have more sense, and would be better Christians." "Ah, well! " the Mother Superior answered him, "choose those whom you wish." "It is not fur me to choose," said *Mamantouensa*, "it is for you who know them. The choice should fall on those who are most attached to God, and who love him most."

You may well imagine, my Reverend Father, how much these holy women were charmed to find in a Savage sentiments so reasonable and Christian. Alas! it will take time and pains to teach the*Tchactas* to think and speak in this way. This indeed can only be the work of him, who knows how, when it pleases him, to change the stones into children of Abraham.

Chikagou guards most carefully, in a bag made expressly for the purpose, the magnificent snuff-box which the late Madame, the Duchess d'Orléans, gave him at Versailles. Notwithstanding all the offers made to him, he has never been willing to part with it, — a degree of consideration very remarkable in a Savage, whose characteristic generally is, to be in a short time disgusted with anything he has, and passionately desire whatever he sees, but does not own.

Everything which *Chikagou* has related to his countrymen, with regard to France, has appeared to them incredible. "They have bribed you," said some to him, "to make us believe all these beautiful fictions." "We are willing to believe," said his relatives, and those by whom his sincerity was least doubted, "that you have really seen all that you tell us, but there must have been some charm which fascinated your eyes, for it is not possible that France can be such as you have painted it." When he told them that in France they were accustomed to have five cabins, one on top of the other, and that they were as high as the tallest trees, that there were as many people in the streets of Paris, as there were blades of grass on the prairies, or mosquitoes in the woods, and that they rode about there and even made long journeys in moving cabins of leather, they did not credit it any more than when he added that he had seen long cabins full of sick people, where skillful Surgeons performed the most wonderful cures. "Hear!" he would say to them in sport, "you may lose an arm, a leg, an eye, a tooth, a breast, if you are in France, and they will supply you with others, so that it will not be noticed." What most embarrassed *Mamantouensa*, when he saw the ships, was to know how it was possible to launch them into the water after they had been built 012 land, where arms enough could be found for this purpose, and above all to raise the anchors with their enormous weights. They explained both these points to him, and he admired the genius of the French who were capable of such beautiful inventions.

The Illinois departed on the last day of June; they were to unite with the *Akensas*, for the purpose of falling upon the *Yazous* and upon the *Corroys*. These last having set out on their retreat to the*Tchikactas*, whither they were carrying the French scalps they had taken, were met on the way by the *Tchatchoumas* and by some *Tckactas*, who in their contest with them took eighteen scalps and delivered some French women with their children. Some time afterward, they were again attacked by a party of the *Akensas*, who took from them four scalps, and made many of their women prisoners. These good Savages encountered on their return two pirogues of French hunters; they passed their hands over them from head to foot, according to their custom, in testifying their sorrow for the death of the French, and of their Father in Jesus Christ. They made a solemn oath that, while one *Akensa* should be remaining in the world, the *Natchez* and the *Yazous* should never be without an enemy. They showed a bell and some books, which they were taking home, they said, for the first black Chief who should come to their Village. These were all that they had found in the cabin of Father Souel.

I was in pain to learn what these barbarians had done with the body of this Missionary, but a French woman who was then their slave, has informed me that she at last induced them to give it burial. "I saw him," she would often say to me, "lying on his back in the canes very near his house; they had not taken from him anything but his cassock. Although he had been dead fifteen days, his skin was still as white, and his cheeks as red as if he were merely sleeping. I was tempted to examine where he had received the fatal blow, but respect stopped my curiosity; I placed myself a moment at his knees, and have brought away his handkerchief which was near him."

The faithful *Akensas* mourned every day in their Village the death of Father du Poisson, and with the most earnest entreaties, demanded another Missionary. We could not excuse ourselves from granting this request to a Nation so amicable, and at all times so attached to the French, possessing, too, a degree of modesty of which the other Nations were ignorant, and among whom there exists no peculiar obstacle to Christianity, except their extreme attachment to jugglery,

But we have endeavored, my Reverend Father, to console ourselves in our grief with an argument of which you would never think, It is, that we may congratulate ourselves that our loss has not been more general. In fact, the two dear Missionaries for whom we mourn, did not appear to be by any means as much exposed to the cruelty of the Savages as are many others, particularly Father de Guyenne, and still more Father Baudouin.

The latter is without any defense in the midst of the great Nation of the *Tchactas*. We have always had a great distrust of these Savages, even at the time when they were making war for us upon the*Natchez*. Now they have become so inflated with their pretended victory, that we have much more need of troops to repress their insolence, and to keep them in their duty, than to finish the destruction of our open enemies.

Father de Guyenne, after much opposition on the part of the Savages in the neighborhood of Carolina, succeeded in building two cabins in two different Villages, to be near at hand to learn their language and to instruct them; but they were both demolished. He will be obliged at last to confine his zeal to the French Fort of the *Alibamons*, or to seek a more abundant harvest on the banks of the Mississipi.

It only remains, My Reverend Father, to inform you of the situation of our enemies, They are united near the river of the *Oachitas*, on which they have three forts. We believe that the *Natchez*are as yet in number about 500 warriors, without counting their women and children; they were scarcely more than 700 before the war. Among the *Yazous* and the *Corroys* there are not more than forty warriors. They have planted their corn between two little rivers which run near their forts. It would only be necessary to cut off this corn, to starve them during the winter, but the thing is not easy to effect, from what the smaller Tribes inform us, who harass them continually. The Country is cut up by *Bayouks* [bayous], and filled with canebrakes, where the inconceivable quantity of mosquitoes would not permit an ambuscade to be established for any length of time.

The *Natchez*, who were shut up in their forts since the last expedition, have begun again to show themselves. Incensed that a party from *Oumas* and *Bayagoulas* had captured one of their pirogues, in which were seven men, a woman, and two children, they went in great numbers near a small fort, where they have surprised ten Frenchmen and twenty Negroes, There was but one small Soldier with two Negroes who were able to save themselves. He had formerly escaped the massacre made by the *Natchez* by concealing himself in an oven, and this time he escaped by hiding in the trunk of a tree.

You can well believe, my Reverend Father, that this war has retarded the French colony; nevertheless, we flatter ourselves that this misfortune will be productive of benefit, by determining the

Court to send the forces necessary to tranquilize the Colony and render it flourishing. Although they have nothing to fear at *New Orleans,* either from the smaller neighboring Tribes, whom our Negroes alone could finish in a single morning, or even from the *Tckactas,* who would not dare to expose themselves on the Lake in any great numbers, yet a panic terror has spread itself over almost every spirit, particularly with the women. They will, however, be reassured by the arrival of the first troops from France, whom we are now constantly expecting. As far as our Missionaries are concerned, they are very tranquil. The perils to which they see themselves exposed seem to increase their joy and animate their zeal. Be mindful then of them and of me in your holy Sacrifices, in the union with which I am, with respect, etc.

Appendix Four
The Marriage Contract of Pierre Mayeux & Marie Manne[1]

February 27, 1739

Marriage Contract
Executed by and between

Sr. Pierre Mieux,
A resident of Pointe Coupee,
Formerly widower of Marrie Cellier
And
Dame Marie Francoise Mane,
Formerly widow of Sr. Laurent David.

The parties promise to take each other in lawful marriage, to be solemnized in the Holy Catholic Church.

They agree that they shall pay their respective debts before marriage, neither of the parties to be responsible for the debts of the other contracted before their marriage.

The parties agree to the community of acquets and gains according to the Custom of Paris.

The dowry of the future wife is valued at 2000 lives, consisting of "a house" in the city, household furniture and furnishings and clothes. One-third the value of said dowry shall fall into the community, the remaining two-thirds to be reserved for any children who may be born of the future marriage.

The future husband makes a marriage settlement of 300 lives, the principal of which shall be reserved for the children who may be born of said marriage.

The parties agree to a preciput of 150 lives.

(Signed)
Daublin
Maieux
Thomas Lege
Roumier
Henry, Notary

The future wife declares that she does not know how to write or sign her name.

[1] Louisiana Historical Quarterly, Vol. 6, #2, April 1923, p. 302

Bibliography

Arnold, Morris S., *Colonial Arkansas 1686-1804: A Social and Cultural History*, Fayetteville, University of Arkansas Press, 1991

Arnold, Morris S., *The Rumble Of A Distant Drum: The Quapaws and Old World Newcomers*, 1673-1804, Fayetteville, University of Arkansas Press, 2000

Arnold, Morris S., *Unequal Laws Unto A Savage Race: European Legal Traditions In Arkansas, 1686-1836*, Fayetteville, University of Arkansas Press, 1983

Axelrod, Alan, *A Savage Empire: Trappers, Traders, Tribes, and Wars That Made America*, New York, MacMillan, 2011

Barnett, James F., Jr., *The Natchez Indians: A History to 1735*, Jackson, University Press of Mississippi, 2007

Barry, John M., *Rising Tide: The Great Mississippi Flood of 1927 and How It Changed America*, New York, Simon and Schuster, 1997

Bourgeois, Lillian, *Cabanocey: The History, Customs, and Folklore of St. James Parish*, Gretna, Firebird Press, 1999

Caillot, Marc-Antoine, *A Company Man: The Remarkable French-Atlantic Voyage of a Clerk for the Company of the Indies*, edited by Erin M. Greenwald, New Orleans, The Historic New Orleans Collection, 2013

Charlevoix, Pierre F. X., *Charlevoix's Louisiana: Selections from the History and the Journal*, edited by Charles E. O'Neill, Baton Rouge, Louisiana State University Press, 1977, originally published 1744

Clark, Emily, *Masterless Mistresses: The New Orleans Ursulines and the Development of a New World Society, 1727-1834*, Chapel Hill, University of North Carolina Press, 2007

Coleman, Roger E., *The Arkansas Post Story*, Fort Washington, PA, Eastern National, National Park Service, Department of the Interior, 2009

Costello, Brian J., *A History of Pointe Coupee Parish*, Louisiana, Donaldville, LA, Margaret Media, 2010

d'Artaguiette, Diron, in *Travels In The American Colonies*, Toronto, MacMillan of Canada, 1916

Davis, Robert, Christian Slaves, Muslim Masters: White Slavery in the Mediterranean, The Barbary Coast, and Italy, 1500-1800, Macmillan, New York, 2004

De La Clue, Bertet, *A Voyage to Dauphin Island in 1720,* edited by Francis Escoffier and Jay Higgenbotham, Mobile, Museum of the City of Mobile, 1974

De Laye, *Relation of the Massacre of the French at Natchez and the War Against the Indians,* 1730; translated by Dave Cottrell, 2016

Deiler, J. Hanno, *The Settlement of the German Coast of Louisiana and the Creoles of German Descent,* Miami, HardPress, ND, originally published 1909

Dumont, Jean-Francois-Benjamin, *The Memoir of Lieutenant Dumont, 1715-1747: A Sojourner In The French Atlantic,* Chapel Hill, Univeristy of North Carolina Press, 2012

Du Pratz, Le Page, *History of Louisiana,* BiblioBazaar reproduction, ND, originally published 1758

Elliott, Jack D., *The Fort of Natchez and the Colonial Origins of Mississippi,* Fort Washington, PA, Eastern National, 2013

French, Benjamin Franklin, *Historical Collections of Louisiana*, British Library Historical Print Edition, ND, originally published 1851

French, Benjamin Franklin, *Historical Memoirs of Louisiana, from the First Settlement of the Colony to the Departure of Governor O'Reilly in 1770*, Nabu Press, 2011, originally published in 1853

Galloway, Patricia Kay, *La Salle and His Legacy*, Jackson, University of Mississippi Press, 2012

Garvey, Joan B., and Mary Lou Widmer, *Beautiful Crescent: A History of New Orleans*, Gretna, Pelican Publishing, 2013

Gayarré, Charles, *Louisiana: Its Colonial History and Romance*, New York, Harper and Sons, 1851

Giraud, Marcel, *A History of French Louisiana, Volume Five: The Company of the Indies, 1723-1731*, Baton Rouge, Louisiana State University Press, 1987

Gleeson, Janet, *Millionaire: The Philanderer, Gambler, and Duelist Who Invented Modern Finance*, New York, Simon & Schuster, 1999

Goodspeed, *Biographical and Historical Memoirs of Louisiana*, two volumes, Chicago, Goodspeed Publishing Company, 1892

Gould, Philip, *et al*, *Natchitoches And Louisiana's Timeless Cane River*, Baton Rouge, LSU Press, 2002

Hall, Gwendolyn Midlo, *Africans in Colonial Louisiana*, Baton Rouge, LSU Press, 1992

Hudson, Charles, *Knights of Spain, Warriors of the Sun: Hernando de Soto and the South's Ancient Chiefdoms*, Athens, University of Georgia Press, 1992

Johnson, Larry, *Tar Creek: A History of the Quapah Indians, the World's Largest Lead and Zinc Discovery, and the Tar Creek Superfund Site*, Mustang, OK, Tate Publishing, 2009

Keddy, Paul, *Water, Earth, Fire: Louisiana's Natural Heritage*, Bloomington, Xlibris Corporation, 2008

Matrana, Marc R., *Lost Plantation: The Rise And Fall Of Seven Oaks*, Jackson, University Press of Mississippi, 2011

Merrill, Ellen C., *Germans of Louisiana*, Gretna, Pelican Publishers, 2005

Milne, George Edward, *Natchez Country: Indians, Colonists, and the Landscapes of Race in French Louisiana*, Atlanta, University of Georgia Press, 2015

Powell, Laurence N., *The Accidental City: Improvising New Orleans*, Cambridge, Harvard, 2012

Proulx, Gilles, *Between France and New France: Life Aboard the Tall Sailing Ships*, Toronto, Dundurn, 1984

Riffel, Judy, *A History of Pointe Coupee Parish And Its Families*, Baton Rouge, Le Comité Des Archives De La Louisiane, 1983

Sabo, George, *Historic Indians of Arkansas*, Fayetteville, Arkansas Archeological Survey, 1992

Saucier, Corinne L., *History of Avoyelles Parish*, Gretna, Pelican Press, 1998

Surrey, Nancy Maria Miller, *The Commerce of Louisiana During The French Regime, 1699-1763*, Kensinger Publishing, ND, originally published 1916

Swanton, John R., *Indian Tribes of the Lower Mississippi Valley*, Mineola, Dover, 1998, originally published 1911

Thwaites, Rueben Gold, *The Jesuit Relations and Allied Documents, Volume XLVII, Lower Canada, Crees, Louisiana, 1720-1736*, Cleveland, The Burrows Brothers Company, 1899

Whayne, Jeannie M., *et al*, *Arkansas: A Narrative History*, Fayetteville, University of Arkansas Press, 2003

CPSIA information can be obtained
at www.ICGtesting.com
Printed in the USA
LVHW050032170120
643872LV00008B/321